21076

THE BRITISH REVOLUTION
VOLUME ONE

Lord Randolph Churchill
An Introduction to the House of Commons
Rosebery
Gallipoli
Chips: The Diaries of Sir Henry Channon
Memoirs of a Conservative: J. C. C. Davidson's Memoirs and Papers
Churchill: A Study in Failure 1900–39
Ambitions and Realities: British Politics 1964–70

The Complete Speeches of Sir Winston Churchill, 1897–1963
Victor Cazalet: A Portrait

ROBERT RHODES JAMES

THE BRITISH REVOLUTION

BRITISH POLITICS, 1880–1939

VOLUME ONE
FROM GLADSTONE TO ASQUITH
1880-1914

HAMISH HAMILTON
LONDON

First published in Great Britain 1976
by Hamish Hamilton Ltd.
90 Great Russell Street, London WC1B 3PT

Copyright © 1976 by Robert Rhodes James

SBN 241 89459 X

Printed in Great Britain by
Western Printing Services Ltd., Bristol

For
ANDREW MORGAN
A small repayment for a considerable debt

CONTENTS

ILLUSTRATIONS

Between pages 66 *and* 67

Between pages 98 *and* 99

Between pages 194 *and* 195

Between pages 226 *and* 227

Nos. 1, 2, 3, 4, 6, 7, 14, 15 and 16 are reproduced by permission of the Mansell Collection; nos. 5, 8, 9, 13 and 17 by permission of the Radio Times Hulton Picture Library; nos. 10 and 12 by permission of the National Portrait Gallery; no. 11 by permission of the Scottish National Portrait Gallery and of the Dowager Countess Rosebery.

PREFACE

LORD ROSEBERY HAS written that the political ocean is never quiescent and that its most serene temper is the calm before the storm, 'often more awful than the storm itself'. To carry this apposite image further, the principal difficulty for the political historian is to determine between the surface waves and the deep tides and, most difficult of all, to deduce their true relationship and mutual significance. Politics are often depicted in terms of conflicts between individuals and factions whose results determine events in which, as Sorel has written, 'chance seems to be modifying the whole course'. Other historians, not enamoured of this interpretation, give priority to those deeper forces which they see as being far beyond the control and even influence of politicians and factions, which the latter do not comprehend or which they ignore until they are swept away by them to prosperity, oblivion, or ignominy. It is not often appreciated that these opposing views are, in fact, reconcilable.

The period of sixty years covered by these two volumes is one of the most tumultuous and complex in British history. The narrative itself opens with the General Election of 1880, when the profession of politics was severely limited, the privilege of the vote was confined to a minority of the adult male population, the secret ballot was still a suspected novely—robustly denounced by Lord Palmerston in 1852 as 'a course unconstitutional and unworthy of the character of straightforward and honest Englishmen'—many hallowed corrupt practices still flourished, and the hustings, open voting, and practices immortalised by Charles Dickens in his account of the Eatanswill Election in *The Pickwick Papers* were very recent memories. Queen Victoria had nearly twenty years of her long reign and life before her. William Gladstone, who as a child had heard the guns triumphantly thundering in celebration of the victory at Waterloo, was beginning his second

Premiership, with two more to follow; Benjamin Disraeli—now adorned as the Earl of Beaconsfield—had just relinquished office for the last time, and memories of Lord Palmerston and Lord John Russell were very fresh.

By 1939 full universal suffrage had been achieved, which was in itself one evidence of the remarkable political and social revolution which is the theme of this work. Winston Churchill—born in 1874, six years before this narrative opens—lamented in 1929 that 'the leadership of the privileged has passed away'. As a statement of absolute fact that this was open to challenge, but no one could seriously question that there had been large and dramatic transformations in the character of national politics and, indeed, in the structure of the society of this remarkable nation.

There had been many other influences and changes not only in Britain itself but far from its shores, which had made their impact upon the development of its history. The Boer farmers, the Irish nationalists, the followers of Arabi in Egypt, of Gandhi in India, of Kemal in Turkey, of Lenin in Russia and of Hitler in Germany, had all played roles in what I have described as The British Revolution. British wealth and power, so substantial and so taken for granted in 1880 were, by 1939, so severely diminished that the nation was entering a desperate struggle for its very survival. This work is, in reality, the account of many revolutions, and indeed of some counter-revolutions as well, as the British nation moved from the relative calm and power of the nineteenth century into the unexpected storms, tumults, and perils of the twentieth.

My purpose has been to produce a narrative of tolerable length and balance which adequately describes and covers events and developments of considerable complexity and controversy, and to discern the 'waves' and 'tides' and their mutual significance. It might be argued that initially it gives undue prominence to the House of Commons and to its principal personalities, and to the varying fluctuations of what can be loosely called 'London politics'. It is true that to depict British politics in this first period simply as a gladiatorial contest between a few notables cheered on by an anonymous and ignored multitude would unquestionably omit certain significant elements. But in my judgement it is the case that until 1914 the real political decisions and struggles took place within a remarkably small segment of the population. This does not mean that the struggles were unreal or unimportant. If the principal cast was small and the electorate was a relatively limited participating audience, the active interest and involvement of that audience is not a nostalgic fiction. Politics was an eagerly followed drama, and the rise and fall of reputations at Westminister had a real public impact. This became less true after 1914, as the electorate widened greatly, the issues altered, the problems became more ominous, and new methods of public communication were created. It will be seen in the second volume that the balance of emphasis and attention changes, reflecting my interpretation of the subtle but very important differences in the character and structure of British politics and society during this period.

Both volumes concentrate primarily upon domestic politics. Thus, examination of foreign affairs and foreign policy is confined to those occasions when they had a direct relevance to, and impact upon, domestic politics. The range and detail of this period are so substantial that through necessity much has had to be omitted, and several important episodes have had to be handled somewhat swiftly. As always, I have found the problem of references a very difficult one. I have tried to keep all footnotes to a minimum, and to present a bibliography that—although necessarily selective—may be of real value to the reader. The Index contains brief biographies of the most significant individuals. This is, as I well know, a compromise, but I trust it may be recognised as a sincere endeavour to meet the requirements of the scholar and the concerns of the non-specialist reader.

I would not expect the balance of my priorities to be accepted by all historians, but my dominant purpose has been to try to bring the individuals and the struggles of the past to life again, and to convey to the contemporary reader some element of the human dramas, achievements, failures, and perversities which, at different times and in different contexts, enthralled or enraged their forebears, and which contributed to substantive changes not only to the course of British history but which are of a much wider modern significance.

*

This work has been in preparation for so long that the list of those individuals to whom I am indebted is so extensive that I hope they will accept a general statement of my profound gratitude. Furthermore, in my bibliography and footnotes I have been able to mention only some of the books and articles and manuscript collections which have been of such value to me. Thus, in saying, in Chaucer's valediction, 'Farwel my book and my devocion', I pay my grateful thanks to all who have helped me and who have shown me so many warm kindnesses throughout its extended journey.

But some have a very particular place in my gratitude. My beloved Father, who was born in 1886 and died in 1972, was always gently impatient for the completion of this work, having been personally involved in some of the episodes I have described, and eager to read his youngest son's interpretation of them. Andrew Morgan unwittingly began the course of this book when he was a young history teacher and I his nervous pupil in 1948, and it is to him that it is dedicated in all gratitude and regard. To my wife, whose entire married life has had the shades of politics—ancient and modern, national and international —heavily in its background, my debt is beyond gratitude or expression.

It is given to few writers to say that they have lived and written in happiness and serenity, and have always been surrounded by kindness and understanding. For all who have provided me with these circum-stances I can only say that this book truly belongs to them.

ROBERT RHODES JAMES

CHAPTER ONE

PRELUDE, 1860–1880

IN THE year 1547 the House of Commons, which had previously assembled in various buildings in the fragmented history of its nascent but severely limited existence and influence, was given by the Protector Somerset the use of the exquisite, long-neglected, and deliberately impoverished Chapel of St. Stephen's in the Royal Palace of Westminster, hard by the swift-flowing Thames. It was appropriate to the mood of the time that a secular and subservient body should have been instructed to occupy, and thereby to humiliate further, one of the most beautiful of all buildings raised in England to the Glory of God, and which had brought to stone and mortar the soaring genius of the Perpendicular Style, of which King's College Chapel, Cambridge—almost certainly the work of the same hands— remains as evidence of what was lost by the desecration, and then destruction, of St. Stephen's.

The representatives of the *communes* took their places in the choir-stalls, which ran on either side of the Chapel, removed the altar and placed the Speaker's Chair in its place, with a bare table before it for the Clerk. St. Stephen's was sixty feet long and thirty feet wide. This tiny area was to be the meeting place of the House of Commons for nearly three hundred years, with constant complaints by generations of Members at the contrast between their miserable accommodation and the great houses in which the servants of the Sovereign and other grandees resided. As William Cobbett complained in 1833: 'Why are we squeezed into so small a space that it is absolutely impossible that there should be calm and regular discussion, even from that circumstance alone? Why do we live in this hubbub? Why are we exposed to these inconveniences?' One observer commented that 'When an important debate occurred . . . the Members were really to be pitied; they were literally crammed together, and the heat of the House

I

rendered it in some degree a second edition of the Black Hole of Calcutta.'

As the significance of the Commons rose, the asperity of these comments became more sharp, but the arrangements in St. Stephen's were little altered. The statues and carvings were callously mutilated, then the walls hidden by tapestries, and then, in the early years of the eighteenth century, covered with wooden panelling. Sir Christopher Wren added narrow galleries, and the great East Window was transformed into three tall, blank, windows. But the essentials remained, and endure to this day. The choir-stalls were converted into benches, but they still faced each other across the Floor, the Speaker's Chair still stood on the altar steps at the East End, with the Clerks' table before it.

It was an intimate place, oppressively stifling when filled, and compared by Macaulay with the hold of a slave ship, but convenient for the transaction of Parliamentary business, and for the purpose of Parliamentary revolution. It was to this rudely converted chapel that King Charles I came to attempt to seize the Five Members, and in it that Cromwell carried the Grand Remonstrance, and the Reform Bill of 1832 was passed. Here spoke Cromwell, Pym, Hampden, Walpole, the two Pitts and the two Foxes, Burke and Sheridan, Castlereagh and Canning, the young Robert Peel and the even younger William Gladstone. Here Samuel Johnson—resolved that the Whig dogs should not get the better of it—and the young Charles Dickens observed and reported. As the influence and power of the Commons increased and that of the monarchy and the Lords waned, the realities of political power increasingly moved towards this physically inadequate but politically enthralling room.

On the night of October 16th 1834, the Palace of Westminster was largely destroyed by a spectacular fire—long anticipated by experts—which drew admiring throngs in London and was watched with awe from the hill-tops of Surrey and Middlesex. Westminster Hall, which adjoined St. Stephen's, was saved, but St. Stephen's itself was gutted, only the lower chapel surviving. The two Houses of Parliament moved into temporary quarters while, in the usual atmosphere of bickering, jealousies, anguish and bitterness which invariably seem to mark the raising of significant edifices, the new Palace of Westminster arose on the site of the old. The combined genius of Charles Barry and Augustus Welby Pugin—at the outset 39 and 22 years of age respectively—

created a monument to the Gothic Revival yet which had, particularly in its proportions, a very English personality. From the clock-tower at the north end to the Victoria Tower at the south, they established one of the most remarkable silhouettes in nineteenth-century architecture. The unknown artisans, by their detailed workmanship, themselves created a monument to the standards of their age.

The new House of Commons was notably larger than St. Stephen's with larger galleries—that for the Ladies being hidden behind a steel grill—and more handsome artefacts, but the general arrangements were identical, and it could seat less than half of its full membership. The chief complaints of Members when they took possession in 1852 concerned acoustics and lighting. Over the protests of Barry, who felt so deeply about the matter that he never set foot in the Chamber again, the House ordered a glass ceiling to cover the ornately carved roof on which Barry and Pugin had devoted so much attention. Gas-flares, which burnt above this new ceiling, provided illumination. Members remained so dissatisfied with this cramped and poorly ventilated room that plans were prepared in 1868 for a much grander Chamber, almost double in size, in which every Member would have a seat, to be built in the adjoining Speaker's Court. But, thankfully, the plans were never executed, and the Members became increasingly reconciled.

This dank, tawny, room was to be, until it was destroyed by German bombs in May 1941, the home of the House of Commons. It inherited and incorporated not only the physical features of St. Stephen's but the customs which had grown up in the Chapel. The practice had been established from the earliest days that the Ministers and supporters of the King's Government sat on the benches to the right of the Speaker, with its critics and independents sitting opposite them. Although of a later growth, the concept of 'the Loyal Opposition' had also been established before St. Stephen's had been destroyed and the Commons had acquired their new abode.

*

The period between the formation of the Administration of Sir Robert Peel in 1842 and the death of Lord Palmerston in 1865 had been one of extreme political confusion, and by the mid-1860s the development of political parties as opposed to random groupings had not reached a level of much sophistication. But out of this complex struggle for mastery in which there had been few fixed points, there had mysteriously but definitely emerged the canalising of a number of interests into two general, if not as yet truly formalised, parties. Thus, by the middle of the 1860s the Liberal and Conservative Parties were uneasy coalitions, drawn together with relative degrees of discomfort and by thinly defined concepts of common interest, and liable to swift and easy fragmentation.

Leadership remained essentially dependent upon personal factors. Peel's Conservative coalition of the late 1830s and early 1840s had been shattered by the schism over the repeal of the Corn Laws in 1846 and the extraordinary but devastating combination of Benjamin Disraeli and Lord George Bentinck in vehement opposition to Peel's apostasy. From that trauma the Conservatives had taken more than twenty years to recover their bearings and develop any common philosophy. In this period of political fluidity Palmerston had exercised his formidable gifts of fusion, persuasion, personal style and great public popularity to establish a Liberal coalition which, as has been written, 'was primarily formed from an amalgam of old Whiggery and new radicalism, together with certain eccentric strains of Canningite toryism and Peelite conservatism.'[1] Lord Shaftesbury, one of the most significant of all nineteenth century social reformers, wrote after the election of 1857 that 'There seemed to be no measure, no principle, no cry, to influence men's minds and determine elections; it is simply "Were you or were you not? Are you, or are you not, for Palmerston?"'.

It was this coalition to which W. E. Gladstone, the erstwhile tormented Peelite, gave further cohesion and leadership after Palmerston's death in 1865. Meanwhile the Conservative coalition, whose Parliamentary strength lay primarily in the counties, had gradually fallen—not without considerable misgivings—under the control and guidance of Disraeli. These two exceptionally gifted men drew around them supporters and allies, and their duels gave to politics an excitement and drama which accentuated the divisions between their parties, and which remained primarily historical and personal rather than ideological. There were differences between these parties, but none could be described as fundamental. Both were cautiously committed to social reform, and both were irrevocably committed to the cause of Free Trade. But although the divisions might be subsequently regarded as minimal, at the time they loomed very

[1] Norman Gash: *Politics In The Age of Peel*, xii–xiii.

large and the political disputes were conducted with an intense vehemence and passion.

The passage of the Second Reform Act of 1867 by the first Disraeli government had been a substantial political gamble which had, at least temporarily, failed, and the Liberals had swept to a comfortable victory in the 1868 General Election. But, as they began to show clear signs of disintegration after 1871, the eloquence, philosophies, and personal magnetism of Disraeli held the Conservative coalition together and gave it hope for the future.

The structure of British politics had been changed in subtle but crucial ways in the 1860s and early 1870s. The electorate, although considerably enlarged after 1867, still represented only a small proportion of the adult male population, and there is good cause to regard the 1867 Reform Act as a spectacular exercise in calculated gerrymandering intended for the benefit of the Conservatives rather than as a mighty leap in the dark in the general direction of democracy. But the introduction of the secret ballot in 1872, urged by the Chartists forty years before, was a genuinely revolutionary change, whose implications were formidable. The hallowed and very expensive methods of bribery, intimidation, 'treating', imported electors, and other devices whereby the people's will had been signified were no longer guaranteed to deliver the desired results. Furthermore, the introduction of two-member constituencies and plural voting made it evident to at least some politicians—and notably a young and ambitious Birmingham businessman, Joseph Chamberlain—that entirely new organisational methods would have to be introduced. Disraeli also perceived this, and the Conservatives had taken the first serious steps towards a form of national organisation which was still very crude and inefficient, but which laid significant foundations for the future.

It was to be some time before these developments were to have clearly discernible consequences, but by 1880 several had already become apparent and were to become dominant. The Corrupt Practices Act of 1883 and the 1885 Reform Act were to be crucial in developing these processes, but it would be wrong to assume that the political structure and practices of generations changed overnight. Bribery in certain constituencies was still remarkably enduring: in Gloucester in 1880 it was estimated that out of 4,904 electors 2,756 were bribed. The Commissioners who examined a by-election at Sandwich in 1880 reported that 'it did not appear that the mode of taking votes by ballot had the slightest effect in checking bribery. On the contrary, while it enabled many voters to take bribes on both sides, it did not, as far as we could ascertain, render a single person unwilling to bribe for fear of bribery in vain.'[1]

Nonetheless, the General Election of 1880 was the last in which corrupt practices on the old brazen lines were widely attempted, and it was significant that great efforts were made to conceal them.[2] Gladstone rode to triumph in the constituency of Midlothian with the assistance of voters who had been hurriedly lured into the constituency, placed on the register, and not ill-rewarded for their civic virtue in a ferocious contest for votes between the Buccleuch and Rosebery interests and money. The agents of the Duke of Marlborough had to work hard to secure the re-election in Woodstock of the Duke's younger son, Lord Randolph Churchill. The practice of spreading the word, particularly in rural areas, that the ballot was not all that secret was still prevalent, and still not without impact.

But the old rules had changed, and were to change much more and very quickly. No single event or act had achieved this, rather a combination of events in which the seriousness and willingness to make changes in the quest for improvement, which was now so marked a feature of the mid-Victorian period, played a part which it is difficult to categorise or describe with precision, yet which was such a marked characteristic of the age. Joseph Arch wrote in his autobiography (published in 1898) that 'as a lad, every time I earned a penny by doing odd jobs or running an errand, I would buy some old papers. . . . I would read Gladstone's and Bright's speeches and from them formed my opinions'. Such opinions were in the direction of reform, usually vaguely defined, and based on the foundation of self-help.

Disraeli, in his later years, observed that England, being a land subject to fogs and possessed of a powerful middle class, required grave statesman. This had certainly not been his impression earlier in his career, but he adapted himself with great skill to the new mood and circumstances. Palmerston's timing in his death had been characteristically felicitous. Politics, and England, had become more serious. The political adventurer now had to be more careful. Politics had

---

[1] H. J. Hanham; *Elections and Party Management—Politics in the Time of Disraeli and Gladstone*, 267.

[2] It can also be genuinely described as a truly 'general' election. In 1859, 374 seats had not been contested; the number fell to 210 in 1868, 187 in 1874, and 110 in 1880.

gradually ceased to be the part-time occupation of only an aristocratic
or nouveau-riche élite. The new prosperity had created new cities,
new wealths, and new men, to whom London and the House of
Commons were the goal of their new ambitions. Bagehot wrote in 1872
that 'The spirit of our present House of Commons is plutocratic . . . its
most prominent statesmen are men mostly of substantial means, but
they are mostly, too, connected more or less closely with the new
trading wealth'. As a generalisation this was capable of refinement and
was not the whole truth, but it contained a very strong element of the
truth. As G. J. Holyoake commented in 1868, 'the House of Commons,
like the London Tavern, is only open to those who can pay the tariff.
. . . All that the sons of labour have gained, at present, is the advantage
of being consulted.' The situation was still basically the same as it had
been in the 1830s, when Macaulay had written to his sister that 'Every
day shows me more and more strongly how necessary a competence is
to a man who desires to be either great or useful'. Leslie Stephen
wrote in 1867 that 'England is still an aristocratic country; not
because the nobility have certain privileges, or possess influence in
certain boroughs. A power resting upon such a basis would be very
fragile and would go to pieces at the first strain upon the Constitution.
The country is aristocratic, because the whole upper and middle, and
a great part of the lower, classes have still an instinctive liking for the
established order of things; because innumerable social ties bind us
together spontaneously, so as to give to the aristocracy a position
tolerably corresponding to their political privileges'.[1]

For a man who wished to enter politics and had the financial
resources to undertake a political career, securing a seat in Parliament
could be surprisingly easy, and no longer required the obligatory
heavy expenditure which had in the past made contested elections of
such financial benefit to the electors.[2] After 1883, although elements of
corrupt practices continued in some areas, and the wealth of hopeful
Members of Parliament was no disability to them, money by itself was
no longer enough, and a young man no longer needed, as the young

[1] Quoted in H. J. Hanham op. cit.
[2] At St. Albans, between 1832 and 1852 some £24,000 was spent on corrupt
practices, for a total electorate of less than 500. In Canterbury, between 1841 and
1852 £18,000 was spent on bribery. It was not to be wondered at that the electors of
Barnstaple, appalled by the prospect of an uncontested election, tried to advertise
for a candidate in *The Times*. For these and many other examples of corrupt practices
see Charles Seymour: *Electoral Reform in England and Wales*.

Gladstone had done, a wealthy patron such as the Duke of Newcastle. For this, a certain price had to be paid. The development of local party associations gave them the power of selecting candidates; the fact that they were usually very susceptible to suggestions from the regional and national organisations did not remove this new influence. The balance of patronage had changed: now it was not the former grandees but the parties that were beginning to exercise it. The manner in which Chamberlain's 'caucus' ran Birmingham politics, and the fact that the pledge to Parnell was crucial to success in Ireland in 1885, were the first examples of tight control over candidates in a manner that was to develop rapidly in the early 1900s.

But in the 1870s and early 1880s, although the balance was changing, influence and wealth were often the decisive factors, and the position of the party associations and the central organisation often very weak. In 1874 Lord Randolph Churchill and Arthur Balfour virtually inherited family constituencies—Woodstock and Hertford—but although the practice continued for a suprisingly long time, the days of the virtual ownership of constituencies by the great families were passing. In Lancashire Conservatism the favour or frown of Lord Derby was critical to aspirants up to the Second World War, the Chamberlains dominated Birmingham for two generations, and no Rothschild ever met problems in the Vale of Evesham. But, as the electorate expanded, the importance of substantial personal wealth declined and the role of the central party organisations became more significant, and accordingly the possibilities for men of relatively modest means greatly improved. When Arthur Lee determined to enter Parliament as a Conservative in 1900 he went to the office of the formidable 'Captain' Middleton, of whom more will be heard, and was at once proffered the opportunity of a safe seat in Hampshire. Three days later he was the candidate, as he has related:

> An emergency meeting of the constituency Association was called for the Thursday afternoon. This took place at the Town Hall, Fareham, and at 3 o'clock on a fine summer's day I found myself turned loose like a young bull into a ring of some 50 mature, if not crusted, local Conservative leaders, many of whom were resentful at being thus hustled, and highly suspicious of the whole proceeding. By an almost miraculous coincidence it had emerged that my grandfather Sir Theophilus Lee had for many years lived in the district, at

Bedhampton, and that my own father had been buried there. This had been quite unknown to me until the day before, but it at once made me a 'local man' and I did not fail to give so opportune a circumstance its full electoral value. Then I 'stated my views' on the political questions of the day at impressive length and with as much assurance as I could command . . . I found it comparatively easy to suggest easy familiarity with such problems as 'Home Rule', 'Local Veto', 'Church Dis-establishment' and 'Agricultural Reform'. Anyhow I succeeded in passing muster, and even in generating sufficient enthusiasm to enable my adoption to be carried by a unanimous vote.[1]

Lee had been lucky, but not exceptionally so. Good connections were all-important in that very close-knit political-social world. A blatant outsider like the Canadian self-made millionaire, Max Aitken, would have had considerable difficulties until he had worked his passage if he had not become the close friend of the Conservative leader, Bonar Law, who in 1910 drew the attention of the Unionist leaders of Ashton-under-Lyne to 'a young friend of mine . . . [who] now wants to stand for Parliament'. Aitken was swiftly accepted, and duly elected. In 1923 Victor Cazalet, not yet 26, was eagerly adopted as Conservative candidate for Chippenham on the basis of warm recommendations from London. The situation was more complicated for the Liberals, but not much different in practice. In the 1880s H. H. Asquith, Augustine Birrell, Edward Grey and R. B. Haldane experienced relatively little difficulty in securing good seats at the first attempt and with little local influence.

Although the Member was expected to contribute to local party expenses, which varied very considerably and could be very formidable, his actual presence in the constituency between elections was not required save on special occasions. The great leaders would, from time to time, descend upon their constituencies as in a cloud of fire, deliver a major and lengthy address, and depart for London. Lesser breeds, particularly at the beginning of their careers, usually had to appear more often, but by modern standards the requirements of most constituencies in their demands on the attention of their Member were modest indeed. His biographer relates that Sir Henry Campbell-Bannerman, Liberal Member for the Stirling Burghs for forty years

[1] Alan Clark: '*A Good Innings*'; *The Private Papers of Lord Lee of Fareham*, 78.

between 1868 and 1908, 'paid an annual visit to the five burghs to hold what he called a "colloquy" with his constituents, having a public meeting in each and meeting the leading citizens informally at the house of a prominent supporter. In those days the annual meetings between a Member and his constituents were serious affairs. His supporters described him as a model Member, taking trouble to understand their problems alive to their prejudices and always ready to support their interests. But he spent very little time in the constituency and sometimes he found it hard going . . . in a letter to Bryce he said: "I hardened my heart and thoroughly *did* my constituency which is a good thing over".' On one occasion there was a complaint by the secretary of the Liberal Association in Dunfermline, a Mr. Ireland, of Campbell-Bannerman's 'cavalier' treatment of his constituents, 'contenting yourself with one flying visit in the year of an hour or two's duration which is the only intercourse you have had with your constituents for some years', but Campbell-Bannerman took no notice and did not change his ways. His constituents regularly returned him, usually unopposed.[1]

This lofty approach was beginning to change in the 1920s, but only marginally. Unless the political winds were blowing very harshly against the party of one's choice, and barring total disasters, the process of actually getting into Parliament was not very difficult, and the burdens of Parliamentary life were not severe. The House of Commons did not often meet for more than six months in the year, and politicians of a later age are struck by the enormous volume of political correspondence conducted in Parliamentary Recesses, usually from large country-houses.

Until the activities of the Irish Nationalists made them necessary in the 1880s, the House of Commons had very few written rules and had had no need of them. It was governed by traditions which were instilled into the new Member with great severity and which he flaunted at his peril. The memory of Disraeli's disastrous maiden speech was still vivid. Presumptuousness was not tolerated. At the end of a major debate, after the final leading speakers had spoken, the House voted, and any Member who attempted to continue the debate would be silenced with bellows of 'Divide!'. 'The good sense and the good taste of the House of Commons', Disraeli had written, 'will be found on the whole to be the best regulators of the duration

[1] John Wilson: '*C-B*', 44–5 and 154.

of a debate.' The institution of Parliamentary Questions was in its infancy, and had to be regulated after the Irish seized this opportunity for further obstruction. But, as the 1880s continued, even the Irish became more respectful of the hallowed traditions of the House and swift to censure any infringement of them.

The late Victorian House of Commons had high standards. It had gradually lost the raucous vulgarity which so shocked visitors earlier in the century, but it remained a very masculine and irreverent assembly, swift to mock pomposity, generous to sincerity and ability, but with a certain cruelty and a suspicion of outside reputations that made it such a formidable and incalculable body. 'It is a nerve-wracking place for the ambitious man', Lee later wrote; 'he lives a jungle-life existence, carrying his political life in his hand and knowing that if he slips the denizens will tear him in pieces without any sort of compunction. I was always conscious of this and although I sat in the Commons for 18 years I never faced the ordeal of speaking without anxiety and apprehension.'[1] Disraeli described it as 'the most chilling and nerve-destroying audience in the world.'

It was here, not in the country, that political reputations were made or destroyed, because this was the national political stage. It had drama, and the possibility of fame. It was here that Gladstone, Disraeli, Palmerston, Lord John Russell, Lord Randolph Churchill, Chamberlain, Charles Stewart Parnell, and Arthur Balfour made their national reputations. The development of the railways had not only revolutionised physical communications but also the availability of national newspapers. These, during this period, paid considerable attention to politics and particularly to Parliament, and this fact greatly and significantly enhanced the national importance of a Parliamentary reputation. F. E. Smith was to call Parliament 'the microcosm of the talent of Great Britain' and urged that 'no man conscious of great powers should ever, willingly, be excluded from it.' In the nineteenth century this was indeed true, or at least was generally believed to be the truth. The House of Commons was the goal that lured them from all parts of the nation—David Lloyd George from Wales, Parnell from Ireland, Andrew Bonar Law from Glasgow, Keir Hardie from West Ham *via* Scotland, Asquith from Yorkshire, and Chamberlain from the Midlands. Here, in this small Chamber, and in the ornate intimacies of the Palace of Westminster, the men of politics gathered to

[1] Clark, op. cit., 79–80.

further their reputations, to ply their trade, some to participate with eagerness, others considering themselves as privileged inside observers of the great game.

Often described as a club, it was in reality more like a theatre, in which the drama was always changing yet was always absorbing, and where new actors rose—and often fell—and in which chance and odd circumstance were expected and eagerly awaited. If, by the standards of later years, it was in many respects a leisurely life, for those who were privileged to belong to it, it was their real and their full life, and which they pursued with ardour and with style. When Sir William Harcourt said that his objective was 'to stand well with the House of Commons' he expressed a very widely held ambition.

But the real lure was the sheer excitement of politics, in which the rewards for the few were so considerable, when Office did indeed contain Power, and in which fortunes could fluctuate so dizzyingly. The civil service was in its infancy, a new creation, unsure of itself and of its relationship with its political masters. The philosophy that 'the Government governs best when it governs least' was widely believed, and the structure of Government was at best flimsy and insecure, in most aspects hardly advanced in expertise and experience than in the days of Pepys. And the world of the fledgling civil service was also the world of the politicians, that of family linkages, social ties, discussions at dinner-parties or at country week-ends. Official positions of significance were no longer at the disposal of Ministers as they had been in the past, but the relationship between political masters and public servants was close, intimate, and on the same level. Edward Hamilton, the close friend of Rosebery, served Conservative Governments. His week-end engagements covered Liberal and Conservative establishments and friends. He was, unconsciously, the bridge between the old partisan concept and the subsequent complete anonymity of the professional civil service. But in his time the official world was as small as, and as intimately linked with, the political and social world of London.

For the Victorian politician, the House of Commons was his place of business, his home of pleasure, his hope of fame. As Disraeli sardonically observed, the first requisite for success in the House of Commons was to be there. For those who were determined and had the financial resources, getting there did not provide major difficulties.

Succeeding there, and remaining there, were much more hazardous to achieve.

*

It is difficult, and invariably perilous, to endeavour to draw the portrait of a particular age. No period of British society until then is as copiously documented as nineteenth century England, but the historian, confronted by the extraordinary contrasts of accounts and approaches and the infinite variety of the contemporary experience of this turbulent period, emerges more with a quantity of contradictory conceptions than with a clear picture and understanding of the spirit, driving-power, doubts, uneasiness and momentum of Victorian Britain.

The physical results are themselves very contradictory, ranging from the superlative engineering feats of Brunel, the great new civic buildings in London and the major cities to the unplanned and squalid development of the towns, and the less happy manifestations of the Gothic Revival. Save in the Crimea, Britain was not involved at all in major conflicts since the Napoleonic Wars, and it had escaped—however narrowly—the violent internal social revolutions which characterised most European countries in the first part of the century.

But although the reality of Victorian society was not, on inspection, as serene as it later appeared, the contrast between the vast changes made on the face of Britain by the Industrial Revolution and the relatively small impact upon the basic structure of that society is very striking. There were agitations, difficulties, and change, but in reality the balance of power had not shifted dramatically. The historian, confronted with these and many other contrasts, gains piercing insights into sectors, and not least from the great contemporary fictional observers of society, but finds it difficult to see the whole. To describe mid- and late-Victorian England as a confused, exciting, and fascinating paradox is not to escape into banal generality but to advance in understanding.

But, clearly, there were ingredients in that paradox which were of central significance. The most important were the balm of wealth and power that Britain had acquired and continued to acquire from the beginning of the century. Either in commercial or in military power there was no real challenger close at hand. And while the most notable characteristics of the age were a seething dynamism, self-confidence and energy, yet these were also tempered by caution, apprehension, and by an instinctive self-protective belief in established institutions. For this society was much less confident and far less complacent than it was later depicted. It could see serious problems present or looming at home and abroad, and these concerns constituted the principal meaning, relevance, and content of contemporary politics.

But, after the turmoils and dangers of the first half of the century, by the 1860s it had appeared that Britain had entered into a period of almost indefinite prosperity and wealth. This mood of buoyant optimism had been reflected in the Report of the Census Commissioners in 1871 which had recalled and invoked the words of Milton:

> Lords and Commons of England, consider what nation it is whereof ye are, and whereof ye are the governors; a nation not slow and dull, but of a quick, ingenious and piercing spirit; acute to invent, subtile and sinewy to discourse, not beyond the reach of any point the highest that human capacity can soar to.

The period of British supremacy had been very brief indeed. Until the early 1870s, although Britain had developed rapidly into a major industrial nation, agriculture had remained the largest single industry. Now this major industry was suddenly and fatally stricken by the combination of a series of bad harvests and the availability of cheap American wheat. Although there was a temporary recovery in the 1880s, the blow was to be mortal. Between 1841 and 1901 some four million people left the land and moved into the towns and cities, increasing the proportion of urban dwellers from half the population in the 1850s to three-quarters by the beginning of the twentieth century; by 1914 nearly eighty per cent of the population of England and Wales lived in the towns and cities, and the bulk of the land fell into poverty and neglect. The extraordinary emptiness of the English countryside was to be, subsequently, one of the most vivid memories of those who remembered this period. Land under cultivation fell from some 17 million acres in the 1870s to less than $13\frac{1}{2}$ millions by 1913, and Britain became a substantial food-importing nation for the first time in her history.

Up to the 1860s exports had provided a national bonus; from this time onwards, with a steadily mounting population, national economic survival depended upon the export of goods and services at a time when two new industrial giants—America and Germany—were

developing rapidly as formidable rivals. The *Annual Register* had
warned in 1867 that 'England . . . owes her great influence not to
military successes, but to her commanding position in the arena of
industry and commerce. If she forgets this, she is lost. . . . The signs,
for those who can read, are present, and can be plainly seen.' By 1880
they were to be even more clearly seen, but the response was insufficient. Britain was a very rich nation—in 1885 Sir Robert Giffen
estimated the value of British investments abroad at £1,302 millions—
and the value of its foreign possessions was beyond calculation. British
workmanship and technology were unequalled. But the brief hour of
supremacy had passed, as had the mood of buoyant optimism. The
'Great Depression' of the late 1870s may indeed, be, in retrospect, a
myth[1], but it was not regarded as such by contemporaries. Events such
as the collapse of the City of Glasgow Bank in 1878 were taken very
seriously indeed, and the agricultural depression was plain to see.

Macaulay had claimed in 1848 that 'the history of our country
during the last hundred and sixty years is entirely the history of
physical, of moral, and of intellectual improvement.' But by the end
of the 1870s there were some who were seriously questioning the
validity of these confident assumptions. The unexpected depression
created a revived awareness of the harsh squalor and misery that lay
so close to the surface of national prosperity, and which made the
contrast between the affluence of the few and the existence of the many
so glaring and painful. Laissez-faire and Free Trade were still
sacrosanct articles of national faith, virtually unchallenged and un-
challengeable, but although there had been few signs of serious
industrial trouble there were indications of new stirrings in areas which
had been quiescent since the Hungry Forties. Joseph Chamberlain
had transformed Birmingham by a programme of energetic and
enlightened civic reform, and the new County Council was, in the
1890s, to do much for London. But social reform was sporadic, and
even major advances such as the 1870 Education Act in reality only
marked the beginnings of dealing with a much more profound problem,
which was that the great majority of the population of this powerful
nation lived in poverty, or near poverty, without education, and were
the first victims of any economic depression, while a small minority
enjoyed power and great affluence. The meek acceptance by the
deprived of this situation was still a dominant attitude, and the

[1] See S. B. Saul: *The Myth of the Great Depression 1873–1896.*

historian surveying the reality can only marvel at the passivity of the afflicted, and share Cobden's astonishment that 'the people at large' were so 'tacit in their submission to the perpetuation of the feudal system in this country.' But this was being challenged. The decline of Britain as a church-going nation, which had been taking place since the 1850s, was in itself a portent. In the 1880s these stirrings were to develop into something much more significant.

Of this teeming nation, whose population rose from 12 million in 1811 to over 40 million by the end of the century, and this in spite of massive emigration from Ireland, the vote in 1880 was the prerogative of two and a half million adult males. The electorate had more than doubled as a result of the 1867 Reform Act, but it was still a relatively small fragment of the nation. The programme of the Chartists in the 1840s had been only partly implemented, but not entirely forgotten, and the continuation of a situation in which the great majority of the population had not even this modest degree of influence over its destiny was bound to cause trouble.

Although much had changed since the 1840s, Britain still remained Disraeli's Two Nations, and the first regarded the latter with a deep apprehension. It was once remarked of the Liberal Lord Rosebery that he felt of democracy as though he were holding a wolf by the ears, and Rosebery was not alone. The sanctity of Property was the religion of the old and new moneyed classes. The London mob which had aroused such terrors in the past now only emerged very occasionally, and with little of the ferocity of the past, but its potentialities were vivid, as the Hyde Park riots of May 1866 had demonstrated. For all its surface glitter and apparent self-confidence, and which so impressed wealthy foreign visitors, the First Nation wielded its power with fear in its heart. It did not share that contempt for the docility of the British working class which so bewildered and angered Marx and Engels.

The dominant question for the First Nation was how to preserve its power without inviting its destruction. To what point could social reform be achieved without disturbing the basic structure of difference and division? Disraeli had persuaded the Conservatives to recognise the necessity of Reform in the 1860s by instilling into them the realisation that a policy of gradual and controlled reform, conducted by them on their own terms and at their own timing, contained the key. 'In a progressive country', he remarked, 'change is constant, and the question is not whether you should resist change which is inevitable, but whether that change should be carried out in deference to the manners, the customs, the laws and the traditions of the people, or whether it should be carried out in deference to abstract principles and arbitrary and general doctrines.'

But to have this opportunity required the necessity of Office. It was as this fact inexorably sank in that the far-flung Conservative coalition had begun to merge into something much more national and formidable. It could be said of Disraeli as Lord Beaverbrook wrote of Lloyd George many year later, that 'he did not seem to care which way he travelled provided he was in the driver's seat'. It was this message that he conveyed to his party, and it was in reality his most enduring memorial. The vital requisite for controlled reform was to be in the driver's seat. The doctrine of Imperialism abroad and social reform at home had seemed romantic and impractible when it was enunciated by Disraeli in the early 1870s, but by 1880 the Conservatives were beginning to see the point. Power was henceforth the ideology of their party—Power to preserve power, to control movements which, if ignored or alienated, could sweep them away. From this conclusion it was a very short step indeed to the conviction that for the Conservatives to be out of power would lead to national catastrophe. This belief gave to the Conservative Party a passion, a venom, a cohesion and an unscrupulousness which was to make it a dominant force, in office or out of it, for the next sixty years.

It would not be difficult to mock at these pretensions, but they provided the cement which bound the Conservative Coalition together and enabled it to expand its appeal so dramatically. Not only the Conservatives were apprehensive. Radicalism was a fine luxury for the established in good times but a dangerous plaything in bad. Gladstone in 1885 was alarmed by a tendency in Liberals to 'take into the hands of the State the business of the individual man'. When Chamberlain campaigned for this 'unauthorised programme' in the same year he was denounced as a revolutionary, yet he was very careful to emphasise that 'I am opposed to confiscation in every shape and form' and that 'nothing would be more undesirable than that we should remove the stimulus to industry and thrift and exertion which is afforded by the security given to every man in the enjoyment of the fruits of his own individual exertions.' As will be seen, other issues caused the great Liberal split of 1886, but a major element in the movement of the anti-Gladstone Liberals into the embrace of the

Conservatives was to be the fear of extra-Parliamentary forces which could cast down the accumulated wealth and influence of three generations. The horror of Joseph Chamberlain at land legislation in 1882, which he denounced as 'veiled confiscation', emphasised a belief in the rights of property which he was to demonstrate in his assaults on Gladstone's 'Newcastle Programme' of nearly a decade later, and were to make him and the Whig Lord Hartington natural recruits into the Conservative ranks.

In contrast to the Conservatives, the Liberal Coalition was in the 1870s a very curious amalgam indeed, and it was difficult to detect any cement at all in its haphazard structure. It had no lack of war-cries—indeed, a super-abundance of them—nor of talent, but it was riven in personalities and dogmas. It had no particular idea about what exactly it wanted to reform, or how. The old Whig element, which remained strong, had little interest in reform at all. Among those who termed themselves Radicals there was a very wide spectrum of objectives and philosophies, and it was this 'sectionalism' which most concerned Gladstone in the 1870s, and of which he wrote in 1877 that 'no more ingenious recipe could be found in a self-governing country for solving the problem, apparently so hopeless, how to devise a method under which, where the majority prevails by law, the minority shall be in fact supreme.' Gladstone himself, who described himself as 'an out-and-out inegalitarian' and 'a firm believer in the aristocratic principle—the rule of the best', responded to causes and problems, often with genius and deep perception, but he was at root a *responder*. In his old age he wrote that he perceived his most 'striking gift' as 'an insight into the facts of particular eras, and their relations one to another, which generates in the mind a conviction that the materials exist for forming a public opinion, and for directing it to a particular end.' The fact that his response usually emerged suddenly out of a process of deep thought and personal communion made him a highly uncomfortable colleague and leader. As he himself wrote:

For years and years, well into advanced middle life, I seem to have considered actions simply as they were in themselves, and did not take into account the way in which they would be taken or understood by others. . . . The dominant tendencies of my mind were those of a recluse, and I might, in most respects with ease, have accommodated myself to the education of the cloister.

Gladstone was so complex a man that it is perilous to describe him in a brief compass, but this self-portrait held true throughout his life. As Lord Selborne wrote, 'He can hardly be brought to interest himself at all in matters (even when they are really great matters) in which he is not carried away by some too strong attraction; and, when he is carried away, he does not sympathise, or take counsel with, those whose point of view is at all different from his own.' After the Liberals fell to defeat in the General Election of 1874 he allegedly retired from public life, but his persistent eruptions—most dramatically over the Bulgarian Atrocities in 1876—had compromised the authority of the nominal leaders, Lord Hartington in the Commons and Lord Granville in the Lords, and had confirmed in the eyes of his admirers that he *was* the Liberal Party.

Gladstone had not only developed into the greatest public orator of his day, who could hold vast multitudes enthralled like the great preachers of old—and the comparison is a real one—but after Disraeli's departure to the Lords in 1876 he was also the most formidable and experienced Parliamentarian in public life. He had made his maiden speech in St. Stephen's Chapel, had passed through the agonies of the Corn Law schism and its aftermath, and in the swirling confusions of the 1850s had held his own through sheer ability and force of personality. His opponents, even Disraeli who affected to regard him with contempt, were afraid of him. His followers were awed by his powers and by his huge following, particularly in the North. Some of them considered him as the most valuable safeguard against the latent powers of the multitude, a kind of spectacular lightning-conductor for bitter feelings which, but for Gladstone, would have become highly and practically dangerous. Others were fearful of his unpredictability, and were baffled by the processes by which he suddenly and unexpectedly soared across ravines at whose edge he had trembled for years. Some regarded him as a true Radical, whose entire life had been a glorious progression from implacable Tory to root-and-branch reformer. But the political fact was that, however and for whatever reasons they had come to this conclusion, Gladstone was regarded by the bulk of Liberals as the holder of the true faith of Liberalism and of the Liberal cause. Thus, to a dangerous degree, it was *he* who provided the cement in the Liberal Coalition, and he alone. This fact was to dominate the policies and fortunes of the Liberals for the next fourteen years, and even beyond them.

*

Other movements had developed in the 1860s and early 1870s whose impact was not clearly apparent by 1880, but which were to have most profound consequences on the development of Britain over the next twenty years.

Viewed in calm retrospect, it is evident that the period 1870 to 1900 should be described as the Age of Imperialism. In these years the five major Imperial Powers—Britain, France, Germany, Belgium and Portugal—acquired by various methods some 12 million square miles of new territory. In 1900 it was estimated that the British Empire consisted of over 13 million square miles and 366,793,000 persons; the nearest challenger was France, with 3,740,756 square miles and over 56 million people; and Germany, with 1,027,120 square miles and over 14 million people. The bulk of the British, French and German acquisitions occurred in the years 1884–1900, in which the British acquired nearly three and three-quarter million square miles of territory and nearly fifty-seven and a half million people, and most of these new possessions came in the 'scramble for Africa' which was the principal phenomenon of these years.

This had been very difficult to foresee, so far as the British had been concerned, in the 1860s. India was recovering slowly from the after-effects of the Mutiny. Canada, given a new federated status, the six Australian colonies, and New Zealand, were far away. British possessions in Africa consisted of the Cape Colony, Sierra Leone, the Gambia, Lagos, and the Gold Coast settlement. The prevalent mood in high political circles in Britain was far from imperialistic, in the sense of expanding existing possessions. Even in radical circles the balance of argument had moved from the advocacy of separatism, and of abandonment of what Disraeli described as 'these Colonial dead-weights which we do not govern', to how best they should be administered. By the early 1860s no leading politician—with the possible exception of Lord Granville—could be described as a separatist, and Colonial Reform was one of the dominant themes in political discussion.

It was true that Cobden had spoken of 'the bloodstained fetish of Empire', and that John Stuart Mill had written that 'such a thing as the government of one people by another does not and cannot exist'. It was also the case that the very word Empire had a foreign, and, above all, a dictatorial connotation. As late as 1879 the Colonial Secretary, Lord Carnarvon, declared that 'I have heard of Imperial policy and Imperial interests, but Imperialism, as such, is a newly coined word to me', which he disliked 'for the obvious reasons that it suggests uncomfortable Continental associations'.[1] In 1876, when Queen Victoria assumed the title of Empress of India, *Punch* commented that:

> And, age by age, that name accurst
> Has still from first to latest
> Implied of Monarchies the worst,
> But ne'er with us the greatest.

But the subject of Empire was slowly becoming of revived interest to many Victorians. Huskisson's comment of 1828 that 'England cannot afford to be little. She must be what she is, or nothing' had perhaps an even greater significance in the 1860s, when the belief that a dynamic society must expand had many more adherents, and was well expressed by Adam Smith: 'It is a sort of instinctive feeling to us all, that the destiny of our name and nation is not here, in this narrow island which we occupy; that the spirit of England is volatile, not fixed.' Cobden had made it clear that he was not opposed to the *principle* of Colonies, but to the manner in which they were administered; in private correspondence he was more critical of the principle, but it was significant that latterly he kept such views to himself.

Matthew Arnold expressed a distaste for a narrow and insular mentality when he wrote in support of Heine's strictures on the British spirit in *Heine's Grave*:

> Yes, we arraign her! but she
> The weary Titan! with deaf
> Ears and labour-dimmed eyes,
> Regarding neither to right
> Nor left, goes passively by,
> Staggering on to her goal.[2]

At Eton, the schoolmaster William Johnson (who subsequently changed his name to Cory), dwelt heavily upon the grandeurs of the

---

[1] See Richard Koebner and Helmut Dan Schmidt: *Imperialism: the story and significance of a political word, 1840–1960*, for a detailed examination of this aspect of imperial thought and controversy.

[2] The metaphor became a popular one. As late as the Colonial Conference of 1902 Joseph Chamberlain spoke of 'the weary Titan' struggling under 'the too vast orb of its fate.'

past and the feebleness of the present. Among his pupils was a future Prime Minister, Lord Rosebery. As another pupil, Sir Henry Newbolt, wrote of Johnson:

> Beyond the book his teaching sped,
> He left on whom he taught the trace
> Of kinship with the deathless dead,
> And faith in all the Island Race.

The problem confronting the British in the 1860s was neatly expressed in the opening words of a pamphlet written by Joseph Howe in 1866 called 'The Organisation of Empire':

> Under the Providence of God, after centuries of laborious cultivation, the sacrifice of much heroic blood, the expenditures of a vast amount of treasure, the British Empire, as it stands, has been got together, and the question which is presented to us, in some form of Parliamentary or newspaper disputation almost every week is, *what is now to be done with it?*

If Howe's solution—responsible administration in the Colonies and representation at Westminster in a 'Parliament of the Empire'—was too extensive (and too vague) for contemporary appetite, the question that he posed was becoming a very real one.

The Radicals had found particular difficulty in determining their attitude to Empire, and the very existence of the colonies perplexed and divided them. By the 1860s few of the successors of Adam Smith and Jeremy Bentham could fully accept the philosophy of emancipation, and the argument that the desertion of the Colonies would be a worse crime than their seizure became more widespread. Many argued that they were an encumbrance—an opinion shared by Disraeli when he was Chancellor of the Exchequer in 1852—but what was to be done with them? Attention was accordingly given more to the task of improving the lot of the colonies than to abandoning them. Reform rather than Abandonment increasingly marked the Radical attitudes. The vision of Major John Cartwright—'the father of Reform'—a century before of 'a firm and brotherly league' of free and equal states with co-ordinated legislation and a common Crown became more attractive and comforting. It was extremely significant that when the severe repressive measures of Governor Edward Eyre of Jamaica aroused radical wrath in the 1860s, John Bright spoke at Rochdale of 'the legal putting to death of *subjects of the Queen and citizens of the Empire*.'[1]

In the middle and later 1860s this interest increased remarkably. A book by a young radical baronet, Sir Charles Wentworth Dilke, was published in 1869. Entitled *Greater Britain*, it attracted immediate attention and enjoyed a considerable success. 'The idea which in all the length of my travels has been at once my fellow and my guide—a key wherewith to unlock the hidden things of strange new lands—is a conception, however imperfect, of the grandeur of our race, already girdling the earth, which it is destined perhaps eventually to over-spread.' Dilke's book and his portrayal of the glowing future of the Anglo-Saxon race—for Dilke was thinking as much of America as of Britain—was warmly approved by the Radical Liberal W. E. Forster and by the historian J. A. Froude.

The year before, the Colonial Society was launched in London with the motto 'United Empire', and Gladstone and the Colonial Secretary, Granville, had attended its inaugural dinner. The aged but still influential ex-Premier Earl Russell wrote in a foreword to an edition of his speeches published later in the same year that his objective was 'the consolidation of the British Empire. In my eyes it would be a sad spectacle, it would be a spectacle for gods and men to weep at, to see this brilliant luminary cut up into spangles.' Froude, in his rectorial address at St. Andrew's University in March 1869, declared that 'Britain may yet have a future before it grander than its past; instead of a country standing alone, complete in itself, it may become the metropolis of an enormous and coherent Empire'. In a series of articles in *Fraser's Magazine* he had excoriated the old Manchester School and its narrow and insular outlook. Sir Charles Adderly, who had been under-secretary for the Colonies and who had played some part in the creation of the Dominion of Canada, delivered a robust assault on the old concept of the paternal role of the small Colonial Office, as personified to some by Sir James Stephen, Permanent Secretary from 1836–47, and derided as 'Mr. Mother-Country'. Adderly envisaged an Empire of self-governing dominion states, enjoying common citizenship, rights and duties; but it was significant that those colonies settled by aliens and military stations would be excluded from this process. Although little noticed at the time, the retirement of Frederick Rogers (later Lord Blachford) from the permanent-secretaryship of the

[1] Author's italics.

Colonial Office in 1871 marked the end of the direct influence of an individual who believed firmly in the inevitable disintegration of the Empire into autonomous states.[1]

It is important to emphasise the part played in the education of the men who were destined to be the chief apostles of the new expansionist conception of Empire in the 1880s and 1890s by influential leaders like William Johnson, Froude and Ruskin.

Froude's influence was considerable, and Ruskin's inaugural lecture as Professor of Fine Arts at Oxford, delivered in 1869, was one of the most significant and interesting of all contemporary utterances on the new expansionist vision of Empire. Among his audience on that occasion was Cecil John Rhodes, who had returned from farming cotton in Natal and working in the Kimberley diamond fields, to study at Oxford. An extract from Ruskin's lecture should be given:

> There is a destiny now possible to us, the highest ever set before a nation to be accepted or refused. We are still undegenerate in race; a race mingled of the best northern blood. We are not yet dissolute in temper, but still have the firmness to govern and the grace to obey. . . .
>
> This is what England must either do or perish; she must found colonies as fast and as far as she is able, formed of her most energetic and worthiest men; seizing every piece of fruitful waste ground she can set her foot on, and there teaching these her colonists that their chief virtue is to be fidelity to their country, and their first aim is to advance the power of England by land or sea; and that, though they live on a distant plot of land, they are no more to consider themselves therefore disfranchised from their native land than the sailors of her fleets do because they float on distant seas. If we can get men, for little pay, to cast themselves against cannon-mouths for love of England, we may find men also who will plough and sow for her, who will behave kindly and righteously for her, and who will bring up their children to love her.

The impact of this passionate declaration of faith on an audience of eager and impressionable young men was profound. When Rhodes declared at the age of twenty-four that 'I contend that we are the first race in the world, and that the more of the world we inhabit, the

[1] For a detailed study of the Colonial Office, see Chapter XIX (by R. B. Pugh) of *The Cambridge History of the British Empire*, Volume III.

better it is for the human race', he was already engaging upon that subtle but crucial extension of Ruskin's vision which was to bring it to the extreme racial faith of subsequent generations of imperialists, personified by Alfred Milner and Leo Amery. At its best, it was something larger and better, but when it fell below that level it degenerated swiftly into an arrogant racialism. But to men like David Livingstone, Charles Gordon, Evelyn Baring, Milner and Amery the concept of racial superiority had as its definite and absolute corollary responsibility and toil. It was *faith* in their race which acted as their driving force. Towards the end of his life Milner wrote what he called his 'Credo—key to my position', which may be inserted at this point to illustrate the development of the arguments with which Ruskin had amazed and inspired his undergraduate audience.

I am a Nationalist and not a cosmopolitan. . . . I am a British (indeed primarily an English) Nationalist. If I am also an Imperialist, it is because the destiny of the English race, owing to its insular position and long supremacy at sea, has been to strike roots in different parts of the world. I am an Imperialist and not a Little Englander because I am a British Race Patriot. . . . The British State must follow the race. . . . If the swarms constantly being thrown off by the parent hive are lost to the State, the State is irreparably weakened.

It was, characteristically, Disraeli who had first perceived the political importance of the new and marked change of intellectual attitudes towards Empire. When he rose to speak at the Crystal Palace on June 24th 1872, his audience had no foreknowledge of the message he was to deliver, for the cause and idea of the British Empire had never occupied Disraeli's attention or interest to any noticeable extent. Henceforward, it was to be the last great theme of his long and extraordinary career, that career which had seen the transformation of the cynical arriviste libertine to the solemn champion of the Conservative Party and the harbinger of Imperialism.

Reduced to its essentials, the Crystal Palace speech deliberately represented the Liberals as the destoyers of Empire and the Conservatives as its champion. 'The issue', Disraeli stated, 'is not a mean one. It is whether you will be content to be a comfortable England, modelled and moulded upon Continental principles and meeting in due course an inevitable fate, or whether you would be a great country, an Imperial country, a country where your sons, when they rise, rise to paramount positions, and obtain not merely the esteem of their countrymen, but command the respect of the world.' 'England', he declared, 'has outgrown the Continent of Europe. England is the metropolis of a great maritime Empire extending to the boundaries of the farthest Ocean.' The re-establishment of the Conservatives as the 'patriotic' and 'national' party was to pay important political dividends in the 1880s and 1890s.

But the immediate impact of Disraeli's speech was small, and the events of 1874–9 were to demonstrate that he had seen a possible political advantage in an Imperialistic doctrine before that doctrine had gained general acceptance or even recognition.

At the General Election of February 1874 the issues were primarily domestic. Gladstone's first (and incomparably greatest) Government had lost its reforming impetus. The animosity that it had aroused had out-weighed the approval. The party itself was divided on its future course. The Education Act of 1870 had aroused the fierce opposition of Midland Nonconformity, poised for the final blow against the influence of the Church in education, and angrily disillusioned by the compromise contained in the Act. The Nonconformist opposition to the Government first brought to national attention the name of Joseph Chamberlain, who had established himself in Birmingham as the forceful exponent of a new conception of civic administration and reform. The first Gladstone Government had disestablished the Irish Church, made the first venture into Irish land reform, opened the civil service to competitive examination, ended the purchase of commissions in the Army, introduced the secret ballot, established the principle of free elementary education, and by the Judicature Act of 1873 had reorganised the law courts and established the court of appeal. But it had also settled the *Alabama* dispute with the United States of America on terms which evoked criticism, and the virtual acceptance of the Russians' unilateral repudiation of the Black Sea clauses in the Treaty of Paris was also deemed unheroic. But the Liberal Government ran out of ideas and luck on domestic matters, and Gladstone himself became exhausted under the strain. Gladstone's election address in 1874 concentrated on the promise of the abolition of income tax, and was a bitter disappointment to the rising generation of Radicals, of whom Chamberlain and Dilke were the most conspicuous.

Chamberlain described Gladstone's manifesto as 'the meanest public document that had ever, in like circumstances, proceeded from the pen of a statesman of the first rank.' Disraeli's appeal was to a respite from 'incessant and harassing legislation', to a restoration of British influence in Europe, and 'to support by every means her imperial sway'. But it is extremely doubtful that the Imperial aspect had much influence. The electorate was bored with the hectic manner of Gladstonian government, and certain elements were responsive to Disraeli's accusation that Liberal reforms 'menaced every institution and every interest, every class and every calling, in the country'. At a time when the vote was substantially the privilege of the upper and propertied middle classes, such warnings had particular effect. And when Chamberlain declared that the Liberal leader was 'hardly in touch with the robust common sense of English liberalism' there were many who agreed with him.

Another element in the Liberal defeat was the unexpected emergence of an Irish Home Rule Party, the direct result of the 1872 Ballot Act and of the ferocious opposition of the Irish Catholic hierarchy led by Cardinal Cullen against the Irish University Bill of 1873, on which the Government had been defeated in the Commons on March 11th–12th 1873. Gladstone had resigned, with the invitation to Disraeli to form a minority government; Disraeli had refused, and the reputation of the Government had been further compromised. A series of minor scandals concerning the Post Office and the conduct of the Postmaster-General (W. Monsell) and Commissioner of Public Works (A. S. Ayrton), had followed. The removal of the Chancellor of the Exchequer, Robert Lowe, and other changes had not stemmed the rising tide of unpopularity that engulfed the Government. In 1874 the Conservatives secured an overall majority of fifty, but it could hardly be said that their victory was the consequence of the introduction of the Imperial issue.

Disraeli's first major Imperial coup came in 1875, when he in effect secured control of the Suez Canal by the purchase of the largest single holding—forty-four per cent—of the shares. Palmerston had strongly opposed the Canal, and Disraeli had described it as 'a most futile attempt and totally impossible to be carried out'. Ferdinand de Lesseps had proved Disraeli's claims incorrect, and the Canal had been completed in 1869. Egypt was part of the Ottoman Empire, but the Khedive Ismail was able to ignore the English protests to the

Sultan. He was less able to handle the financial aspects of the building of the Canal, and by 1869 was deeply in debt. In 1867 he had obtained from the Sultan the style and title of Khedive, and in 1873 he achieved permission to act as an independent ruler and to raise revenue and grant concessions without reference to the Sultan. But Ismail's capacity to spend money was awesome, and his many achievements for Egypt were overwhelmed by his chronic indebtedness. Thus it was that in 1875 he had to sell his 176,602 shares, out of a total of 400,000; with the assistance of the House of Rothschild, Disraeli secured them. Gladstone considered this 'an act of folly fraught with personal danger', but this was not the general reaction in England.

But although this action of Disraeli's was exceedingly popular, the bestowal on the Queen of the title of Empress of India in 1876 was less happily inspired. *The Times*, after initial approval, considered that it threatened the Crown 'with the degradation of a tawdry Imperialism'; Gladstone emerged from his retirement to denounce it as 'theatrical bombast and folly'; even the *Daily Telegraph*, a devout and docile admirer of the Government, expressed doubts, and the Liberals tabled hostile motions in both Houses of Parliament. The Queen was deeply angered by this hostility, and the episode confirmed her in her bias against the Liberal Party, on which Disraeli played with great skill. But the opposition did show that the glamour of Imperialism did not yet have a significant appeal to intelligent opinion. But it was significant that Disraeli had his champions. Edward Dicey—editor of *The Observer*—attacked Gladstone for upholding 'the anti-imperialist theory of British statecraft'. An official of the Madras Service, W. M. Thorburn, published in 1876 a book entitled *The Great Game*, advocating an expansive military Empire of a metropolitan character, which rapidly went through three editions. The first two contained an introductory chapter that deplored the absence of a forceful imperial policy; the third applauded Disraeli for providing one.[1]

A great moral issue arose in 1876. The Middle East crises of 1875–8 lie beyond this narrative, but no study of the movements of Imperialist sentiment in Britain can ignore the controversy over the Bulgarian Atrocities. First reports of the wholesale massacres of men, women and children by groups of armed Turkish irregulars called the Bashi-Bazouks were discounted by the British Government on the advice of the excessively pro-Turkish Ambassador at Constantinople, Sir H.

[1] See Koebner and Schmidt, op. cit.

Elliott. Disastrously, Disraeli tried to laugh off the reports. When Forster questioned him in the House on July 10th, Disraeli said that he doubted that torture had been employed by 'an oriental people' who 'generally terminate their connection with culprits in a more expeditious character'. The Tories leaped and roared at this sally. On July 31st Gladstone himself asked a question; the Prime Minister dismissed the allegations as 'coffee-house babble'. He subsequently blamed Elliott for his 'lamentable want of energy and deficiency of information', but it had been Disraeli himself who had made the most grievous blunder. He was justified in endeavouring to damp down hostility to Turkey at a time when his policy was based on supporting Turkey against Russian ambitions in the Middle East, but by adopting a flippant and contemptuous tone he had laid himself open to accusations of irresponsibility and even callousness.

The violent agitation that now arose owed nothing to Gladstone. In fact he behaved with almost excessive caution, and nearly missed the occasion. One of his biographers has written that 'never had Gladstone's instinct for right-timing been more perfectly exemplified',[1] which is a serious misunderstanding of the events of 1876.[2] It was not until September 6th that his famous pamphlet, 'The Bulgarian Horrors and the Question of the East', was published. It was—and remains— a startling document. One detects in its frenzy Gladstone the theological disputator rather than Gladstone the politician. It was a shrill, impassioned, and grotesquely vitriolic philippic. The Turks were depicted as 'the one great anti-human species of humanity', whose 'abominable and bestial lusts' were such that 'at which Hell itself might almost blush'. There was, however, one magnificent passage of inspired invective:

Let the Turks now carry away their abuses in the only possible manner, namely by carrying off themselves. Their Zaptiehs and their Mudirs, their Bimbashis and their Yuzbachis, their Kaimakams and their Pashas, one and all, bag and baggage, shall, I hope, clear out from the province they have desolated and profaned. This thorough riddance, this most blessed deliverance, is the only reparation we can make to the memory of those heaps on heaps of dead; to the violated purity alike of matron, of maiden, and of child.

[1] P. Magnus, *Gladstone*, 242.
[2] See R. T. Shannon: *Gladstone and the Bulgarian Agitation*.

The last great duel between Gladstone and Disraeli—who in August, went to the Lords as the Earl of Beaconsfield—was in many respects their most significant. Disraeli's policy was, in Gladstone's eyes, not merely immoral in itself, but deliberately provocative. At the Guildhall on November 9th, he threatened Russia with war, and a famous music-hall refrain—'We don't want to fight, but by Jingo if we do,/We've got the ships, we've got the men, we've got the money too!'—had brought a new word into the language of political debate. Both parties were divided. Salisbury, Derby and Carnarvon were as alarmed by Disraeli's speeches as Granville, Hartington and Harcourt were by Gladstone's. The public utterances of both were marked by a personal animosity that was to affect Gladstone's career for the next twenty years. As Sir William Harcourt wrote to Dilke on October 10th, 1876, 'Gladstone and Dizzy seem to cap one another in folly and imprudence, and I don't know which has made the greater ass of himself.'

It seemed that it was Gladstone. His fury at the Turkish atrocities had led him into a series of wild panegyrics of the Russians. When, after a brave resistance, the Turkish armies were fought back almost to the walls of Constantinople itself, British opinion veered round sharply again. In London, Gladstone was vehemently unpopular, but elsewhere—particularly in the north of England and Scotland—his earnestness and fervour had made an immense impression. Froude, Ruskin, Carlyle and Tennyson gave him public support. But the events of 1878, culminating in the Congress of Berlin and 'Peace with Honour', seemed to give the victory to Beaconsfield.[1] In the speech from the Throne that ended the Session of 1877 there was a significant phrase:

> If, in the course of the contest, the rights of my Empire should be assailed or endangered, I should confidently rely on your help to vindicate and maintain them.

In the Lords (April 8th, 1878) Beaconsfield set out his new Imperial philosophy:

---

[1] But note should be taken of his letter to Salisbury, September 17th, 1878: 'So long as the country thought they had obtained "Peace with Honour" the conduct of Her Majesty's Government was popular, but if the country finds there is no peace they will be apt to conclude there is no honour.'

I have ever considered that Her Majesty's Government—of whatever party formed—are the trustees of that Empire. That Empire
was formed by the enterprise and energy of your ancestors, my
lords, and it is one of a very peculiar character. I know of no
example of it, either in ancient or modern history. No Caesar or
Charlemagne ever presided over a dominion so peculiar. Its flag
floats on many waters; it has provinces in every zone, they are
inhabited by persons of different races, different religions, different
laws, manners, customs. Some of these are bound to us by the ties
of liberty, fully conscious that without their connection with the
metropolis they have no security for public freedom and self-
government; others are bound to us by flesh and blood and by
material as well as moral considerations. There are millions who are
bound to us by our military sway, and they bow to that sway because
they know that they are indebted to it for order and justice. All these
communities agree in recognising the commanding spirit of these
islands that has formed and fashioned in such a manner so great a
portion of the globe.

This ideological basis for Imperialism aroused fierce controversy
and hostility from the Liberals. Robert Lowe declared that 'when
anything very foolish is to be done we are always told that it is an
Imperial matter . . . Rome . . . was so imperial that its people were
robbed to sustain the imperial policy'. The comparison with Rome
was current. The banker and historian Frederick Seebohm urged that
Britain should be the Athens, and not the Rome, of the English-
speaking world.[1] Other comparisons lay at hand. Sir William Harcourt
described the policy of the Government as 'an Imperial policy—a
servile imitation of the imperialism of the Second Empire'; Gladstone
declared that 'we do not want Bosnian submissions', and accused the
nation of neglecting affairs at home 'to amuse herself everywhere else
in stalking phantoms'. A. J. Mundella warned a Sheffield audience
against being led captive by 'a sham imperialism'. 'What does
imperialism mean?' Lowe enquired. 'It means the assertion of absolute
force over others'.

Beaconsfield responded that there was only one responsibility from

[1] *Imperialism and Socialism* (1880) Seebohm's main contention—that imperialism
was the banner of revolutionaries and radicals and thus threatened social order—
was less characteristic.

which he shrank, 'that of handing to our successors a weakened or diminished Empire'. Lord Salisbury said that 'we are striving to pick up the thread—the broken thread—of England's old Imperial traditions'. He went on to produce another argument, which was just beginning to have a real attraction in certain circles: 'The commerce of a great commercial country like this will only flourish—history attests it again and again—under the shadow of Empire, and those who give up Empire to make commerce prosper will end by losing both.' This recalled Disraeli's own statement in 1863 that 'there may be grave questions as to the best mode of obtaining wealth . . . but there can be no question . . . that the best mode of preserving wealth is power'.

But the debate was not merely one that concerned theoreticians and politicians in Britain. In South Africa, the British High Commissioner, Sir Henry Barkly, and his Colonial Secretary, Richard Southey, urged upon the Colonial Office a policy of blatant acquisition. The Boers who had left Cape Colony on the Great Trek in the 1830s were now established in the Transvaal and the Orange Free State, a devout, independent, and sternly puritanical farming community. The discovery of diamonds at Kimberley in 1870 not only attracted some ten thousand prospectors to a hitherto deserted area but also made South Africa appear to be a kind of nineteenth-century El Dorado. Southey had been responsible for a very quick and sharp acquisition of the diamond fields by buying the disputed area of Griqualand West from the local chieftain. This gave the Boers a very real grievance, which was not diminished by the payment of £90,000 in compensation. Barkly and Southey now worked towards the annexation of the Transvaal itself, in the firm conviction that, as Barkly wrote to the Conservative Colonial Secretary, Lord Carnarvon, on May 25th 1874, Britain 'has only plainly and firmly to indicate her will, in order to seek submission to it'. Carnarvon, who at first favoured reconciliation with the Transvaal, was gradually propelled towards annexation. 'These South African questions', he wrote, 'are a terrible labyrinth of which it is very hard to find the clue'. Carnarvon had sponsored the Act of 1867 that had federated Canada; a similar federation of South Africa was a gleaming prospect.

The annexation of the Transvaal was in the event absurdly simple. The President, Burgers, was weak. The Republic was insolvent. There were unending, and increasingly menacing, disputes with native tribes. In 1875 the Boers suffered a severe defeat at the hands of the

Bantu, and turned to a force of desperadoes led by a Prussian ex-officer who received no pay but were permitted to take what plunder they could. They acted with great efficiency and brutality, and the prospect of a major war between white and black became grimly nearer as the Zulus, led by their monarch, Cetawayo, cried out for revenge.

Carnarvon's representative was Sir Theophilus Shepstone, the Minister for native affairs in Natal, an attractive, courageous and knowledgeable man with a deep affection for, and understanding of, the Zulus. Carnarvon sent him to Pretoria to discuss confederation with Burgers, and with the discretion to propose bringing the Republic under the British flag. He reached Pretoria early in 1877 to find the treasury bankrupt and the President desperate for assistance. Burgers and his colleagues were prepared to accept annexation on the conditions that they should receive pensions or positions and that they should be permitted to make a public protest against the annexation. Shepstone accepted both conditions, even approving the draft of Burger's statement of protest. At the time it seemed to be a matter of no significance, but Shepstone had ensured the re-establishment of a spirit of Boer nationalism at a time when the Republic was on the verge of collapse. The emergence of Paul Kruger—Burgers's putative opponent at the next Presidential election—as the champion of this nationalism was the first result of the annexation. The resentment against the Griqualand West coup and the incursion of exploiting outsiders into the Veld had already been seen in many ways. Perhaps of most significance had been the movement to restore the Afrikaans tongue, initiated by Arnoldus Panneris, a Hollander schoolmaster, and which had made surprising headway since 1873. The publication of the principles of the Afrikander Bond on July 4th 1879, showed that annexation had sharply quickened the pace of Boer nationalism. But these straws in the wind went utterly unperceived at the time in Government circles in Cape Town and in London.

Shepstone's annexation came as an unwelcome shock to the new High Commissioner, Sir Bartle Frere, on his arrival in South Africa at the end of April 1877. The fact that Carnarvon had empowered Shepstone to undertake a task of such importance undoubtedly undermined the authority of the High Commissioner. He proceeded to direct his attention exclusively to the Zulu problem, and came quickly to the conclusion that, as war was inevitable, it should be swiftly undertaken. He and the local Commander-In-Chief—General Thesiger (who succeeded to the title of Lord Chelmsford in December 1878)—appealed to the home Government for military reinforcements. The Cabinet urged Frere to handle the problem by negotiation, but eventually authorised the dispatch of troops. Frere delivered an ultimatum to Cetawayo on December 11th and deliberately launched the Zulu War.

This venture came at a moment when the glitter had begun to fall off what Wilfrid Blunt called 'Dizzy's suit of imperial spangles'. In reality, Beaconsfield had been extremely cautious in foreign policy; purchasing the Canal shares was one thing, direct intervention in Egypt's affairs, urged on him in 1878, was quite another. But in politics appearances are often as important as facts. Beaconsfield had rhetorically linked himself with a 'forward', 'patriotic', 'imperial' and 'national' foreign policy, and was now neatly caught on his own phrases. The combination of apparent flamboyant and unsuccessful adventures abroad and economic depression at home gave the Liberals—and particularly Gladstone—a magnificent target which they assailed with a rare unanimity. The issue of the Bulgarian Atrocities had aroused a very real passion which, as has been emphasised, owed nothing to Gladstone but which he exploited just before the outcry had faded. The despatch of the Mediterranean Fleet to Besika Bay and then through the Dardanelles left more enduring memories of recklessness than the alleged triumph of the Congress of Berlin. And then Beaconsfield's critics were given additional ammunition.

Contrary to Frere's expectations, the Zulu War was neither swift nor successful. On January 22nd 1879 Chelmsford suffered, at Isandhlwana, a shattering disaster. Misled by a Zulu feint, he took most of his force away from the main camp; when it returned it discovered that 52 British officers, 806 troops, nearly 500 natives and some non-combatants had been overwhelmed and killed. The news reached England on February 11th, and brought a storm of criticism down upon the Government. Even the reports of the epic defence of Rorke's Drift immediately afterwards, where a force of just over 100 men repulsed an immense Zulu attack, could not affect the political impact of the Isandhlwana disaster. Large reinforcements were dispatched, and the Government defended Chelmsford and Frere against severe Liberal criticisms. Sir Garnet Wolseley was sent out to replace

Chelmsford, and arrived just as Chelmsford was about to defeat the Zulus at Ulundi (July 1879). Cetawayo was deported and his territory divided up into eight principalities. The total cost to the British of this lamentable foray had been 76 white officers, over 1,000 men and over 600 native troops killed in action; this included the Prince Imperial of France (the only son of Napoleon III). Seventeen white officers and 330 men had died of disease, and a further 99 officers and 1,286 men invalided; 37 officers, 206 white troops, and 57 native troops had been wounded in action—an astonishingly small figure compared with the deaths suffered in action, and which illustrates the fierceness of the fighting and the valour of the Zulus. The cost in financial terms was over £5 million.[1]

Unhappily, Frere was not the only representative of the Government who had ambitions. Lord Lytton had been appointed Viceroy of India in 1876 with specific instructions to induce Sher Ali, the Amir of Afghanistan, to receive a friendly mission to his country. The negotiations at Peshawar early in 1877 foundered on the British condition that their agents should be admitted to the frontier positions. In July 1878 a Russian mission arrived in the capital of Kabul, and a British mission was turned back at the frontier. Lytton now urged military intervention on the Cabinet, which received the request badly. But Beaconsfield and Salisbury—the main advocates of a careful and restrained policy—eventually agreed, after an unexpectedly impassioned appeal by the Secretary for India, Lord Cranbrook, to leave matters to Lytton's judgement.

The dismal consequences were much the same as in South Africa. Lytton issued an imperious ultimatum and then invaded Afghanistan with three armies, one of which was commanded by Major-General Frederick Roberts V.C. Sher Ali was overwhelmed, and his son ceded the principal British demands in May 1879. The peace was brief. On September 3rd the British mission at Kabul was killed to a man, and the war had to begin all over again, in one of the most difficult regions for military operations in the world. Roberts' march to Kabul restored the military situation and made him a national hero, but the evil effects of Isandhlwana and Kabul combined to

---

[1] *Narrative of the Field Operations Connected with the Zulu War of 1879* (H.M.S.O., 1881). Gladstone's private comment may be noted: 'It is very sad, but so it is that in these guilty wars it is the business of *paying* which appears to be the most effective means of awakening the conscience.'

increase resentment at the apparent aggressive and costly nature of Beaconsfield's Imperialism.

If this was not entirely fair, neither was it wholly unjust. Beaconsfield had given encouragement to those tendencies which animated Frere and Lytton to act as they thought was now required and approved. When Beaconsfield developed his theme of 'Imperium et Libertas' in a speech at the Mansion House in November 1879, Gladstone categorised it as 'liberty for ourselves, Empire over the rest of mankind'. Imperialism had become a highly pejorative term in Liberal mouths. 'What is especially desirable to make clear', Joseph Chamberlain wrote to the editor of the influential *Fortnightly Review*, 'is that this infernal Afghan business is the natural consequence of Jingoism, Imperialism, "British interests" and all the other phrasing of this mountebank Government'. In one of those brilliant phrases that occasionally illuminate British domestic politics, Henry Dunckley (editor of *The Manchester Examiner and Times*) described Beaconsfield as an exponent of a system of government that was 'an absolute monarchy tempered by sacerdotalism'.

What was not perceived at the time was that the subject of Empire had become intellectually respectable, even in the most radical circles; that the public interest had been definitely aroused; and that forces out of the control of parties of governments were building up rapidly. Even at this stage, however, remarkably few were talking of the *expansion* of Empire. The first voice to argue that with real effect was J. R. Seeley, in 1881, following the path laid by Ruskin and Froude.

*

In 1876 Disraeli, confident that Gladstone's retirement was a definite fact, went to the House of Lords with the title of Lord Beaconsfield. Although he could still have his occasions, he had become a totem of past glories and was an old and lonely man, depicted by the young Max Beerbohm 'with his lustreless eyes and face like some Hebraic parchment'. 'Power!' he remarked. 'It has come to me too late. There were days when, on waking, I felt I could move dynasties and governments; but that has passed away.' It was difficult to discern in that pallid, sphinx-like and black-suited cynic sitting impassively for hours, arms enfolded, in that great gilded barn the House of Lords, the outrageous political and literary adventurer of the 1830s, the scourge of Peel in 1845–6 who, if he had leaned forward and had flicked his victim with a thong could not have devastated him more acutely or immediately, the self-styled educator of his Party, the great survivor, the brilliant, despised, and eventually revered opportunist of the '50s and '60s. Now, adulated by the Sovereign who had at first disliked him so greatly—and with such good cause!—and reverenced by his Party, Lord Beaconsfield was sinking into gloom-filled lethargy and seigneurial pessimism. The deplorable young Disraeli had moved, by careful and deliberate metamorphosis, into the respectable Disraeli, the saviour of the Conservative cause, and now into the immortal Lord Beaconsfield. As he faded, so did his Administration.

This was particularly evident in the House of Commons, where the Chancellor of the Exchequer, Sir Stafford Northcote, was worthy but not inspiriting, and the Home Secretary, R. A. Cross, despite considerable administrative talents, lacked authority. The real Conservative talents lay in the Lords, where Lord Salisbury, then aged 50 and who as the young Lord Cranborne in the 1860s had attacked Disraeli for his apostasy, and who had written of him that 'he is an adventurer; as I have too good reason to know, he is without principles and honesty . . . in an age of singularly reckless statesmen he is I think beyond question the one who is least restrained by fear or scruple', and had championed the cause of the old Conservatism with the passion of a Junius, had now found his destiny in the conduct of foreign affairs.

It was indeed fortunate for the Administration that Gladstone's appearances were only occasional, and that the Liberal leadership was flaccid. Lord Hartington, heir to the Duke of Devonshire, and who hardly represented the rising tide of Radicalism, was an angular man of middle age, who had entered Parliament in 1857, a Whig member of an historic Whig family, with a considerable capacity for silence. His position depended principally upon his great name, his not inconsiderable wealth, and the well-merited belief that he was not only shrewd but possessed that most rare of human qualities, common sense. But neither he nor his Party could rid themselves of the conviction that he was merely a *locum tenens*, awaiting an announcement of the return from Hawarden.[1]

---

[1] As the country estates of the leading politicians in this period were of some political interest, those of the most significant should be mentioned. Gladstone's home was Hawarden Castle, in Flint, just over the Welsh border from Chester. Beaconsfield's was Hughenden, close to High Wycombe, Buckinghamshire;

Beside him on the front bench sat Sir William Harcourt, an eager, opinionated, intensely warm and intensely insensitive politician-lawyer on the make. Harcourt's principal merit was gusto, plunging with zest and usually without too much thought into the most intricate and complex of problems. Harcourt loved politics with an all-consuming enthusiasm, blustering, shouting, red-faced, outraged, and yet also caressingly gentle and kind. Unhappily, he had a marked tendency to stamp upon his colleagues' toes with greater zeal and more manifest pleasure than on those of his political opponents. The Liberals, fearful of his temper and troubled about his judgement, yet impressed by his spirit, intellect, and capacity for hard work, eyed him with uneasy esteem.

More interest was shown in the rising Liberals, of whom Joseph Chamberlain, who entered the House in a by-election in 1876, was by far the most arresting.

Chamberlain had risen from a strict Unitarian family in London which had moved to Birmingham, where he had made his fortune and his name. The fortune came from the manufacture of screws and other larger enterprises; the name came from his progressive record as Mayor of Birmingham, his part in the National Education League's battles against the 1870 Education Act, his radical declarations, which included some faintly anti-royalist and Republican observations which aroused disproportionate dismay and opprobrium, and the creation of an organisation, the National Liberal Federation, which was compared to the American Caucus and was viewed with re-pugnance, alarm, or awed respect. The organisation was initially the response to the two-member constituency and the introduction of

Salisbury lived at Hatfield House, in Hertfordshire; Lord Rosebery moved between Dalmeny House, near Edinburgh, Mentmore, in Buckinghamshire, and The Durdans at Epsom, in Surrey; Joseph Chamberlain's home was at Highbury, near Birmingham; Hartington's was Holker Hall, Cartmel, in north Lancashire; Lord Spencer resided at Althorp, in Northamptonshire; Sir William Harcourt had a substantial residence in the New Forest (Hampshire) as did Arthur Balfour at Whittingehame, near Edinburgh, and Sir Stafford Northcote at Pynes, near Exeter in Devon. Many of these were inherited properties, and varied in size and luxury, the mansions of Rosebery and Salisbury being the most impressive and Chamberlain's probably the least. All of them had London houses as well, but it is striking how often these were regarded as regrettable necessities, and how eagerly the political world would quit London when Parliament adjourned and conducted political business through copious correspondence and visits to colleagues far away from the House of Commons.

plural voting, but it was developed into something more formidable than machinery for ensuring that party followers knew whom to vote for. The Federation, blessed at its birth by Gladstone personally, was clearly not only a vehicle for Chamberlain's ambitions but potentially a very formidable take-over bid for the entire Party organisation. Thus, although he sat on the back benches, a cold, carefully dressed, monocled newcomer to Parliament, he was at once recognised as a politician of the front rank. The House, and particularly the Liberals, had greeted him with bleak suspicion. There was, even at this stage, something chilling and implacable about him.

As John Morley was to write of him, 'his politics came to him, now and always, from a penetrating observation of things around him as they actually were.' It was evident that unlike most Members, his life was politics and politics was his life. 'The political creed is the whole man', as Beatrice Webb (then Beatrice Potter), who was briefly but deeply in love with him, wrote in 1884; 'the outcome of his peculiar physical and mental temperament, played upon by the experiences of his life.'[1] It was already known that he was of an independent spirit, the kind of man who spoke and acted as though he were on at least level terms of authority and influence with the major politicians of the day. He had not yet had the opportunity nor the facility to demonstrate to the House of Commons the debating style which flourished best when he was under fierce attack, which was slow to mature, and which made men increasingly chary of meeting him head-on in severe controversy. But already the House had seen enough of him to realise his considerable capacities and even more considerable potentialities.

For the Liberals, although they did not like the man, Chamberlain's youth, vigour, and power were in very welcome contrast to the lethargic occupants of the Opposition Front Bench, and indeed the remarkable feature of this Parliament lay in the number of men of future eminence who sat in relative obscurity on the back benches. Lord Randolph Churchill, the younger son of the Duke of Marlborough, had been elected for Woodstock in 1874, but his appearances in the House of Commons had been few. Arthur Balfour, elected for Hertford in the same year, was taking a relaxed approach to his Parliamentary responsibilities. But one back-bencher was neither obscure, nor unknown, nor relaxed, and had already established a

[1] Quoted in Peter Fraser: *Joseph Chamberlain*, p. 116.

unique reputation which even eclipsed the speculation about Chamberlain's future.

Charles Stewart Parnell had entered the House of Commons at a by-election as Member for Meath in 1875. His maiden speech ended with words of which greater notice should have been taken.

Why should Ireland be treated as a geographical fragment of England, as I have heard an ex-Chancellor of the Exchequer call it some time ago? Ireland is not a geographical fragment, but a nation.

When Parnell entered the House, Parliamentary interest in the Irish Question was low. 'The Irish Question' had many definitions imposed upon it by the English. 'That dense population', Disraeli declared, 'in extreme distress inhabits an island where there is an Established Church which is not their Church, and a territorial aristocracy the richest of whom live in distant capitals. Thus, you have a starving population, an absentee aristocracy, and an alien Church, and in addition the weakest executive in the world. *That* is the Irish Question'. But it was The Question only in part. Disraeli—with much greater shrewdness and imagination than the majority of his English contemporaries—had touched upon certain of the more obvious and odious manifestations of English rule in Ireland, which he could well appreciate and comprehend. He knew that similar circumstances in England itself could only lead to bitter discontent and, possibly, revolution. But The Irish Question had a dimension that was un-fathomable and incomprehensible to the English. It was true that agrarian poverty and exploitation lay at the root of much Irish hatred of the English; it was also true that religious factors were of major significance; and that long-hugged myths and jealousies played their part. But the abiding element, which the English could never under-stand, was the passionate desire of the Irish people to mismanage their own affairs in their own way. They also loathed being regarded as children and treated accordingly. This simple fact utterly escaped those Englishmen—many of them worthy and honourable—who endeavoured to resolve The Irish Question. A vast abyss lay between the two peoples, and it was one that no English politician understood, let alone endeavoured to bestride. Therein lay the roots of this vast, and as yet unfinished, tragedy.

The disestablishment of the Irish Church and the Land Act by the

1868–74 Liberal Government had made it a tenet of respectable Irish nationalism that the best hope for Ireland lay in alliance with the Liberals, and in the development of this conviction the roles of Cardinal Cullen and Isaac Butt, the leader of the Parliamentary Party, had been crucial. This enthusiasm had faded abruptly after 1870, and had helped to inspire the formation of the Home Rule Association, not a political party as such but designed, in the words of its founder, Isaac Butt, 'to bring the question before the public mind'. But there was another, and older, strand in the Irish cause, exemplified by the Irish Republican Brotherhood—the Fenians. It was accepted that Ireland had to take one course or the other, that of constitutional methods or that of violence; the possibility that they might be fused into one movement had not been seriously countenanced.

When Parnell made his maiden speech the Irish Parliamentary Party was a courteous and moderate group, anxious not to offend English opinion nor to interrupt the workings of the British Parliament. Butt was an able Dublin lawyer, in his early years a vehement Protestant Conservative and strongly opposed to any suggestion of the repeal of the Act of Union. But in 1852 he was elected for Youghal, and became increasingly the champion of the Irish tenants and Catholic education. It was not until the late 1860s, when he defended Fenians without fee, that he achieved a leading position. He had founded the Home Rule Association in 1870, and then, in 1873, the Home Rule League. But the General Election of 1874 had come too soon for the League, few of his fellow-members in the Irish party in the House were Home Rulers, and his position was precarious. His private life was open to criticism from the Catholic clergy; the Fenians supported him only out of gratitude for past services; the tenant farmers never gave him their full allegiance. Above all, he conspicuously failed to achieve anything tangible. His annual Home Rule Bill, a moderate proposal for limited self-government, was politely introduced, politely debated, and contemptuously voted into oblivion. But he was an eloquent speaker, and in other circumstances might have been highly effective. In introducing the Home Rule proposal for the first time he concluded a speech of one and a half hours with the words:

Give us a new participation in a new compact, carried not by fraud and coercion, but founded on the free sanction of the Irish people. Backed as I am now by sixty representatives of the Irish people, in their name I offer you this compact, and I believe if it is accepted it will be, humanly speaking, eternal.[1]

Although this appeal, and many others, were ignored, Butt persevered along the Parliamentary constitutional road, while impatience grew in Ireland and turned to something considerably worse than impatience when the full impact of the agricultural slump struck in the late 1870s. The establishment of the militant Land League in County Mayo by Michael Davitt in 1879 symbolised the change in mood and temper.

Davitt had been born in 1846, and his childhood was dominated by the harrowing experience of the Great Famine, the inhumanity of landlordism, and the necessity for so many Irish people of the choice of death or emigration. The Davitts had settled in England, where Davitt's real education took place. Unlike most Irishmen of his generation he did not hate England; he hated the conditions under which so many Englishmen lived as much as he hated those under which his fellow-countrymen lived. He himself was a factory child, and at the age of twelve lost his right arm in a factory accident; at the age of nineteen he joined the Fenians. In 1870 he had been arrested and imprisoned first in London, and then in Dartmoor, where he was most evilly treated, and which destroyed his health. When he was released seven years later his weight was 122 pounds, 'not, I think,' he wrote, 'the proper weight for a man six feet high and at the age of thirty-one.' He paid the first of many visits to America where he had enunciated the outlines of his developing new programme, and which matured into the Land League. Davitt had turned aside from the extremism of the Fenians, but he had taken up a weapon which was to prove much more deadly—the cause of the impoverished and exploited Irish tenant-farmer.

By this time Butt had been replaced by Parnell. On the day that the new Member for Meath had taken his seat, the House of Commons had been outraged by a performance of blatant and unprecedented obstructionism committed by a coarse and ill-dressed Belfast provision merchant, Joseph Biggar, who had himself lost patience with English disdain for Irish grievances and the processes of correct Parliamentary practice. Butt had been greatly distressed by Biggar's contempt for the accepted usages of the House, but Parnell had been impressed. The

[1] David Thornely: *Isaac Butt and Home Rule* (1964), 231.

process which Biggar had started was now developed. To Butt's fury and humiliation, Biggar, Parnell, and a handful of Irish Members who shared their views took virtual command of the proceedings of the House of Commons. 'If we are to have Parliamentary action', Parnell had coldly remarked, 'it must not be the action of reconciliation but of retaliation', and proceeded to paralyse the British Parliament and to demonstrate the limitations of unwritten rules and accepted codes of behaviour.

The English stared with astonishment and then with anger at this outrageous spectacle, but were impotent. There was nothing to stop the iconoclasts, and they were wholly untroubled by ridicule or abuse. The Government, faced with a situation which was without precedent, attempted to respond. Two anti-obstructionist measures, passed after prolonged debate, proved to be easily circumvented; a Committee was set up to consider further and more effective measures; Butt un-availingly denounced Parnell's tactics to English cheers but to Irish hostility, and was doomed; in 1879 Northcote moved six resolutions to attempt to meet the problem, but five had to be abandoned and the sixth—after consuming three exhausting nights in debate—proved to be useless. Even the Irish who were most contemptuous of the 'con-stitutional' approach to Home Rule were impressed, and when Parnell publicly stated to the House of Commons that the Fenians who had been hanged for killing a policeman in Manchester in 1867 while attempting to rescue two of their comrades had not committed murder he won powerful new allies. In 1877 he displaced the forlorn Butt (who died in 1879) from the Presidency of the Home Rule Confederation; he was not yet thirty-one.

In appearance Parnell was tall, cold, and aloof, and—save when obstructing—of few words, yet those had an icy clarity that Bryce compared to a freezing wind on a winter's day. All leaders of revolutions are unusual individuals, but Parnell was one of the strangest of all. He was an aristocrat leading a predominantly middle class political party dependent upon the support of a peasant movement; a Protestant landowner at the head of an overwhelmingly Catholic movement bitterly opposed to landlordism; a man of action, he staked everything on constitutional methods sharpened by the threat of violence; super-ficially cold and aloof, not given to bandying civilities with his follow-ers and often openly contemptuous of their inadequacies, he evoked in them an awe and respect which made them suffer much without complaint and to accept his unpredictability, his hauteur, his chilling silences; and he was to destroy himself and—at least for a time—his cause, through a passionate love-affair.

In inheriting Butt's position, Parnell had inherited his problems, and these rapidly became much more acute. The bad harvests of 1877 and 1878 were followed by the failure of the potato crop in 1879, and created a desperate crisis in Ireland—a crisis of stark poverty. Most tenants were liable to eviction if they could not pay their rents, and in the circumstances of 1877–9 this possibility became a grim reality. It was under these circumstances that Davitt had founded the Land League in County Mayo, and whose appeal was immediate and widespread. Although the League's methods were constitutional— Davitt himself favouring 'a policy of parallel action between the revolutionary and constitutional movements'—the implications of its policies were revolutionary, and could well become so in reality if the already hapless condition of the agricultural tenants continued to worsen even further. Parnell, while aware of the obvious dangers which were involved, accepted Davitt's invitation to become President of the Irish National Land League in October 1879. Thus, within four years of entering Parliament with little previous experience or even understanding of politics, Parnell had become a major political figure, and 'the New Departure'—the fusing into one national movement of all the elements of Irish protest and grievance—was created. The next stage was to secure candidates who would follow him personally, and by 1880 he had created a majority of Irish M.P.s sufficient to secure his election as Chairman of the Parliamentary Party.

But the scale and nature of Parnell's rapid rise were lost on the majority of British politicians, who took little interest in Irish affairs unless they were compelled to do so. Gladstone, the author of the disestablishment of the Irish Church and the Irish Land Act of 1870, who had written in 1845 'Ireland, Ireland! That cloud in the west, that coming storm, the minister of God's retribution upon cruel and inveterate and but half-atoned injustice', and who had declared in 1868 that his mission was 'to pacify Ireland', was particularly in-insensitive to the looming peril. When Beaconsfield in his 1880 Manifesto—which took the form of an open letter to the Duke of Marlborough, Viceroy of Ireland—described Home Rule as a menace 'scarcely less disastrous than pestilence and famine', it was denounced by the Liberals as a characteristic manoeuvre to cloud the main issues.[1] But Beaconsfield, who in 1836 had denounced 'this wild, reckless, indolent, uncertain and supersititious race, whose history describes an unbroken circle of bigotry and blood', had never visited Ireland,[2] and had wholly ignored the Irish Question during the six years of his Administration—had belatedly seen the signs. When the young Balfour lamented the defeat of the Government in April 1880, Beaconsfield simply replied, with great emphasis and solemnity, '*Ireland*'.

But the 1880 General Election was fought, outside Ireland, entirely on other issues. Gladstone's retirement had ended dramatically when he announced his candidacy for Midlothian in 1879 and conducted the first—and the greatest—of his campaigns that autumn. Superbly stage-managed by the Earl of Rosebery, the rising star of Scotland and already—at the age of thirty-two—widely spoken of as a future Prime Minister, Gladstone at Midlothian dwelt before vast audiences on the immorality of 'Beaconsfieldism' and on the iniquity of its foreign adventures. Characteristically, he did not offer specific remedies, nor a detailed programme but spoke as an inspired visionary on the attack. The impact in Midlothian in terms of votes was limited,[3] but elsewhere was evidently considerable.

The Conservatives offered feeble resistance. Deceived by two recent by-election victories in Liverpool and Southwark, Beaconsfield had sought the dissolution in March in full expectation of victory. Only too late was it recognised that the rudimentary organisation put together before the 1874 election by John Gorst—who had been ill-rewarded for his work—had been permitted to decline disastrously. The Liberals, in contrast, were far better organised and prepared, and not only in those constituencies where the National Liberal Federation claimed the dominant influence. The result was decisive. The Liberals won 349 seats, the Conservatives fell from 351 to 243, and the Irish Home Rulers numbered 60—of whom 37 could now be accounted Parnellites. The significance of this fact was overlooked in the hour of victory. Gladstone had swept aside Hartington's claims to the Premiership, as the Queen was most reluctantly forced to concede; Chamberlain exultantly claimed sixty Liberal victories for the Liberal

[1] It did little good in Ireland, either. The Home Rule Confederation urged its members to 'vote against Benjamin Disraeli as you would against the mortal enemy of your country and your race.'

[2] Gladstone had, once, for three weeks in 1877.

[3] The result of the election was: Gladstone 1,579; Lord Dalkeith 1,368.

Federation, and was hailed by *The Times* as 'the Carnot of the moment'. Chamberlain did not disagree. To Dilke he wrote that 'the victory which has just been won is the victory of the Radicals. Gladstone and the Caucus have triumphed all along the line.'

The Conservatives were shocked and disconsolate, and cast down by the most sombre forebodings. Salisbury wrote to Balfour that:

> The hurricane that has swept us away is so strange and new a phenomenon that we shall not for some time understand its real meaning. I doubt if so much enthusiasm and such a general unity of action proceeds from any sentimental opinion, or from a more academic judgement. It seems to me to be inspired by some definite desire for change; and means business. It may disappear as rapidly as it came, or it may be the beginning of a serious war of classes.

The Conservatives did not appreciate in that hour of depression how providential had been their defeat, and the Liberals, engaged in the exquisite task of Cabinet-making, had no premonition of the storms that were about to sweep down upon them.

CHAPTER TWO

THE LIBERAL INHERITANCE, 1880-1885

THE FORMATION of Mr. Gladstone's second Administration was not a swift, smooth, or comfortable process.

The more radical elements in the party, convinced that the great victory had been their achievement, sought a substantial influence in the new Cabinet. But in the event they were reduced to the ageing John Bright and the uncongenial W. E. Forster, while upon Chamberlain was bestowed the Board of Trade, justly regarded as the least significant place in the Cabinet; and although Sir Charles Dilke received a senior post in the Government, he was not included in the Cabinet. Gladstone himself took the Exchequer, Lord Granville returned to the Foreign Office, Lord Kimberley went to the Colonial Office, Lord Spencer became Lord President, the Duke of Argyll was Lord Privy Seal, Hartington assumed responsibility for India, Harcourt moved with ponderous relish to the Home Office, Lord Northbrook went to the Admiralty and H. C. E. Childers—at the Admiralty in the 1868-74 Administration—took over the War Office. Rosebery had held himself aloof, although he could probably have been persuaded easily enough to join if Gladstone had taken much trouble over the matter—the first of a series of personal misunderstandings that were to quickly dim the companionship and triumphs of Midlothian.

It was not simply a matter of Gladstone's innate preference for Whigs, as the disgruntled radicals averred, which caused this marked imbalance. Gladstone was now in his seventy-first year; since 1874 he had been very much out of touch with contemporary politics. His appearances in the Commons had been few and brief, and he did not know or understand the new men and the new moods. He accepted Chamberlain with reluctance; the rest of his colleagues were familiar faces from the past—comfortable and proven. The rising Conservatives in 1951 were to experience very similar emotions when they beheld Winston Churchill's last Cabinet.

The radical discontent was at least partially responsible for the mood of the new House of Commons when it assembled at the end of April. As John Morley subsequently wrote:

> Mr. Gladstone found that the ministry of which he stood at the head was a coalition, and what was more, a coalition of that vexatious kind, where those who happened not to agree sometimes seemed to be almost as well pleased with contention as with harmony. . . .[1]

The principal problem was, however, much more profound. The 1868 Liberal Government had had a great deal of unfinished reforms awaiting its attention, and which it was eager to undertake in what Gladstone later nostalgically called 'the era of liberation'. In 1880 the situation was very different. The Liberals had fought the campaign in a purely negative manner, offering an end to 'Beaconsfieldism' but no real alternatives. The leadership had no defined policies or objectives, and no legislative programme at all. This was to haunt the Liberal Government throughout its existence.

Immediately after he had been re-elected Speaker, Mr. Brand noted in his diary that the Liberals were likely to be a difficult team to drive and that many members seemed determined to go their own ways. This was perceptive, but he might also have noted similar tensions in the disheartened and embittered Conservative Opposition.

The position of Sir Stafford Northcote, the Conservative leader in the House of Commons, was acutely unenviable, and cannot be described better than in words used by Disraeli himself in his biography of Bentinck:

> But he who in the Parliamentary field watches over the fortunes of routed troops must be prepared to sit often alone. . . . Adversity is necessarily not a sanguine season, and in this respect a politician is no exception to all other human combinations. In doors and out of doors a disheartened opposition will be querulous and captious. A discouraged multitude have no future. Too depressed to indulge in a large and often hopeful horizon of contemplation, they busy themselves in peevish detail, and by a natural train of sentiment associate their own conviction of ill-luck, incapacity, and failure, with the most responsible member of their confederation.

[1] Morley: *Gladstone*, III, 5.

It was hardly reasonable for the Conservatives to cast the odium for their misfortunes upon the able, genial, and patient Northcote, but Beaconsfield was beyond criticism on his pedestal—and would soon be translated to an even more exalted pedestal to which no criticism may be usefully directed—and the Conservatives were not in a very reasonable mood.

Northcote was competent and likeable, an experienced Minister and an adept Parliamentarian. But Rosebery subsequently put his finger upon his deficiencies as a party leader.

> Where he failed was in manner. His voice, his diction, his delivery, were all inadequate. With real ability, great knowledge, genial kindness, and a sympathetic nature—all the qualities, indeed, which evoke regard and esteem—he had not the spice of devil which is necessary to rouse an Opposition to zeal and elation. . . . When Northcote warmed there was, or seemed to be, a note of apology in his voice; there was also what is known as the academic twang, an inflection which cannot be defined, but which is not agreeable to the House of Commons.[1]

By this stage the bulk of the Conservative Party regarded Gladstone with emotions of fear and detestation which, had they but known it, were passionately shared by the Queen. He was, for one thing, a renegade, one of theirs, who had joined the enemy camp. Their assumption of his motives for this was not charitable, and they recalled with nostalgia the brilliant manner in which Dizzy had held him up to public derision as an unbalanced and unscrupulous fanatic. Disraeli may have actually believed this caricature, but his followers certainly did. They had thought he was finished in 1874, and had watched with anger and mounting horror his campaign against the Bulgarian Atrocities in 1876 and his triumphant renaissance in Midlothian, where he had seemed to them to have trumpeted the cause of class war in his desperate ambition for power. This was how they saw him, and why they hated him. The Conservatives may have been as bereft of policies as the Liberals, but at least they knew what they were *against*.

But they were also afraid of Gladstone. He had been in the House of Commons for nearly half a century and no one—not even Dizzy in his prime—had managed to crush him. He had had set-backs in debate, but they had been followed by devastating counter-attacks and

[1] Rosebery: *Lord Randolph Churchill,* 169.

he was, indeed, 'terrible on the rebound'. To an apprehension that was generally shared by his followers, Northcote added the fatal ingredient of respect. He had served as Gladstone's private secretary many years before and, like so many who had seen him at close quarters, had been impressed. It was Northcote who called Gladstone 'that Grand Old Man'; the phrase stuck, but it was not the kind of enconium that the Conservatives expected from their leader. Thus, when the Tories wanted Gladstone flayed, Northcote was courteously critical. When Gladstone slipped, and the Tories howled for the kill, Northcote issued critical admonitions to which Gladstone had no difficulty in responding with interest. Northcote was in poor health, but in any event he did not possess the qualities of fire and fury which the Opposition craved. The field was open for a challenger, and it was to come from a very unlikely quarter.

Ministers were quickly faced with an extraordinary and unforeseeable test. On May 3rd Charles Bradlaugh, newly elected as one of the two Liberal Members for Northampton, presented himself at the Table of the House and claimed to affirm rather than take the Oath of Allegiance. Bradlaugh was a well-known and courageous advocate of free-thinking, and his lusty denunciations of the Christian religion— 'the blasphemy against humanity, the mockery of humanity [which] has crushed our efforts, has ruined our lives, has poisoned our hearts, and has cursed our hopes'—had made his meetings the scenes of many violent confrontations. He also had advanced views on population control which were generally excoriated as outrageous, and when his reckless fire also fell upon the Monarchy he had succeeded in enraging a very formidable cross-section of public feeling.

The Speaker, confronted by the burly and intransigent figure of Mr. Bradlaugh demanding to affirm the Oath, decided to leave the issue to the House. Affirmation had been permitted in the Courts for a decade, and in Parliament for longer in the cases of 'Quakers, Moravians, and Separatists'. While Bradlaugh clearly did not fit into any of these categories, the principle of the right to affirm had been established, and Speaker Brand should have so ruled. But he did not, and much flowed from that failure.[1] The Government moved for a Select Committee which, by a majority of one, decided that Bradlaugh had to take the Oath. Bradlaugh defiantly announced that he would not, and would take his seat nonetheless.

[1] For an excellent account, see W. L. Arnstein: *The Bradlaugh Case*.

Meanwhile, the fires had begun to glow. Sir Henry Drummond Wolff, one of the Conservative Members for Portsmouth, had seen the opportunity of gravely embarrassing Ministers, and saw also that Bradlaugh's defiance of the Select Committee had aroused strong feelings in the House. On May 21st, when Bradlaugh reappeared, Wolff objected, and an extremely heated debate ensued. On May 24th, when it was resumed, Lord Randolph Churchill, the obscure, slight, and unprepossessing Member for Woodstock, denounced Bradlaugh's atheism and disloyalty, quoted from some of his more inflammatory writings, and—most interestingly of all—concluded with a direct appeal to Gladstone not to lead the Liberal Party through the lobbies 'for the purpose of placing on the benches opposite an avowed atheist and a professedly disloyal person'.

Although Gladstone doggedly maintained his position that the House could not deny a Member his right to take his seat, he was not carrying his supporters with him. Churchill had touched a very responsive chord in the Liberals. Another committee was established 'to search for precedents' and found none. The Government proposed that Bradlaugh be permitted to affirm and the matter be referred to the Courts, but the motion was defeated by 275 votes to 230. When Bradlaugh defiantly reappeared, he was committed to the Clock Tower, was unseated, was triumphantly re-elected, and the storms arose again. These scenes were to be repeated throughout this Parliament. There was something in the spectacle of Bradlaugh that aroused an atavistic reaction from the majority in the House of Commons, and the eloquence of Gladstone and the justice of his cause could not control these passions. It was a lamentable business in itself, but it was also a highly disturbing opening for a new Administration, and a swift check to the eager expectations of the great election victory.

But there were other consequences. Shortly after his speech, Lord Randolph joined Wolff and John Gorst on the front bench below the gangway, and the trio at once demonstrated a skill and independence which caught the attention of the House. Wolff and Gorst were experienced politicians, but Lord Randolph's quickness and self-confidence were a revelation. He was small in stature, slender in build, with a large moustache and rather popping eyes. He spoke with a lisp, and had difficulty in pronouncing the letter 's'. It was indeed difficult to see in this curious young aristocrat the man of whom Max Beerbohm was to write that he was, 'despite his halting speech, foppish mien, and rather coarse fibre of mind . . . the greatest Parlia-mentarian of his day'. Before 1880 he had made only one speech of any note in the previous Parliament—characteristically, it had been a memorable attack on his own Government—and although the details of his involvement in a somewhat discreditable episode involving his brother and the Prince of Wales in 1876 were known only to a few[1], the resulting ostracism of Lord Randolph and his young American wife from London society was common knowledge. He had gone with his father, the Duke of Marlborough—who had been persuaded by Beaconsfield to accept the Irish Viceroyalty in these highly embarrass-ing circumstances—to Dublin, and had been seen seldom at West-minster until the Bradlaugh affair.

But after that he was quickly noticed. 'He has certainly a pretty turn for sarcasm', the shrewd Parliamentary observer H. W. Lucy wrote in June, 'an honest contempt for bumptuous incapacity, and courage amounting to recklessness, which combine to make him equally dangerous, whether as friend or foe.' The three were joined by Arthur Balfour, whose approach to public affairs had been notably relaxed, and whose involvement in this iconoclastic group was as great a surprise as the discovery of Lord Randolph's unexpected skills as a Parliamentarian. Balfour was never, in reality, a total member of what was dubbed 'the Fourth Party' (the Irish being the Third), and which proudly proclaimed itself as such. But for the others there was considerable value in having the nephew of Lord Salisbury in the group, and Balfour himself certainly found it a useful and rewarding introduction to serious politics.

The Fourth Party, created out of the chaos of the Bradlaugh Case, was from the outset a much more serious phenomenon than many realised at the time. Those who regarded it as something on the lines of an undergraduate caper—despite the fact that both Wolff and Gorst were nearer fifty than forty—soon changed their opinion. The Opposition Front Bench became quickly embarrassed and humiliated, Gladstone took the Fourth Party seriously from the beginning, and Beaconsfield was so intrigued that he paid one of his rare visits to the Commons to see the 'Party' in action. They were often irresponsible, enjoyed their sudden fame and worked to maintain it, and had learned much about obstructive tactics from the Irish. But they had a serious core, and developed a serious purpose. Churchill's powers developed

[1] See Philip Magnus: *King Edward VII* for the most complete account.

so rapidly that within three months Northcote asked for a truce and the dissolution of the group, but Beaconsfield, while advising them to 'stick with Northcote, he represents the respectability of the party', went on to remark that 'I wholly sympathise with you, because I never was respectable myself'. Within a remarkably short time the Fourth Party had undermined the authority of Northcote, and Lord Randolph's high ambitions had been born.

*

The bitter consequences of the combination of the agricultural depression, bad harvests, and the neglect of the Conservative Government, now fell terribly upon Ireland. A pall hung over the country, reminiscent of that of the 1840s. 'I saw that for Irishmen to succeed', Davitt later wrote, 'they must be united and that they must have a practical issue to put before Englishmen and the world at large. . . . I made up my mind that the only issue upon which Home Rulers, Nationalists, Obstructionists and each and every shade of opinion existing in Ireland could be united, was the land question.' The vital element in the agrarian discontent which mounted during the summer of 1880 and exploded in the winter of 1880–1 lay in the agrarian poverty and subsequent evictions of defaulting tenants. The Liberals had no Irish policy at all and, indeed, little understanding of the ferocity of the storm which was descending upon them. There had been no reference to Ireland in the Queen's Speech, and it was rapidly evident that the Chief Secretary, Forster, was quite inadequate to the challenge. He took up a measure proposed by an Irish member to compensate those 'disturbed', but, after a stormy passage through the Commons in which the opposition was principally led by Lord Randolph, it was summarily rejected by the Lords. The action of the Lords was deplorable, but Ministers failed to discern its importance until too late. When Parnell asked Forster whether 'he proposes to employ the constabulary and military forces of the Queen for the purpose of assisting at the eviction of tenants who can be proved to be unable to pay their rents,' the Chief Secretary replied that 'we shall protect the officers of the courts of law in the execution of the law'.[1] The evictions mounted; so did the violence of the reaction in Ireland. Forster turned to buckshot; the Irish to more deadly methods.

The first tactic was one of non-co-operation with the landlords.

[1] Conor Cruise O'Brien: *Parnell And His Party*, 51.

Davitt declared in July that 'Today, from east to west, from north to south, not a man can be found who would dare to take the farm of an evicted tenant. If one should be found so recklessly indifferent, it would be simply impossible for him to live in that locality. The people would not buy from him; they would not sell to him; in chapel on Sunday he would have to sit apart by himself.' Parnell endorsed this tactic. Speaking at Ennis, in County Clare, on September 19th, he said:

> When a man takes a farm from which another has been evicted, you must show him on the roadside when you meet him [A Voice: 'Shun him'] in the streets of the town, at the shop counter, in the fair, in the market place, and even in the house of worship, by leaving him severely alone, by putting him into a moral Coventry, by isolating him from his kind as if he were a leper of old; you must show him your detestation of the crime he has committed.

The first, and most dramatic, victim was Captain Boycott. Boycott was an Englishman who leased a thousand acre farm from Lord Erne, and also acted as agent for Lord Erne's Mayo estates. His task was to collect the sum of £430 per annum from thirty-eight tenants, which, as has been written, 'brought Boycott much trouble and about £50 a year'.[1] In County Mayo, the birthplace of Davitt and the Land League, this difficulty was now greatly augmented. First, Boycott's own workers went on strike for higher wages, which Boycott had to concede. Then the tenants demanded a rent reduction of five shillings; Lord Erne offered a two shilling reduction, accompanied by a stern warning as to the consequences of defaulting. The tenants refused to pay, and the process-server had to be protected by the police. Boycott's workers were persuaded to leave him; Lord Erne's seat, Lough Mask House, had to be protected by armed policeman; and on September 25th, on the far side of Lough Mask, Lord Mountmorres was murdered. Boycott and his wife were beleagured, shunned by all. Eventually, after publicity to their plight had been given by the English press, they were rescued by a group of men from Ulster, protected by troops.

The Boycotts were unharmed, but the success of the 'boycotting' spread throughout the country while the asassination of Lord

[1] See T. H. Corfe: 'The Troubles of Captain Boycott', *History Today*, November and December 1964, and Joyce Marlow, *Capiain Boycott*.

Mountmorres had brought dread to all landowners. Boycott had indeed been put 'into a moral Coventry, by isolating him from his kind as if he were a leper of old'. While the League was making the strategy, Parnell was retaining his leadership of the general movement—a very difficult exercise in the ferment of the winter of 1879–80, but made immeasurably easier when he was specifically denounced by Ministers for the mounting chaos in Ireland. 'The landlords fear to evict', as Forster reported to Gladstone. 'Parnell is quite right . . . in saying that the League has stopped evictions, though he ought to have said "the League and its attendant outrages".'

But the evictions did continue, and the violence of the response continued. In the last three months of 1880 the situation reached crisis proportions. The desperate Forster appealed for more troops, more armed police, more buckshot, and the arraignment of the Irish leaders. Parnell and thirteen other members of the League were prosecuted—fruitlessly—for conspiracy, and the Viceroy (Lord Cowper) pressed urgently for the suspension of habeas corpus. With deep reluctance and dismay, the Government turned to coercion. The situation was grimly reminiscent of the 1840s, when Macaulay had asked of Ireland: 'How do you govern it? Not by love but by fear . . . not by the confidence of the people in the laws and their attachment to the Constitution but by the means of armed men and entrenched camps.' The thoughts of the Cabinet had indeed, in Morley's words, been 'violently drawn from Dulcigno and Thessaly, from Batoum and Erzeroum, from the wild squalor of Macedonia and Armenia to squalor not less wild in Connaught and Munster, in Mayo, Galway, Sligo and Kerry.'

At this point it was violently drawn to another inheritance from the Beaconsfield Government.

*

Gladstone, inveighing against the pursuit of 'false phantoms of glory' at Midlothian, and pleading the cause of 'the rights of the savage, as we call him', had also pledged himself to the restoration of the Transvaal to the Boers. The pledge had not been honoured.

The end of the Zulu war had changed the position of the Boers, but the movement for independence and the restoration of the Afrikaans language were signs that few outside heeded. Frere was not immediately recalled. He stood out for a federal solution, but it was only after negotiations with the Boers had failed in June 1880 that he belatedly returned to England. The event was not followed by the repeal of annexation nor even by an offer of self-government under the Crown, which Frere had unavailingly urged on Ministers.

The Government, acutely harassed by Bradlaugh, Ireland, and other unexpected distractions, received reassuring reports from the men on the spot. As late as mid-November the senior British official in Pretoria was confident, and the new Governor of Natal, Sir George Colley, recommended a reduction in the garrisons in the Transvaal. The patience of the Boers, however, had ended. On December 20th they rose, and the four small British detachments were quickly surrounded. Colley called upon the Boers to disperse, and to give urgency to his demand advanced at once to the border with 1,500 men. On January 29th he was, amazingly, beaten back at Laing's Nek. The Cabinet, now dimly aware that things seemed to have changed since 1877, welcomed an invitation from President Kruger to give facilities for a Royal Commission if the British forces withdrew. But Colley was determined to advance, and on February 26th marched to Majuba Hill with 359 men. By the 27th he and ninety of his men were dead, and sixty taken prisoner.

In Britain, national pride was deeply hurt. A British force destroyed by a collection of farmers! But although Gladstone had impetuously declared that an immediate grant of self-government to the Transvaal was out of the question on January 6th, he now chose to negotiate. Indeed, short of entering into a major war in South Africa, he had little choice. But the result was a compromise which dissatisfied all sides. The Pretoria Convention of August 1881 defined the boundaries of the State, gave it 'complete self-government, subject to the suzerainty of Her Majesty', prohibited slavery, and saddled the state with most of the debt accumulated since annexation. It was with great difficulty that Kruger was able to persuade the revived Volksraad to accept the settlement, and then only on the understanding that it was only 'for the time being and provisionally'.

In South Africa and in Britain Gladstone was violently attacked for the settlement, and cries of 'Majuba Hill!' joined the Conservatives' list of charges against him. The death of Beaconsfield early in 1881 had given them good opportunity of comparing his robust and patriotic policies with the pusillanimity of his successor. Majuba Hill gave added material. The 'Imperial' debate in domestic politics, which had swung so heavily against the Conservatives at the end of the 1870s, now began to show signs of moving in their favour.

The real lesson, however, had not been discerned in London by either party. It had been well put by a distinguished historian of South Africa:

> The prestige of the Imperial Government .. was far gone in the eyes of white and black alike. The long-enduring and sorely strained reputation of the handful of redcoats in which Governors had been wont to put their trust had been blown to the winds, Any future intervention in the affairs of Boers, who were satisfied that British soldiers could always be beaten, would have to be in force.[1]

Thus, a handful of Boers had played their part, at present un-recognised, in the overseas British Revolution. But, meanwhile, Ministers were oppressed by revolution, real and immediate, much closer to home.

*

It was characteristic of Gladstone to look beyond the limitations of coercion to the true causes of the Irish crisis, and of which the dominant one concerned the land. Meanwhile, however, the need to restore law and order was urged as paramount by Cowper and Forster, and the Protection of Person and Property (Ireland) Bill passed through the Commons amid scenes of wild disorder and suspensions of Irish Members which led to the introduction of the closure. On February 2nd Speaker Brand ended an historic continuous sitting of forty-one hours by dramatically taking the Chair and putting the Question on his own responsibility on the grounds that 'a crisis has arisen which demands the prompt intervention of the Chair'. On the following day the arrest of Davitt was announced, and in the resultant uproar thirty-six Irish Members were suspended. Many Irish believed that this would lead to the immediate withdrawal of the Home Rulers from Parliament, but Parnell, despite some past cryptic utterances on the possibility, continued the fight in London. Viewed in retrospect, this would have been the ideal moment for secession, but Parnell's developing conception of the most effective course of action involved fighting on several fronts, and Parliament was to remain the principal one.

[1] E. A. Walker: *A History of South Africa*, 393.

On April 7th Gladstone introduced his Land Bill, which provided for the provision of fair rents, fixity of tenure, and the right of the tenant to the free sale of his interest in his holding. It was a notable advance, but it was introduced in the context of coercion and appeared to be another concession to violence. In a sense it was, but it was in reality a response to the success of the Land League, and posed a considerable threat to it. In this difficult situation Parnell did not impede the passage of the Bill, but in Ireland deliberately attacked it. His new organ, *United Ireland*, was particularly virulent, and Gladstone, convinced that Parnell was out to wreck the Act, declared at Leeds on October 7th that 'the resources of civilisation are not yet exhausted'. Parnell retorted by a denunciation of the Prime Minister which categorised him as a man 'prepared to carry fire and sword into your homesteads unless you humbly abase yourselves before him and before the landlords of your country'. On October 12th the Cabinet agreed to Parnell's arrest, and he was seized the next day in Dublin and sent to Kilmainham Jail, Gladstone declaring (Liverpool, October 26th) that Parnell's resolve was to march 'through rapine to the dismemberment of the Empire'. Parnell, when asked what would happen if he were arrested, had replied that 'Captain Moonlight will take my place'. This turned out to be only partly true. The Land League was suppressed. A 'no rent' manifesto was issued by the League's leaders—of whom virtually all were in prison—but although agitation was renewed, it was not on the scale of the previous winter.

Parnell's imprisonment had several advantages for him. It gave him comfortable martyrdom, and removed him from politics at a very difficult moment, when the Land Act was beginning to be effective and the League was beginning to fade. But there were serious disadvantages for the New Departure in having its leaders in jail, and there was accordingly, a real possibility that the painful and difficult fusion of all the elements in the movement would collapse without the unifying personality of Parnell, whose personal prestige and influence were bound to diminish if he were incarcerated for too long. The 'no rent' manifesto, as Parnell had expected, was unsuccessful, and the violence in Ireland demonstrated that his movement was endangered by elements more extreme than the League. This point was not lost on Ministers. Complex negotiations were opened in December 1881 which led to the release of Parnell and his colleagues in May 1882. The Government pledged itself to deal with the question of rent arrears, while Parnell would use his influence against violence. Parnell also accepted that his proposed amendments to the Land Act—to which Ministers agreed—would be considered 'a practical settlement of the land question and would enable us to co-operate cordially for the future with the Liberal party in forwarding liberal principles and measures of general reform'. At the core of the so-called 'Kilmainham Treaty' was the understanding between the parties that while the struggle for Home Rule would be continued, all efforts would be made to curtail the land war and revolutionary activities by the Irish leader if the Government made significant concessions on land legislation.

The Kilmainham Treaty was negotiated principally by Chamberlain on Gladstone's behalf, and also involved Captain W. H. O'Shea, Member of Parliament for County Clare, and his wife.

O'Shea's previous career had been undistinguished. He had been born in Dublin in 1840, and had entered the Army. In 1868 he had married Katherine, the youngest child of Sir John Page Wood; one of her brothers was to become Field Marshal Sir Evelyn Wood, V.C. O'Shea left the Army, and attempted a number of unsuccessful business enterprises; the growing family was in fact maintained by Mrs. O'Shea's aunt, Mrs. Benjamin Wood, who bought for her a house near Eltham, in Kent. It would appear from all accounts that the marriage was not a happy one, although not noticeably strained. O'Shea had been elected for Clare in the 1880 election; in the summer of the same year Mrs. O'Shea had met Parnell, and what was to become one of the most famous and tragic of modern love-affairs had begun.

Although much has been written of the O'Shea–Mrs. O'Shea–Parnell triangle, there remains a great deal of acutely conflicting testimony and evidence, particularly about the extent to which O'Shea was or was not a *mari complaisant*, and, if so, from what time. The judgement of this commentator is that to accept that O'Shea was wholly ignorant of the fact that Parnell was his wife's lover for ten years, in the course of which she gave birth to three children, applies to him depths of stupidity—or to his wife a degree of ruthless and cynical cunning—which are both so improbable as to be unacceptable. To this commentator it is highly significant that at the time of the Kilmainham negotiations the liaison was known to members of the Government, including Gladstone, Chamberlain, Harcourt, Granville and Dilke, which made O'Shea an important channel for negotiation provided that the fact that he was an intermediary was kept secret.

There is no indication from the available material of the sources of the information given to the leading Ministers. When Gladstone received a letter from Mrs. O'Shea in May 1882 he consulted Granville, who noted in reply that 'She is said to be his mistress.' Perhaps of greater significance was the definite comment of Harcourt, the Home Secretary, to the same effect. Parnell's movements had been followed for some time, and it seems very improbable that his letters to Mrs. O'Shea from Kilmainham had not been opened and read.

But although the political world was a small one in 1880, and gossip was an engrossing part of it, it seems hardly credible that the Government would have entrusted so important a negotiation to an obscure and recently elected Irish Nationalist M.P. and determined to keep the fact secret unless they had had good reason to regard him as being in a very special position. Not all historical material is appended to paper. And this leads inevitably to the strong conjecture that it was O'Shea himself who had told them and persuaded them. This would certainly fit in with what we know about O'Shea's high political ambitions and character. His wife was about to give birth to a child (who died shortly afterwards) which he must have known was not his but Parnell's. He was accordingly in an admirable position not only to act as a go-between but to be of value to both sides, for which he fully expected to be rewarded in due course. This is deduction, but, in the judgement of this commentator, a reasonable one.

The announcement of the 'Kilmainham Treaty' provoked severe shocks both in Ireland and in England. Cowper and Forster resigned immediately, and Balfour gave the first indication of his powers with an attack on Gladstone in the Commons in which he described the arrangement as 'standing alone in its infamy'. But it was swiftly overtaken by a more dramatic event.

On May 4th Parnell was released. On May 6th the new Chief Secretary, Lord Frederick Cavendish—Hartington's brother—was assassinated by a group called The Invincibles in Phoenix Park, Dublin, while walking with the Permanent Under-Secretary, W. H. Burke, on the day of the arrival of the new Viceroy, Lord Spencer. The occasion and the manner of the murders—the men were stabbed with long surgical knives and then their throats cut—outraged British and moderate Irish opinion. This was Captain Moonlight in the broad day. Parnell was justifiably shaken, seeing the assassinations as a blow against his authority, and at once issued a strong condemnation.

In fact, the murders strengthened Parnell's position in Ireland. There is in the Irish character an element which has baffled the English down the centuries, and which is impossible to describe precisely. The English see it as a bewildering rapidity from gentleness to cruelty and back to gentleness again, almost in a twinkling. The English, slower to anger and much more cruel when angry, regard themselves—wrongly—as predictable, and the Irish as totally unpredictable. The fact is that both races are chronically unpredictable to each other. Thus, the violence of English reaction to the Phoenix Park Murders, and the fact that so much of it was directed at Parnell personally, caused a counter-reaction in Ireland which swept away the doubts and dismay which the Kilmainham Treaty had created. The murders convinced many Englishmen—not excluding many Liberals—that the Irish were brutal savages. *This* reaction confirmed Irishmen in their opinion of the English. The murders achieved nothing for the extremists—Parnell's condemnation was not challenged in Ireland—but the English reaction strengthened Parnell's position at a time when it could have been in great danger. As Conor Cruise O'Brien has rightly emphasised, 'What injured an Irish politician's reputation in England was likely to help it in Ireland and vice versa.'[1]

But in England this cast an even uglier light upon the Kilmainham Treaty. Forster compelled Gladstone to reveal parts of the arrangement with Parnell for co-operation with the Liberals in a memorable and highly charged exchange in the House of Commons. The Conservatives stormed and the Liberals, utterly baffled by the wildly varying fluctuations of their leaders' Irish policies, were angry and mutinous. To appease them, a new and stiffer Crimes Bill was hurriedly introduced and violently opposed by the Nationalists; the Arrears Bill turned out not to be generous enough, and the wave of crime in Ireland continued. In August an entire family at Maamtrasna— father, mother, three sons, and a daughter—were brutally murdered in their beds, only one little boy surviving. The evil effects of this terrible episode were long-enduring. The cause of those accused of the crime were championed not only by the Irish Nationalists but by Lord Randolph Churchill, to no avail.

But, although few could perceive it at the time, a crucial stage in the Irish crisis had passed. The combination of better harvests, the provisions of the Land Act, and sheer weariness in Ireland at the

[1] O'Brien, op. cit., 82.

passion and cruelty of 1880–2, had made the successful suppression of the Land League possible. The extremists had harmed themselves with their excesses, but the crucial factor was that Parnell offered results through constitutional methods while having proved his independence and courage. This, clearly, was no Isaac Butt. The Irish National League, founded at the end of 1882, was a constitutional body dedicated to the establishment of Irish self-government through legal methods, and dominated by Parnell. The Catholic Church, whose position in the tumults had been definitely ambivalent, was sympathetic and interested. For an institution dedicated to the *status quo*, the Church in Ireland had been torn between that fundamental philosophy and the passionate nationalism of so many of its priests and the majority of its flock. It had executed as difficult and precarious a survival as Parnell had himself, and was thankful to support a movement whose implications were revolutionary but whose methods were not.

Although violence continued, in England as well as in Ireland, it faded sharply after 1882. Sheer exhaustion had played its part, but by no means the only part. Parnell had proved to the Irish that the constitutional approach, when fully backed in Ireland, could produce results. It had produced the Land Act, the Arrears Act—unsatisfactory though it may have been—and had utterly transformed the relationships between tenants and landlords, far beyond anything known in England, a fact which had occasioned the indignant resignation of the Duke of Argyll and the vehement attacks of Salisbury. 'Boycotting' had been more effective than murder, solidarity more effective than the houghing of cattle or burning of ricks. More had been achieved in two years by Parnell's methods than had been achieved in living memory. Bombs continued to go off in the Tower of London and in the House of Commons itself, and the Irish countryside remained dangerous. But these were increasingly regarded as the work of fanatics, and unworthy of a great cause. It was an astonishing transformation of mood, and was to survive longer than even Parnell could have envisaged.

Meanwhile, the Liberals were confronted by the angry Conservative drum-beat of Majuba, Kilmainham, and Maamtrasna. All they could offer in response to the mounting clamours of their opponents was a startling exercise in gun-boat imperialism.

*

British involvement in Egypt had inexorably increased since Disraeli's celebrated coup of 1875. From the purchase of the Canal shares Gladstone had said that this event—condemned as another of Beaconsfield's 'cruel and ruinous misdeeds'—could only result in political and even military involvement in the affairs of Egypt, and he had been right. European interest in Egypt now greatly increased, and the Khedive Ismail accelerated the process by his irresponsibility and profligate expenditure, which had so alarmed the French and the British that in 1878 the latter had sent two representatives to serve on an international commission initiated by the French. One was a Royal Artillery Major, aged 37—Evelyn Baring. A British and a French representative now served in the Khedive's Cabinet, but quickly concluded that the Khedive was incorrigible, and in 1879 the Sultan was induced by Anglo-French pressure to depose Ismail in favour of his son, Tewfik, who proved considerably more malleable. This was as far as the Beaconsfield Government was prepared to go, and Baring's appeals for a more active intervention were unheeded. The British policy followed the maxim of Palmerston that 'we want to trade with Egypt, and to travel through Egypt, but we do not want the burden of governing Egypt'. The British and French financial ministers were converted into permanent advisers, who could not be dismissed without the consent of the respective governments. But the Anglo-French collaboration was already becoming brittle. The Canal was assuming increasing importance to the British, who owned some eighty per cent of the shipping that passed through it, and their realisation of its strategic significance was becoming much stronger. Before the Gladstone Government took office, the 'Dual Control' was demonstrating signs of severe strain, which the French occupation of Tunis early in 1881 did nothing to reduce.

In 1881 a nationalist revolt broke out in Egypt, led by a Colonel Ahmad Arabi, and was successful and popular enough to impose terms upon the Khedive in September which included the dismissal of all ministers, the granting of a constitution, and an increase in the army. Both the British and French governments were nonplussed by this unexpected development, but the former was not anxious to intervene. The Gambetta-Ferry Government favoured intervention, but fell in January 1882. Gladstone turned to the Concert of Europe for guidance and assistance, to the exasperation of Hartington and Northbrook, and it was in its name that he subsequently professed to act.

By the late spring of 1882, in the judgement of the British and the French, the Arabi movement was getting out of control; there were serious riots in Alexandria early in June in which several Europeans were killed, and which Gladstone described as an 'international atrocity'. These were ascribed by the British—almost certainly incorrectly—to deliberate provocation by Arabi. The estimates vary greatly, from 300 killed to less than forty. At the time the higher figures were believed in England.

The Egyptians began to fortify the city against attack from the sea and to install batteries. A joint Anglo-French fleet, sent as a precaution against further outrages against Europeans, floated uneasily offshore. In January, before the fall of his Government, Gambetta had persuaded the British to concur in a Joint Note which pledged the two Governments to support the Khedive 'against the difficulties of various kinds which might interfere with the course of public affairs in Egypt' and to resolve 'to guard by their united efforts against all course of complications, internal or external, which might menace the order of things established in Egypt'. The French were now fading away, but the principle of the Joint Note still obtained strongly in London.

Ministers in London now became very belligerent. Granville was alarmed about the safety of the Canal, Hartington—who had not recovered from the shock of his brother's murder—was not enamoured of nationalist movements that employed methods of violence, and the reports from the British local officials were alarming. But the radicals were now equally aroused. Chamberlain was talking of 'the honour and interests of England' and was described by Granville as 'almost the greatest Jingo' in the Cabinet; Dilke strongly supported him, and Gladstone—who in 1877 had denounced the argument for intervention in Egypt[1]—was now convinced that Arabi was a despot and 'one of the greatest villains alive'. His first instincts had been sympathetic to Arabi—'Egypt for the Egyptians is the sentiment to which I would wish to give scope', he had written to Granville—but he had changed his views. The Khedive urged that the Anglo-French fleet should bombard Alexandria and send troops to destroy the Egyptian army. With the Prime Minister and the two most prominent radicals in this mood, the British Admiral commanding the fleet off Alexandria bombarded the

---

[1] *Nineteenth Century*, August 1877: 'Aggression on Egypt and Freedom In the East'.

city on July 11th. The French meanwhile, had withdrawn, leaving, as it transpired, Egypt to the British. On July 13th the Khedive sought British protection and denounced Arabi.

On July 22nd Gladstone informed the House of Commons that 'we should not fully discharge our duty if we did not endeavour to convert the present interior state of Egypt from anarchy and conflict to peace and order. We shall look . . . to the co-operation of the Powers of civilised Europe. . . . But if every chance of obtaining co-operation is exhausted, the work will be undertaken by the single power of England'. Arabi stated that 'irreconcilable war existed between the Egyptians and the English'. A British army under the command of Wolseley was despatched, a Vote of Credit for over £2 million was voted by the House of Commons, and only old John Bright—who wrote to Gladstone that 'I think on reviewing the doctrines connected with our foreign policy which I have preached and defended during forty years of my public life, you will not be surprised at the decision I am now compelled to take', and who told Rosebery that Gladstone's action was 'simply damnable, worse than anything ever perpetrated by Dizzy'—protested at this 'manifest violation of international and moral law' and resigned. Lord Randolph Churchill, who had sympathised from the outset with Arabi's purposes, joined Bright in his protests, but they were virtually alone. Gladstone informed the House of Commons that 'there is not the smallest rag nor shred of evidence to support [the] contention' that 'the military party was the popular party'. On August 19th Wolseley's army landed on Egyptian soil.

Wolseley's force consisted of some 30,000 men in all, and the fact that such a force had been assembled and transported at such short notice was in itself a remarkable feat. After occupying Port Said, Wolseley took the main part of his force down the Canal to Ismailia, with the purpose of advancing westwards along the Sweet Water Canal and its accompanying railway towards Cairo, so that he could place his army between Cairo and Arabi's force at Alexandria.

Arabi, who had raised a force of some 60,000 men, at once sent about 12,000 to Tel-el-Kebir, between Cairo and Ismailia, to confront the probable line of the British advance. A further 40,000 joined them at this position, which lay about thirty miles west of Ismailia, and began the construction of an ambitious trench-fortification (still visible today) running some twenty miles northward of the Sweet Water

Canal. It was built by hand in two weeks, a most remarkable and impressive feat. The trench consisted of a breastwork which was six feet high in places; although it was a relatively simple construction, with no communication trenches or traverses, it constituted a formidable military obstacle.

The British force was rather 'soft' after three weeks at sea, and the horses had been particularly affected by the voyage. The advance along the Sweet Water Canal and railway was accordingly slow and piecemeal, with a few desultory advance-guard actions. In seventeen days only twenty-five miles were covered. Three outpost positions were captured, and by September 12th Wolseley, with some 17,000 troops, sixty-one guns, and six cavalry regiments, was established around Kassassin, some eleven miles away from Arabi's trench, manned by over 20,000 men.

Wolseley conducted several personal dawn reconnaissances of the Egyptian positions. He noted that the Egyptians did not 'stand to' until 5.45 a.m., and concluded that a night flank march, with a surprise attack at first light was the most practicable method of assault. It was a courageous and almost foolhardy decision. It involved a march of over eleven miles in the dark across almost featureless terrain. In the event Wolseley's confidence in himself, his officers and his men, were fully justified. The Highland Brigade, which led the advance, was only 150 yards from its objective when it was seen by the Egyptians. The battle itself lasted for under an hour, although resistance was fierce in places. Artillery was brought up to enfilade the occupied sectors of the trench, the cavalry came in from the north to sweep the fleeing Egyptians before them, and the battle was over. The British losses were fifty-seven dead and twenty-two missing; the Egyptian casualties were terrible. It was, with the exception of Omdurman, the most devastating British military victory in the nineteenth century.

A company of the Scots Guards, with a divisional commander empowered to open negotiations, reached Cairo in the evening by train. There was no resistance of any kind. Arabi surrendered the Citadel and himself on 14th September; a few days later the Khedive was re-throned. After a great triumphal parade through the capital, Wolseley and his three divisional commanders embarked for England. The campaign had lasted for forty-seven days; it had cost under 450 British casualties. Gladstone ordered victory salutes of guns in Hyde Park and elsewhere to announce the victory of Tel-el-Kebir. The

1 Benjamin Disraeli 1869: by 'Ape', *Vanity Fair*

2 Lord Salisbury 1869: by 'Ape', *Vanity Fair*

3 Charles Stewart Parnell, 1880: by 'T', *Vanity Fair*

4 Lord Randolph Churchill and the Fourth Party, 1880
(John Gorst, Arthur Balfour, Sir Henry Drummond Wolff):
by 'Spy', *Vanity Fair*

British commanders returned to receive heroes' welcomes. The popularity of the Government soared. It was all very odd.

The aftermath was even odder. There was to be no question of annexation, a step which Gladstone described as 'at variance with all the principles and views of the British Government'. Ministers declared that the British occupation was temporary and that no commitments of a long-term nature had been incurred. These repeated assurances were quite genuine but quite unrealistic. Lord Dufferin was sent to examine the situation, and rapidly concluded that it would greatly benefit from major reforms under the supervision of British advisers. He emphasised that the country should not become a 'concealed protectorate', but the clear implication of his advice was that the condition of Egypt was still perilous, and that the same considerations that had inspired intervention still applied to remaining there. Ministers were extremely reluctant to face this fact. A reaction to the military invasion had set in afterwards in radical circles. Lord Randolph Churchill, ever unexpected, and influenced by Wilfred Scawen Blunt, denounced the campaign as 'a bondholders' war' and spoke disparagingly of 'tawdry military glories'. He fought vigorously for the captured Egyptian officers, contributed to the costs of Arabi's defence, and described his revolution as 'the movement of a nation'. The Tories were disconcerted, but, as Lord Randolph's son has remarked, 'They loved their country much; but they hated Gladstone more.'[1] But the Liberal Party was uneasy, and with good cause. When Churchill demanded an enquiry into the circumstances of the Alexandria riots, Ministers temporised. When one of Arabi's officers was sentenced to death after a farce of a trial the Government agreed to make enquiries; while thus engaged, the officer was hanged. The Opposition launched a fierce attack on Ministers; there was much troublement on the countenance of their supporters as they marched through the Lobbies to support them. Baring had returned to Egypt, and was to remain there, using as his mandate the declaration of Dufferin that 'it is absolutely necessary to prevent the fabric we have raised from tumbling to the ground the moment our sustaining hand is withdrawn'. That 'sustaining hand' was to prove of long duration. What Milner was to describe as 'the Veiled Protectorate' had been created.

*

[1] W. S. Churchill: *Lord Randolph Churchill* (one-volume edition, 1951), 214.

A very real dichotomy within the Liberal ranks was now becoming evident, of which Bright's resignation had been a portent, although it did not emerge into public gaze until the formation of the Imperial Federation League in 1884, of which Rosebery and Forster were active members. Whether one liked the fact or not, the British had acquired very substantial areas abroad and the question was exactly what Howe had posed twenty years before—'What is to be done about them?' The abandonment of India was, of course, unthinkable, but the new link to India, the Suez Canal, had led to a new involvement in Egypt which could easily lead to other commitments. The 'scramble for Africa' was just beginning. What should be the British reaction? The question was complicated by domestic political factors. The Conservative Primrose League, founded in 1883, had from the outset a markedly 'Imperial' tone, and its rapid success—it achieved over a million members by the end of the decade—could not be ignored. The popular excitement at Tel-el-Kebir and the fury at Majuba Hill were also significant. The 'imperial' debate, in terms of votes, was clearly changing. The creation of a new Empire in South Africa as a result of the energies of men like Rhodes, Goldie, MacKinnon and Johnston, owed nothing to Government encouragement. 'The Cabinet do not want more niggers', as Lord Kimberley remarked after a Cabinet meeting that had decided (March 22nd, 1884) against any increase in the Zululand Protectorate. Many Ministers viewed the gradual increase of British influence in Africa with regret. As Dilke wrote in 1890 in a sequel to *Greater Britain*, 'The only excuse that one can make is that, if we had not laid hands upon their territory, France or Germany would have done so.'

But there were other Ministers who took a very different line. Chamberlain, speaking about the German occupation of North-East New Guinea, declared that 'the English democracy will stand shoulder to shoulder throughout the world to maintain the honour and the integrity of the Empire'. And Dilke's views were broadly imperialistic. 'I am as great a jingo in Central Asia as I am a scuttler in South Africa', he wrote in 1885.[1] Gladstone told Lord Frederick Cavendish in November 1881 that he had to wage an almost daily battle 'on the side of liberty as opposed to Jingoism'. The niceties of Gladstone's distinctions between his actions in Egypt and elsewhere increasingly grated on his followers. He claimed that the invasion of Egypt had been undertaken 'from a love of peace, and, I may say, on the principle of

[1] Roy Jenkins: *Sir Charles Dilke*, 179.

peace'. Yet he defended himself in the Commons from taking action in the Sudan on the grounds that it would involve 'a war of conquest against a people struggling to be free . . . and rightly struggling to be free'. On that occasion (May 13th, 1883) Forster, by now an implacable foe, remarked that the Prime Minister 'can persuade most people of most things, and above all he can persuade himself of almost anything'. There was a certain truth in this cruel jibe.

The problem of the Sudan was a case in point. Mohammed Ahmed ibn Abdullah declared himself the new messiah—the Mahdi—and had raised the standard of revolt against the brutal and incompetent Egyptian rule. It was a good moment to do it, and his movement had spread rapidly. In 1883 the British Government sanctioned an attempt by the Egyptian Government to re-conquer the Sudan. The force, some 10,000 strong, was commanded by a British officer, General Hicks. On November 5th it was annihilated by the Mahdist army. The remnants of Egyptian authority in this vast area now consisted of a handful of beleaguered garrisons. Those on the Red Sea coast presented no difficulty, but those centred on Khartoum were a different matter. The Government was overwhelmingly in favour of evacuation south of Wadi Halfa. In an evil hour Gladstone acquiesced in the decision of an extra-Cabinet committee consisting of Hartington, Granville, Northbrook and Dilke (the new President of the Local Government Board and a member of the Cabinet) to dispatch General Charles Gordon to report back on the best methods of evacuation.

Gordon had resigned as Governor-General of the Sudan in 1881, and was temporarily without employment, but his glamorous exploits in China and the Sudan attracted the attention of Granville, and the campaign for his appointment included the Liberal *Pall Mall Gazette*. It was an extraordinary choice. Salisbury declared that the Government must have taken leave of its senses. In Cairo, Baring—now recalled from India where he had been sent in 1880 and appointed British agent and consul-general—gave his assent to Gordon's mission with great reluctance. Baring was in a difficult position, as it was he who had advised the Government to send 'an English officer of high authority to Khartoum with full power to withdraw the garrison and to make the best arrangements possible for the future government of that country', but he had not envisaged Gordon. Dilke, it appears, thought that Gordon was being sent to Suakim, on the Red Sea Coast. When he heard on January 21st that Gordon was going to Khartoum he wrote to Granville that 'if he goes up towards Khartoum, and is carried off and held to ransom—we shall have to send a terrible force after him even though he should go without instructions'.[1]

Gordon has been described by a cool and by no means friendly commentator as 'perhaps the finest specimen of the heroic Victorian type—a Bible-taught Evangelical, fearless, tireless, incorruptible; following the call of duty through fields of desperate adventure'.[2] Certainly his contemporaries viewed him in this light. He had served in the Crimean War, taken part in the British capture of Peking in 1860, and had served under the Chinese government from 1863-5 in the successful suppression of the Tai-Ping rebellion, acquiring the sobriquet of 'Chinese Gordon'. He had gone to the Sudan in 1873, and had made a mighty reputation. Recalled in 1881, he had viewed subsequent developments with consternation and wrath. About some matters Gordon had fanatical ideas, notably of the spread of Christianity and good government. His individuality and energy were notorious and his judgement erratic, but his following in Britain was enormous. Even Granville thought of him as 'a genius and a splendid character'. He was seen off from Victoria Station by a concourse of notables, including the Duke of Cambridge—the Commander-in-Chief of the Army—Wolseley, and Granville.

Gladstone quickly had serious doubts about the wisdom of Gordon's mission, but it was too late. Gordon demanded, and received, the title of Governor-General of the Sudan, and arrived in Khartoum on February 18th, 1884. He proceeded to bombard Baring and Ministers with grandiose proposals, and even attempted to propose terms to the Mahdi for ending his rebellion, which were curtly rejected. But in Britain the exasperation of Ministers and officials with this impossible man was overwhelmed by popular excitement at the spectacle of an heroic figure, and as the force of the Mahdi moved closer to Khartoum public apprehension for his safety became stridently expressed. At first Gordon would not withdraw and then he could not; the clamour for a relief expedition became so intense that the fate of the Government was in peril. Eventually, and with deep reluctance, Gladstone agreed in August after Hartington had threatened to resign, but it was not until October that a force of ten thousand left Cairo to undertake the fifteen hundred mile journey up the Nile.

It reached Khartoum at the end of January 1885 to find that it had

[1] Jenkins, op-cit., 180.   [2] R. C. K. Ensor: *England, 1870-1914*, 81.

been too late and that Gordon was dead. When the news reached Britain there was a storm of anger unprecedented since the news of the Buglarian Atrocities nearly a decade earlier, another clear indication that there was a real political and popular strength in the new imperialism. The Queen telegraphed her bitter displeasure *en clair* to Gladstone, the London mob howled for several weeks, and the Government narrowly avoided defeat in the House of Commons. The virulence against Gladstone personally was greater than at any time during his long and not uncontroversial career. The Cabinet, itself deeply divided, and after surviving by only fourteen votes on a Vote of Censure seriously considered resigning, and Gladstone was compelled to state that it was Government policy to crush the Mahdi—a commitment from which he thankfully and skilfully extricated himself in April when he took a startlingly belligerent line against Russian infiltration on the Afghan frontier at the obscure village of Penjdeh. The Russians drew back, the morale of the Liberals was raised, the Conservatives were astonished, and the Sudan was abandoned to the Mahdi. But the real issue had only been postponed. Gladstone was justified in writing immediately after this remarkable episode that the record of his Government 'has been a wild romance of politics with a continual succession of hairbreadth escapes and strange accidents pressing upon one another'.

The question now was how long this performance could endure.

*

The Conservatives, in the meanwhile, had not been without their own difficulties. The death of Beaconsfield had left Northcote and Salisbury as the party leaders, but the arrangement worked neither smoothly nor effectively. Who, in fact, was the leader? Who, in the event of the creation of a Conservative Government, would receive the Queen's Commission to form an Administration? Lord Randolph Churchill, although he had pursued a highly individualistic line on Irish questions and on Egypt—for which he had earned the respect and affection of the Irish—had emerged as a very definite contender for the leadership. His audaciously irreverent assaults on Gladstone ('the Moloch of Midlothian') and Chamberlain ('this Pinchbeck Robespierre') exhilarated large audiences in the country, drawn to his meetings by the rapidly spreading word of his Parliamentary stardom. In October 1882 an article signed 'Two Conservatives' appeared in the *Fortnightly Review* which was a detailed and unsparing attack upon the party leadership and the aloofness of its ruling circle and which was clearly the work of Gorst and Churchill. Shortly afterwards, in the House, Churchill was demanding: 'Is the attitude of the great Tory Democracy, which Lord Beaconsfield's party constructed, to be one of mere clogged opposition? And is it true, what our foes say of us, that Coercion in Ireland and foreign war is to be the "be-all and end-all" of Tory Ministers?'

Churchill's developing theme of 'Tory Democracy' was an early example of his particular genius for arresting and dramatic phrases. Although much derided at the time, it subsequently caught on, as did the even vaguer doctrine of 'Fair Trade', which provoked Chamberlain to a series of speeches in defence of Free Trade which sowed the first seeds of doubt in his mind about the sanctity of *laissez-faire*. Churchill did not push this particular heresy very far, and it faded from his speeches after January 1884, but it was characteristic of his originality that he was prepared to ask some highly uncomfortable questions about this particular shibboleth.

Churchill's great attraction to Conservatives was that he was always on the attack and afraid of no one, least of all Gladstone. 'I see no good object to be gained', he informed a deputation of Manchester Conservatives who were earnestly urging him to contest one of the constituencies in that city in December 1882, 'by concealing my opinion that the constitutional function of an Opposition is to oppose and not support the Government, and that this function during the three sessions of this Parliament has been either systematically neglected or defectively carried out'. T. P. O'Connor wrote shortly afterwards, with truth, that 'everybody now recognises that all the spirit and go which exist in the Conservative Party have been infused into it by this dashing, irrepressible, and, at first sight, frivolous youth. He has lived down the ridicule which used to be cast upon him by his friends as well as his foes, and at thirty-four he stands out as perhaps the one man of unblemished promise in his party.' Everybody, it may be added, except the Conservative hierarchy.

In his exuberance at the realisation of his developing powers, Churchill trampled recklessly on the sensitivities of older and less sparkling intellects. He mocked not only Northcote—labelled 'The Goat'—but his more earnest colleagues. He was not wise to describe W. H. Smith and Sir Richard Cross as 'Marshall and Snelgrove', nor to poke fun at 'the lords of suburban villas, of the owners of vineries and pineries'. He derided 'old men crooning over the fire at the Carlton Club', jeered at the 'old gang', and was imperious in his relations with those he did not respect. He held them up to ridicule in the House of Commons, at public meetings or cheerful dinner-parties, and he snubbed them in the Lobbies. As he advanced, an ever-increasing army of offended politicians viewed him with mounting uneasiness and personal resentments.

Although Churchill's rapid rise was viewed with dismay by the Opposition Front Bench and those 'respectable' elements in the Party about which Beaconsfield had warned him, Salisbury, from afar, had more mixed emotions. The relentless destruction of Northcote was certainly not opposed to his own ambitions, but the emergence of so formidable a challenger certainly was. Furthermore, Churchill's demagogery and the whole business of 'Tory Democracy' were un-congenial to him. Churchill, in two fiery letters to *The Times* and an article entitled 'Elijah's Mantle' in May 1883 clearly expressed his preference for Salisbury, but a reference to 'a statesman who fears not to meet and who knows how to sway immense masses of the working classes and who either by his genius or his eloquence, or by all the varied influences of an ancient name, can "move the hearts of house-holds" ' was regarded less as a tribute to Salisbury—who, despite an ancient name, was not known for his enthusiasm to meet immense masses of the working classes—than a blatant attempt to put Churchill's name in the list of contenders for Beaconsfield's mantle. The estab-lishment by Churchill and Wolff of the Primrose League later in the year, which had immediate success, and which Northcote and Salisbury joined with considerable reluctance, made the point clearer.

Salisbury was fifty-three years of age in 1883. Born in Hatfield House, he had endured a largely unhappy and unsuccessful childhood, dogged by poor health. After a visit to South Africa and Australia, he had become Conservative M.P. for the pocket borough of Stamford in 1853. Throughout his entire period of fifteen years in the House of Commons, he never fought a contested election, and after he succeeded as Marquess of Salisbury in 1868 he never visited the Commons again, and never gave evidence of any regrets for being removed from its atmosphere.

First as Lord Robert Cecil, and then, after the death of his elder

brother in 1865, as Lord Cranborne, Salisbury had established himself
as a serious Conservative journalist, writing principally in the
Quarterly Review and *Saturday Review* for money as much as for recognition. He married, very happily, Miss Georgina Alderson in 1857
in the teeth of his father's objections, and gradually was less tormented
by the periods of acute depression, accompanied by severe physical
lassitude, which had been a marked characteristic. But he had been an
obscure and solitary back-bencher, aloof, shy, and invariably shabbily
dressed. He despised what he described as 'the world of conclaves and
conspiracies, of pulse-feeling and thumb-screwing, of slippery intrigues
and abortive stratagems', and wrote of Disraeli that 'he is bewitched
by the demon of low dodging'.

Salisbury was a genuine intellectual, a Fellow of All Souls and of the
Royal Society in his own right, deeply religious, suspicious of rhetoric
and novelty, yet himself eloquent and pragmatic. Appointed Secretary
of State for India in 1866, he resigned when it was evident that
Disraeli's Reform proposals included household suffrage and redistribution. He refused to join Disraeli's government in January 1868
after denouncing the Reform Act with a vehemence that had personal
as well as public motivations. Of Disraeli he wrote that 'he is an
adventurer, and, as I have good cause to know, he is without principles
or honesty'. His return to the India Office in 1874 had, accordingly,
been very reluctant.

The key to Salisbury's increasing hold on the Conservative Party
lay less in the fact that he was a grandee and a devout believer in the
fundamentals of Toryism than in his blunt common sense and
scepticism. Thus, in October 1871:

> We live in an age of blood and iron. If we mean to escape misery and
> dishonour, we must trust to no consciousness of a righteous cause,
> to no moral influence, to no fancied restraints of civilisation. These
> bulwarks may be of use when the millennium draws near; they are
> empty verbiage now. We must trust to our power of self-defence,
> and to no earthly aid.

Or, April 1881:

> To those who have found breakfast with difficulty, and do not know
> where to find dinner, intricate questions of politics are a matter of
> comparatively secondary interest.

And then, October 1884:

> If you will study history, you will find that freedom, when it has been destroyed, has always been destroyed by those who shelter themselves under the cover of its forms and who speak its language with eloquence and vigor.

Salisbury disliked public speaking—'This duty of making political speeches is an aggravation of the labours of your Majesty's servants which we owe entirely to Mr. Gladstone' he wrote on one occasion to the Queen—but from the beginning of 1881 he became one of the most active and conspicuous of the Conservative speakers, delivering more than seventy major speeches in the next four years. These were trenchant, well-prepared, and well received. The principal Conservative provincial leaders—Arthur Forwood in Liverpool, Sir William Houldsworth in Manchester, and Satchell Hopkins in Birmingham—were particularly grateful and impressed. To his reputation in foreign affairs Salisbury had now added a party following outside London which was greater than that of Northcote, and acted as a powerful, if less spectacular, counterweight to Randolph Churchill's meteoric campaign. Thus he was, in experience, intellect, and following increasingly seen as the natural successor to Beaconsfield, and was quietly consolidating this position. Its full strength was not to be demonstrated until December 1886.

*

At the end of 1883 the situation for the 'Dual Control' became much more serious when Churchill set out to capture the National Union of Conservative Associations. The National Union, founded in 1867, never occupied a very significant position and possessed virtually no funds. But it was in existence, its Council was elective, it did have an annual conference, and Churchill, with Chamberlain's example very much in his mind, saw in this moribund organisation considerable potentialities.

After the 1880 debacle Beaconsfield had established a Central Committee to reorganise the party organisation. It had not been notably successful, and Gorst—recalled to give it the benefit of his neglected experience—had soon resigned in disgust. The Central Committee, in its membership and approach, was the personification of 'the old gang', but it did have access to, and disbursed, the central party funds. It was Churchill's strategy at the end of 1883 to take the annual conference of the National Union by storm, to secure the election to the Council of his friends and allies, and to secure for it 'all power and finance'. 'This will be a bold step', he wrote to Wolff, 'the Austerlitz of the Fourth Party.' The combination of Churchill in his best demagogic form—'If you want to gain the confidence of the working classes, let them have a share and a large share—a real share and not a sham share—in your party councils and in your party government'—and careful polling of the delegates, nearly achieved the victory, but in the end Churchill's group only secured a fractional majority.

But it was enough for the moment. The new Council appointed an Organisation Committee with Churchill as its chairman, and promptly sought an interview with Salisbury. The implications were clear, and were made even clearer when Churchill embarked on a speaking tour in the Provinces which drew immense audiences and were reported at great length; to fervent applause Churchill then announced his intention of fighting John Bright in his citadel in Birmingham at the next election, a gesture of superb dramatic self-confidence and aggressiveness. Salisbury and Balfour—whose tenuous connection with the Fourth Party had now ended—viewed these developments with concern but decided on caution. In February 1884 Lord Randolph was elected chairman of the Council, and promptly demanded the surrender of the Central Committee, threatening public warfare unless the point was conceded. At this point Salisbury and Northcote decided to force the issue themselves, and Churchill resolved to fight. The tone of his letters to Salisbury now became sharp and at times personally offensive. The lines of battle were clearly drawn; on the one side, the voice of democratic involvement in party affairs, on the other an 'aristocratic and privileged' grouping consisting of 'certain irresponsible persons who find favour in your [Salisbury's] eyes'. This dispute was carried to the country, where Churchill declared that 'Governments will go wrong, Parliaments will go wrong, classes will go wrong, London Society and the Pall Mall clubs always go wrong, but the people do not go wrong' and stated that his political philosophy was 'Trust the people' and that 'I have no fear of democracy'. Salisbury, believing that he had a case for accusing Churchill of bad faith in the negotiations for a settlement, broke them off. Churchill promptly resigned from his chairmanship, and there was much excitement among the substantial elements in the Parliamentary Party which loathed and feared this impossible and disloyal young man with his brazen ambitions.

But the reaction outside London was quite different, and Churchill's wooing of the Provincial party leaders now paid great dividends. On May 16th he was unanimously re-elected Chairman, and Salisbury resolved to come to terms.

Gorst was not present at these negotiations (nor was Northcote), and was deeply embittered by what his son subsequently called 'the great surrender'. Churchill and Salisbury, recognising each other tacitly as equals, agreed that they would work in harmony, that the Central Committee would be abolished, that Sir Michael Hicks-Beach, in whom each had confidence, would become chairman of the Council, and that the Primrose League would be officially recognised. Gorst believed that Churchill had lost a great opportunity, and he rightly foresaw that the National Union would be put to sleep again. But Churchill's objectives had been more limited. It had become clear to him that the battle to win full control over the National Union was going to be a long and divisive one, and one that he might not have won in the long run. An election was close, and it was time to mend bridges. The Salisbury–Churchill pact doomed Northcote's ambition, and established a new duumvirate.

These acute divisions in the Opposition ranks had coincided with the relaxing of the immediate crisis in Ireland and the seizing of the initiative by the Government in the passage of a new Reform Bill which brought to the agricultural workers the extensions of the franchise given to the town artisans in 1867. This was Chamberlain's contribution, and it caught the Conservatives off-balance. The Conservatives refused to accept franchise reform without a simultaneous redistribution of seats, and for a time feelings ran high. The removal of the distinction between borough and county franchise in Ireland also alarmed the Conservatives, but they dared not press this matter too far. Although it appeared as though the issue would be 'the Peers against the People', as Chamberlain hoped, in the end party agreement was reached. Some two million new voters were enfranchised, there was a considerable redistribution, and the principle of 'one man one vote' was established, together with the abolition of the plural-member system. Of even greater immediate significance was the fact that the Act extended the franchise to Ireland on the same terms, increasing the Irish electorate by over half a million voters, and thus giving Parnell his opportunity for a clear Home Rule sweep outside Ulster. Given Parnell's ascendancy by this stage, it is doubtful whether this made much difference in terms of seats in Ireland, but it greatly improved his position in bargaining terms in England.

But this success for the Government was clouded by the disasters in the Sudan and severe internal differences over Ireland. The Crimes Act was due to expire in August, and Ministers were divided on its renewal. Chamberlain proposed a scheme of devolution introducing elective county boards with defined local responsibilities and a national council, a Central Board, which would assume many of the responsibilities borne by the Dublin administration. The Central Board Scheme split the Cabinet, was defeated by one vote on May 9th, 1885, and Chamberlain and Dilke resigned. Their resignations were not made public, and the search for a modus vivendi was continuing when, on June 9th, the Government was defeated in the House of Commons and thankfully resigned.

The Central Board Scheme was unacceptable to Parnell as an alternative to Home Rule, and, whether or not Chamberlain was deceived by the O'Shea who again acted as emissary[1] or not, it was a fatal misreading of Parnell's position to infer that such a watered-down version could be acceptable. In a dark moment for his cause, Parnell negotiated with Churchill—in itself a remarkable indication of how far and how high Lord Randolph had travelled over the previous five years. The discussion was confined to the issue of Coercion. Churchill said that if he were a member of the Government he would oppose the renewal of the Crimes Act. 'In that case', Parnell replied, 'you will have the Irish vote at the elections.'[2] The understanding was confirmed at least in one other meeting between the two. This episode demonstrated the Irish Nationalists' respect for Churchill's positions on the Irish Question, including his early denunciations of coercion and his fierce opposition to the introduction of the Closure in 1881. He was indeed, not only clearly the rising star of the Conservative Party but also the only one who had revealed any sensitivity to their cause. Northcote was not taken seriously by the Irish, and Salisbury's attitude towards Ireland was notoriously antipathetic. 'On Tory

[1] The claim is strongly denied by Henry Harrison in *Parnell, Joseph Chamberlain and Mr. Garvin.*
[2] W. S. Churchill; *Lord Randolph Churchill*, 395.

principles', he had written more than a decade earlier, 'the case presents much that is painful, but no perplexity whatever. Ireland must be kept, like India, at all hazards: by persuasion, if possible; if not, by force.' There were no indications that Salisbury had changed his mind on this matter, and he had been vehemently opposed to the principles of tenants' rights contained in the Land and Arrears Act. Churchill was accordingly the natural Conservative for Parnell to do business with. He subsequently claimed that 'there was no compact or bargain of any kind', but, as Rosebery has pointed out, when one man pledges action in a certain eventuality in return for certain favours it is difficult to describe it otherwise. The Conservatives did not renew the Crimes Act, and in November Parnell did advise Irish voters in Britain to vote Conservative.

On June 8th the Opposition moved an amendment to the Budget condemning the proposed increase in duties on beer and spirits. It was a torpid debate, until it became apparent that the Government was treating it as, in Dilke's words 'a question of life and death', a phrase repeated by Gladstone himself. At half past one in the morning of June 9th the division was taken, and amid scenes of tumult and cries of 'Buckshot!' and 'Coercion!' from the Irish it was announced that the Government had been defeated by twelve votes. Lord Randolph joyously leaped onto the bench to lead the Conservative exultations while Gladstone sat quietly writing to the Queen to inform her of the fall of his Government.

It was a curious incident which, as the Liberal Sir Wilfred Lawson remarked, reminded him of the verdict of a Dorset jury: 'Died on the visitation of God under suspicious circumstances.' Sixty-two Liberals had been absent, of whom only fourteen had been paired, while four had voted for the Opposition amendment. The Irish had combined with the Conservatives. As Conor Cruise O'Brien has commented, 'the unusually large muster of Parnellites on the decisive vote certainly suggests advance planning'.[1] On an issue of confidence the Liberal whips had either been exceptionally negligent or had been advised not to try too hard. The evidence strongly points to the latter conclusion.

Certainly, Ministers were delighted. Chamberlain confessed to a 'spirit of exultation' and wrote that 'the Tories have relieved us from a position of almost intolerable embarrassment'. Gladstone described it as 'a great personal relief'. The evidence of Gladstone's reaction is

[1] O'Brien, op. cit., 98.

ambiguous. His son wrote that 'Father I am sure knew nothing of the probability of defeat until the last moment. Tories taken aback, except Randolph who danced madly about like a Cherokee on the war path.' Mrs. Gladstone recorded that when her husband returned to Downing Street 'it had been a blow, he had gone in to win' but that 'before he fell asleep, came the lovely calm, the words coming from his lips, "All praise to God for his mercies".'[1]

Thus, under distinctly curious circumstances, ended the life of the Administration which had entered office with such high hopes little more than five years previously, which had endured so much, and which now gladly made way for the Conservatives while hopefully awaiting the election which, under the provisions of the Reform Act, could not come until November.

---

[1] Quoted in A. B. Cooke and John Vincent: *The Governing Passion*, 251.

CHAPTER THREE

THE HOME RULE CRISIS, 1885-1886

IN ATTEMPTING to dissect and describe a major political crisis the historian must be careful not to impose order and coherence, either in actions or individual motives, upon a human and confused business. This warning has particular application to the series of events which occurred between June 8th, 1885 and June 8th, 1886, and which together may be described as The Home Rule Crisis. No one at the time could forecast its course or outcome. Few, with the exception of Parnell—who nonetheless made at least one major miscalculation—took a consistent course. It can only be seen as a hectic struggle for political superiority in circumstances which no one had anticipated and which were unfamiliar to all participants. It brought old opponents into unexpected and uncomfortable alliance; it permanently ruptured former associations; and it transformed the nature of modern British politics. But few who were actually involved in the battle appreciated the scale of the stakes until it was over. The Conservatives won, and on balance narrowly deserved to, but were left with problems even greater than they had faced at the outset.

By June 1885, when the Gladstone Government was defeated, the political situation still greatly favoured the Liberals, and it was widely assumed that the increase in the franchise would increase this advantage when the General Election came in November. The Liberal organisation had decayed badly since 1880, but that of the Conservatives was in even worse condition; the appointment of 'Captain' Middleton[1] as National Agent in March 1885 was to produce considerable results, but these were not yet evident. In terms of policy, both major parties were divided and leaderless. No one knew how long Gladstone would continue in public life, nor how serious were his

---

[1] Richard William Evelyn Middleton, 1846–1905. Served in the Royal Navy 1860–77. Conservative Agent for West Kent 1883–4.

81

frequently expressed yearnings for retirement. The Conservatives had no leader at all. Salisbury was unknown quantity in many respects, and his particular brand of patrician High Church Conservatism seemed highly inappropriate to the new conditions. Northcote was clearly out of the running, although he himself did not realise it. Churchill was too young and too new, and aroused at least as much antipathy as enthusiasm. The remaining relics of the Beaconsfield era evoked little interest, excitement, or respect. The Liberals at least had considerable talent, while in these terms the condition of the Conservatives appeared absolutely forlorn. Through a series of startling circumstances this balance was to be dramatically transformed.

Few of the Conservative leaders shared Lord Randolph's exaltation at the fall of the Liberal Administration, and Churchill himself quickly had second thoughts. Salisbury was particularly unenthusiastic. 'To have to govern six months with a hostile but dying Parliament', he had written on June 7th, 'is the very worst thing that can happen to us.' When the Government was defeated and Gladstone announced his intention to resign he wrote to Cranbrook that 'The prospect before us is very serious. The vote on Monday night was anything but a subject for congratulation.' The Conservative recollections of the events of 1873 were very sharp, when Gladstone had resigned but Disraeli had declined to form an Administration and the Liberals had resumed office, and had lurched towards ignominious defeat. The general inclination of the Conservative leaders—with the exception of Northcote—was to follow Disraeli's example, but recognised that it would be difficult to do so if the Queen asked them to form a Government and Gladstone adamantly persisted in his resignation. Furthermore, there was the factor of the rank and file, exhilarated by its achievement and eager for office under almost any circumstances. And there was also the unspoken but real query about what Lord Randolph would do and say if the chance were not taken.

In spite of Salisbury's hesitations, it is clear that by June 11th he had made up his mind to accept the Queen's Commission if it came to him, as come it did. Northcote, who had believed until that moment that he would be called to Balmoral, could not conceal his mortification. Northcote had some reason for his chagrin. The Queen had written to him on May 15th, 1881 to say that '*she* will look on Sir Stafford Northcote as the Leader of the great Conservative Party, though it may not be necessary to *announce* this *now*, and she wished that Sir

Stafford, who is so old and kind a friend, should *know* this'. But, as the Queen herself recognised, the situation had changed greatly by 1885. At Balmoral, Salisbury was very careful not to refuse to form a Government, while emphasising the difficulties under which a minority government would have to work. He returned to London to endeavour to form an administration.

The principal difficulty concerned Northcote and Churchill. The latter, who at this stage went into virtual seclusion, would accept no office if Northcote remained in the Commons, and Sir Michael Hicks-Beach—albeit with considerable unhappiness—supported him. Churchill cancelled all engagements and was virtually incommunicado. Faced with this impasse, some of the leading Conservatives argued that the 1873 option should be tried again, but Salisbury described such a course as 'abandoning the Queen'. At this point, on June 15th, Northcote suffered a major humiliation when Churchill, Gorst, and Wolff refused to accept his guidance on the Lords' amendments to the Redistribution Bill, arguing that they could not be considered until the ministerial crisis was resolved. Beach supported them—almost certainly without realising the full implications—and in the ensuing division the Opposition was hopelessly split. Northcote's bitterness and depression are fully understandable; 'the Queen's passing me over without a word of sympathy or regret is not pleasant'. In his diary he wrote: 'I have offered either to do this [First Lord and Leader of the House of Commons] or go to the Upper House, taking the India Office. I have offered to do whatever he [Salisbury] thinks best. I have not much heart in the matter. This has apparently been my last night in the House of Commons.'

It was obvious that things could not go on in this chaotic manner. On the following morning Churchill ended his period of withdrawal and saw Salisbury. Matters were settled to the satisfaction of both. Churchill would take the India Office, Salisbury would be Foreign Secretary as well as Prime Minister, Northcote would go to the Lords as First Lord of the Treasury, with the title of the Earl of Iddesleigh, Beach would lead the Commons, and Lord Carnarvon—whom Churchill had wanted excluded—would become Viceroy of Ireland. Northcote wrote of Churchill that 'he has practically got rid of me, and now he will prove a thorn in the side of Salisbury and Beach'. Salisbury had handled the crisis with considerable skill, but had not enjoyed the experience, which he described to G. E. Buckle as 'a revelation to me of the baser side of human nature'; to Cranbrook he was even more frank, and not least about the performance of Lord Randolph Churchill.

The final difficulty concerned arrangements with the Liberals for the passage of essential business, and the putative Conservative Government nearly never took office at all while these matters were being argued. But on June 23rd, two weeks after the fateful division on the Budget, the matter was settled, and what Chamberlain derided as 'the Ministry of Caretakers' formally took office.

From this point there was a very striking change in Irish attitudes. Churchill was an avowed opponent of the Crimes Bill, which was allowed to lapse. Carnarvon's ideas on resolving the Irish Question not only involved a policy of greater conciliation but were not dissimilar to Chamberlain's aborted 'Central Board' scheme and, indeed, went further. Salisbury was very uneasy, but permitted Carnarvon to continue his discussions.

In this atmosphere the Irish attitude towards the Liberals, and particularly Chamberlain, notably hardened. *United Ireland*, which had described Chamberlain as 'a sort of shop-keeping Danton' now strongly opposed a proposed visit to Ireland by Chamberlain and Dilke in insulting terms, and Cardinal Manning was cold to the idea. Archbishop Walsh, the new Archbishop of Dublin, refused to arrange any introductions as this 'would be interpreted as hostile to the excellent tenor and promise of Lord Carnarvon's conservative regime'. It was a very curt rebuff, and Chamberlain reacted sharply. He was preparing his own radical programme, the celebrated 'unauthorised programme', and as an immediate response to the way the Irish had treated him he dropped local self-government for Ireland from the list of his reforms. Chamberlain was a dangerous man to cross, as the Irish were to discover.

Meanwhile, Carnarvon was making some apparent progress. On August 1st he saw Parnell in an empty house in Mayfair (15 Hill Street), and found the Irish leader 'singularly moderate'. These discussions also impressed Parnell, and paved the way to his public advice on November 21st for the Irish voters 'to vote against the men who coerced Ireland'. Salisbury and Churchill, however, were becoming very uneasy. Salisbury—who had written, and firmly believed, that Home Rule threatened 'the highest interests of the Empire'—wrote to the Queen that 'he entirely agrees with Your Majesty in thinking that the nationalists cannot be trusted and that any bargain with them would be full of danger'.

Churchill was not aware of the extent of Carnarvon's discussions, and although he was a strong advocate of conciliation he baulked at anything approaching Home Rule. He was also acutely aware of the tactical political situation, and was convinced that the Nationalist movement contained so many mutually antagonistic elements that it could not hold together for long. Carnarvon was a highly intelligent and sensitive man, and as a result of his experience with the Canadian federation, and despite the failure of the federal proposal in South Africa, was a convinced believer in the concept of self-government within carefully prescribed limits. In other circumstances his venture might have had some chance of success; in the atmosphere of 1885, after all that had happened since 1880, and with a General Election imminent, there was very little. Nonetheless, the tone of his public statements and his conduct in Dublin led many people—and not excluding Gladstone—to believe that the Conservative Government was embarked upon a major change of British policy.

This impression was confirmed on July 17th, when Parnell moved for a new enquiry into the Maamtrasna murders of 1882. Beach was extremely cautious, but Gorst and Churchill made inflammatory speeches which were condemnatory of Spencer's administration and which particularly aroused the Ulster Conservatives, who were becoming very unhappy indeed about the trend of Government attitudes. Carnarvon was indignant, the Queen was dismayed, and Salisbury's diplomacy was exercised to calm them down. To the agitated Liberals, unaware of the divisions within the Government, this episode appeared to be clear evidence of a compact between the Conservatives and the Irish. On the same day Lord Ashbourne introduced a new Land Purchase Bill for Ireland which provided grants from the exchequer for tenants wishing to borrow money at relatively low interest for the purchase of their land. It was, as Ashbourne admitted, a modest proposal, but it was welcomed by Parnell and seemed to the increasingly alarmed Liberals to be another significant indication. The Irish Educational Endowments Bill and the Labourers' Bill, both of which became law before the end of the session, deeply confirmed this impression.

These overtures, far from being the Machiavellian intrigue that the Liberals believed them to be, were in fact unco-ordinated and formed no part of an agreed and coherent strategy. Ministers were, in fact, deeply divided, and confused. Churchill, for example, did not know of the Carnarvon-Parnell meeting until 1887, and Salisbury informed neither the Queen nor the Cabinet of this discussion. Parnell, reasonably, had assumed that Carnarvon was speaking with much greater authority than he had been. The revival of agrarian crime in Ireland alarmed Ministers, and particularly Ashbourne, but Carnarvon persistently minimised its significance. The 1885 harvest had been disastrous in parts of Ireland, and the old methods of refusal to pay rents, boycotting, and houghing of cattle had been revived.

The Conservatives began to feel trapped. Many believed that an unequivocal denunciation of Home Rule was essential if their supporters and the Ulster Conservatives were not to stampede. Salisbury personally agreed with the principle, but had his eye on the election. Carnarvon did not even agree with the principle. Churchill was obsessed by the tactical possibilities. Ashbourne and Cranbrook had become converts to coercion. On October 7th Salisbury delivered a major speech at Newport which was a classic of vagueness on Irish matters, and in which he spoke with calculated ambiguity of the creation of 'a large central authority' to prevent injustices from being perpetrated on the minorities by the Catholic majority. He had not endorsed Home Rule nor the principle of an Irish Parliament, but his studied imprecision persuaded the Liberals that he had and the Conservatives that he had not.

Gladstone had observed these movements with care, but ascribed to them a greater coherence of policy than in fact existed. Carnarvon had now become a devotee of a form of Home Rule, but there was no possibility of putting this past Salisbury, let alone the Cabinet. Carnarvon offered his resignation, but Salisbury was able to stall any decision. Gladstone resolved upon inaction, and to wait upon events. 'It is right I should say', he had written to Mrs. O'Shea on August 8th, 'that into any counter-bidding of any sort against Lord R. Churchill I for one cannot enter.' There was very little he could offer short of a full-blooded commitment to Home Rule, which had been already denounced by the improbable coalition of Chamberlain and Hartington.

*

Historians have often pondered on what Gladstone's preoccupations and concerns were in the six months which elapsed between the resignation of his second Government and his actions in December 1885. He spent virtually all of this period at Hawarden, was studiously occupied in research and correspondence which had little connection with contemporary politics, and what public observations he made were carefully Delphic. He made no public speech at all between the beginning of July and the beginning of November. Visitors came to Hawarden, but they were treated with great caution. His colleagues were baffled and offended, his opponents increasingly alarmed.

The truth was much less complicated. As has been emphasised before, Gladstone was not an innovator but a responder, and in 1885 he was temporarily lost—an affliction which strikes politicians of far less sensitivity than Gladstone at regular intervals. He entertained no dark schemes nor nourished any deep jealousies. Lost and puzzled, he waited upon events, and in the meanwhile employed his enormous energies in intellectual pursuits while awaiting political events. He was politically obsessed by Ireland, but this was not his only political preoccupation in these difficult months.

His relationship with Chamberlain had never been smooth. Although Chamberlain had proved himself an able and imaginative Minister, and had been one of the few real successes of the Liberal Government, the gulf of attitude and philosophy between the two man had markedly widened since 1880. It was not simply that Chamberlain was evidently hard, cold, ambitious, and coveted Gladstone's position. Gladstone was a political realist, and understood such matters. Nor was it only a matter of age, or of differing viewpoints on public affairs. It came down to a question of personal dislike. Gladstone did not like Chamberlain, nor did he trust him; at this time, furthermore, he underestimated him. Gladstone was sceptical of Chamberlain's integrity and capacity, and had already come to the conclusion that he was an opportunist without principle. This opinion was now fortified by Chamberlain's 'unauthorised programme', which was set forth in *The Radical Programme* and blazoned in a series of massively attended and widely reported speeches.

These were very good speeches indeed, delivered with a belligerence and style which Chamberlain had never achieved before. Much of the belligerence was delivered against his colleagues, notably Hartington, who was compared to Rip Van Winkle. 'If we cannot convince our allies of the justice and reasonableness of our views, then, with whatever reluctance, we must part company; we will fight alone; we will appeal unto Caesar; we will go to the people from whom we came and whose cause we plead.' In the midst of assaults upon his colleagues and 'the convenient cant of selfish wealth' there was a strong denunciation of Parnell (Warrington, September 8th) which was the first public sign of Chamberlain's anger at the rebuff that he had received.

The trouble was that the 'unauthorised programme', although cautious in its strategy—as Chamberlain explained, 'I am putting the rights of property on the only firm and defensible basis. I believe that the danger to property lies in its abuses'—was couched in vehement language, and some of its proposals were appalling to other Liberals. Items such as free primary education and local government for the counties were controversial—particularly the former—but the concept of much greater State intervention and the implicit abolition of laissez-faire were rather different. Iddesleigh, rather unexpectedly, denounced Chamberlain as 'Jack Cade', and Salisbury described him as 'a Sicilian bandit'. What was more ominous was the silence from Hawarden, broken by a manifesto which on the land issue demonstrated much more sympathy with the viewpoint of Hartington than of Chamberlain.

Chamberlain had launched his great effort without consultation with Gladstone, and by his language had achieved the alienation both of Parnell and Hartington. With the election looming, such conduct could only be interpreted by the Liberal leader in a hostile sense, and it was thus interpreted. Chamberlain, like many overtly ambitious self-made men on the make, was acutely sensitive. He was keenly resentful of any slight, real or imagined, and he hugged his grievances fiercely. He was vain and egotistical. But, as Beatrice Webb has rightly remarked, his 'intense sensitiveness to his own wrongs was not tempered by a corresponding sensitiveness to the feelings and the rights of others'. In Chamberlain's complex character the element of self-righteousness was very strong. His mind ranged neither wide nor deep. It was a precise instrument for dealing with defined problems and providing defined solutions. He was not a man given to doubts or qualifications. His private letters faithfully echo his public speeches. He simplified issues not because he was capable of making complex matters clear, but because his own understanding of them was simplistic. He was thus able to present them starkly and dramatically, because he saw them thus. The 'unauthorised programme' was a crude personal manifesto, but in the absence of any other one it achieved considerable attention. Chamberlain's vanity had been bitterly wounded by the Parnellite rejection; it was now inflamed by his large and enthusiastic audiences. These blinded him to the fact of his increasing isolation.

A visit to Hawarden early in October emphasised the gulf between Gladstone and Chamberlain. Nothing of real importance was discussed, both men were courteous but very careful. Gladstone had not liked the 'unauthorised programme', indeed he had a dislike for political programmes, preferring to discover some great central cause—as in the assault on 'Beaconsfieldism' in 1879–80—rather than a detailed programme which involved prior commitments. 'The unforeseen sometimes does much in politics', he wrote several years later, and in October 1885 it is clear that Gladstone was cautiously waiting upon events, increasingly convinced that 'a question of Irish government may come up with such force and magnitude as to assert its precedence over everything else'. But, although he told Chamberlain that 'he had an instinct that Irish questions might elbow out all others', he did not confide in him. Indeed, it is doubtful whether he had himself come to a definite conclusion at that stage. Gladstone wrote to the Queen that he 'recently thought it would be well to invite him [Chamberlain] to Hawarden, with a view to personal communication, which has now been effected, he thinks with advantage'.

It was a wary, uncomfortable, formality. Chamberlain's supporters subsequently blamed Gladstone harshly for not letting the younger man into his confidence, and not revealing the trend of his thinking. Throughout his life, Gladstone had been solitary when coming to momentous decisions; at this time he could have seen little value in exchanging confidences with a man who had launched his own campaign without discussion, let alone approval, on the eve of a major election. But Chamberlain's admirers, like Chamberlain himself, wanted it both ways. It was not the least of the factors that made Gladstone so suspicious and uneasy in Chamberlain's presence.

Meanwhile, the Unauthorised Programme blazed across the empty Liberal firmament, excoriated by Tory and Whig alike, and then, on November 21st, Parnell made his advice to the Irish electors plain. It was not to vote for the Conservatives, but to vote against the Liberals. With that declaration the plans both of Gladstone and Chamberlain had to be severely revised.

*

Chamberlain's political isolation was now augmented by a startling event.

Dilke's reputation had been considerably enhanced in office, and although he lacked the power-base of Chamberlain or the glamour of Rosebery, he was, like them, spoken of widely as a possible future Liberal leader. Dilke was in many respects an unattractive man, lacking intellectual or political originality, and was certainly a dull speaker, but he was very able, an assiduous worker and had a genuine following. Asquith wrote of him that 'his memory was over-stocked with detail, and there was a lack of the sense of proportion in his voluminous encyclopedia of political knowledge . . . this often gave an air of pedantry to really good stuff'.[1] He was not particularly liked by his colleagues, but he clearly was a force to be reckoned with among the rising Liberals.

In August 1885 Donald Crawford, Liberal M.P. for Lanark, instituted divorce proceedings against his young wife, citing Dilke as co-respondent on his wife's confession of adultery with him. Dilke described it as 'a false charge . . . made by conspiracy and careful preparation', and there were certainly some very suspicious elements involved. Mrs. Crawford's mother (Mrs. Eustace Smith) had once been Dilke's lover and her sister was the widow of Dilke's brother. Crawford's solicitor was the brother of a Mrs. Rogerson, who adjudged herself wronged by Dilke and who had written one of the anonymous letters that had caused Crawford's confrontation with his wife. There seems little doubt that Mrs. Crawford was a consummate liar in the witness box, and that she was also protecting another lover. But although this combination of women and one man who knew a great deal about Dilke and had good cause to wish to destroy him points to a conspiracy, Dilke's life was not unblemished. He was widely known as a man with 'a reputation'. Edward Hamilton wrote in his diary when the rumours of the divorce were circulating that 'it does not surprise anyone who knows Dilke. He is extraordinary free and easy with ladies'.

When the case came up in February 1886 the evidence against Dilke —the sole alleged co-respondent—was dismissed with costs, but Crawford was given his decree nisi, a decision which may have been justified in law but which baffled observers. Far more serious had been the decision of Dilke's counsel not to put him into the witness-box, on

[1] Earl of Oxford and Asquith: *Memories and Reflections*, pp. 154–5.

the grounds that 'in the life of any man there may be found to have been some indiscretions'. The implications of this explanation were clear, and Dilke found that although acquitted by the Court he had been condemned outside it. In these circumstances there could be no question of him being offered office in a Liberal Government, and he was advised to invoke the intervention of the Queen's Proctor to re-open the case. This second case, held in July, was disastrous. The burden of proof was now on Dilke, and he and his counsel were unable to shake Mrs. Crawford's detailed and sensational account of their relationship. The jury took only fifteen minutes to decide that they believed Mrs. Crawford's version, and Dilke was ruined. He had just lost his Chelsea seat, and for a time there was even talk of him being removed from the list of Privy Councillors and arraigned for perjury. Although he returned to the House of Commons in 1892 for the Forest of Dean and remained a Member until his death in 1911, he never again held office nor exerted any political influence.

While it is difficult to disagree with the verdict of Dilke's most recent biographer that 'he was the victim of a conspiracy, the main lines of which (and, indeed, the identity of the other participants in which) are shrouded in mystery and are likely always so to remain',[1] the strong probability is that it was not a political but a personal conspiracy. It is also possible that although the bulk of Mrs. Crawford's story may have been false, the basic fact that Dilke had seduced her may well have been true—which would help to explain why she never withdrew her story after she had undergone a religious conversion to Catholicism and devoted herself to a life of good works.

To contemporaries, the matter was clear. Dilke had denied on oath that he had been Mrs. Crawford's lover; a jury had decided otherwise. He was branded as an adulterer and a perjurer and was, for practical political purposes, finished. Chamberlain's one major ally in the Liberal leadership had been removed.

*

The precise impact of the Irish vote outside Ireland on the 1885 General Election remains a matter of conjecture and controversy. To a remarkable degree, in the light of later events, Ireland was hardly

[1] Roy Jenkins: *Sir Charles Dilke—A Victorian Tragedy*. The question of the alleged involvement of the Roseberys in a conspiracy is discussed in the author's biography of Rosebery, pp. 181–9.

mentioned at all in the English, Scottish, and Welsh campaigns and manifestos. Gladstone's Manifesto read:

> To maintain the supremacy of the Crown, the unity of the Empire, and all the authority of Parliament necessary for the conservation of that unity is the first duty of every representative of the people. Subject to this governing principle, every grant to portions of the county of enlarged powers for the management of their own affairs is, in my view, not a source of danger but a means of averting it, and is in the nature of a new guarantee for increased cohesion, happiness, and strength. History will consign to disgrace the name of every man who, having it in his power, does not aid but prevents or retards an equitable settlement between Ireland and Great Britain.

Three days before Parnell's pronouncement, the Bishop of Neath issued a denunciation of the Radicals as being 'fanatically anti-Christian', seizing upon the Chamberlainite advocacy of 'free schools' which had also aroused the condemnation of Cardinal Manning. There seems no reason to doubt the validity of the argument that these influences were very strong in the anti-Liberal vote in the cities in the election.[1] With Gladstone uncharacteristically quiescent—although calling in Midlothian for a majority independent of the Irish Nationalists—and with Chamberlain and Hartington in dispute, the Conservatives had an advantage which they seized in the cities.

Lord Randolph's campaign against Bright in Birmingham aroused the greatest excitement, and although Churchill was defeated (he was elected for South Paddington in the same election) and Birmingham remained solidly Liberal, elsewhere the Conservatives did very well, winning 116 out of the 226 borough constituencies, and there were high expectations of an overall Conservative victory. In the counties, however, the results of the new Reform Act strongly favoured the Liberals, and the pledge for free allotments—'Three acres and a cow', as it was derided by the Conservatives—played a part.[2] It was a considerable, and very significant reversal of the previous pattern. The final result was deadlock, with Parnell holding the balance. The

---

[1] See C. H. D. Howard, 'The Parnell Manifesto of 21 November 1885 and the Schools Question', *English Historical Review*, January 1947.

[2] Although probably not as great as was believed at the time (see H. Pelling: *Popular Politics and Society in Late Victorian Britain*, pp. 6–7.)

Conservatives were 249, the Liberals 335, and the Parnellite Irish 86.
This time the latter were all Parnellites; by an overwhelming majority,
Ireland had voted for Home Rule. Not a single Liberal was returned
for an Irish constituency, sixteen Ulster Conservatives winning in the
North.

A very confused period followed, while the politicians endeavoured
to analyse the significance of the results and their immediate implications. Salisbury and Churchill, now increasingly concerned by
Carnarvon's activities, were not enthusiastic for remaining in office
unless they could attract some of the leading Liberals, notably
Hartington and G. J. Goschen, but Salisbury—unlike Churchill—was
firmly opposed to the idea of a coalition. Salisbury's opinion of
Gladstone was that he was 'mad to take office, and that this will force
him into some line of conduct which will be discreditable to him and
disastrous, if we do not prematurely gratify his hunger'. Churchill also
flirted seriously with Chamberlain—or, at least, made it seem serious
—while in the Liberal ranks there was comparable confusion.
Hartington, who had accused Parnell of exercising 'a grinding and
widespread despotism' in Ireland, had now been the putative Liberal
Prime Minister for ten years, and the strain was showing. Chamberlain's ambitions were very high. Goschen was intriguing actively for
the creation of a new coalition party. The only event of major significance achieved by the Government—and it was almost ignored at the
time—was the British annexation of Upper Burma in December after
a swift military operation which had deposed King Theebaw and put
his supporters to flight. This brought the whole of Burma under
British rule, and was a significant extension of British power and
influence in Asia and a check to French ambitions in Burma. For the
Minister responsible it was another triumph, and Lord Randolph's
reputation had risen further.

At this point Gladstone broke—or appeared to do so—his long and
baffling silence on the Irish Question. On December 16th his son
Herbert, sharing the suspicions of Chamberlain's motives and ambitions felt by Wemyss Reid, editor of the *Leeds Mercury*, gave the
National Press Agency information concerning his father's altered
views on Ireland and which implied that he had become converted to
the principle of accepting Home Rule. It was stated that Gladstone
would take office 'with a view to the creation of an Irish Parliament to
be entrusted with the entire management of all legislative and

administrative affairs, securities being taken for the representation of minorities and for an equitable partition of all imperial changes'.

Gladstone issued a denial that was so ambiguous, no doubt intentionally, that the confusion was augmented. Chamberlain and Hartington disassociated themselves publicly from this solution. Home Rule, in Salisbury's words, was converted at once from a chimera into a blazing issue. It completely eclipsed the Unauthorised Programme. The 'Hawarden Kite' did not greatly clarify the situation, but it gave the Conservatives their opportunity to depict Gladstone as a desperate man, intent on office at all costs. Chamberlain wrote to Dilke that 'my view is that Mr. G's Irish scheme is death and damnation; that we must try and stop it—that we must not openly commit ourselves against it yet—that we must let the situation shape itself before we finally decide'. Hartington complained to Granville in similar terms: 'Did any leader ever treat a Party in such a way as he has done?' Churchill and Salisbury, seeing the prospects before them suddenly becoming clearer, were resolved to pin Gladstone with Home Rule. From his close links with several Liberals—notably Labouchere— Churchill drew the conclusion, as he informed Salisbury, that 'the Radicals and the Irish want Home Rule, they know they cannot get it without Gladstone, Gladstone will give it and they go for him with all their strength and without risk of losing Joe and they calculate that their Whig falling off will be more than compensated for by the eighty-seven (sic) Irish votes'. This was a fair summation of a very confused situation. 'I fancy that a large number, perhaps the majority, of Liberals will support *any* scheme of Mr. G's', Chamberlain wrote to Dilke.

On December 15th Gladstone had gone to Eaton Hall, the grandiosely Gothic and gloomy seat of the Duke of Westminster, to see Balfour, who was a house-guest. His purpose was to urge a non-partisan approach to the Irish Question, with the co-operation on the Reform Act very much in mind. In this assumption he had been seriously misled by Canon Malcolm MacColl, the intermediary in the Reform Bill negotiations, that Salisbury was 'prepared to go as far probably as yourself on the question of Home Rule, but he seemed hopeless as to the prospect of carrying his party with him.' MacColl had himself not realised that Gladstone favoured an Irish Parliament— a key factor in the fundamental misunderstanding which led Gladstone to make his overture.

Gladstone argued to Balfour in his Eaton Hall discussion and in later correspondence that Home Rule had to be granted to prevent a resurgence of violence in Ireland, that the matter should not 'fall into the lines of party conflict', and that the Government should deal with the question.

There was no question of the Conservatives falling into what they regarded as a crude and obvious trap. Salisbury was intent on averting a break-up of his party, which he foresaw—rightly—as the obvious consequence of endorsing a policy of separation; Churchill had always made it clear that, although very prepared to conciliate Ireland, and to go a considerable distance in meeting legitimate Irish aspirations for self-government, Home Rule was an impossibility. The Conservative Party would not tolerate it, and he knew that the Protestants in Ulster would not.

Churchill was subsequently often blamed for discovering, if not actually creating, the Ulster hostility to Home Rule. The fact was that he was one of the very few English politicians who knew anything about Irish politics, and his brilliant exploitation of the simmering anger in the North was only that. He wrote to his old friend Justice FitzGibbon on February 16th that 'I decided some time ago that if the G.O.M. went for Home Rule, the Orange card would be the one to play. Please God it may turn out the ace of trumps and not the two'. This has been often seized upon to demonstrate Churchill's cynical irresponsibility in declaring that 'Ulster will fight, Ulster will be right'. What he did in fact was to give English Conservative leadership to a movement which would have found its leader in any event, and his action was to link the Ulster cause with that of his party for generations, as was Gladstone's espousal of Home Rule to link the Liberals with the Nationalists. In the context of 1886 it was only one element in the battle to defeat Home Rule; its full significance only emerged later.

If the Conservative leaders now saw their way clear, it was very largely because of their gleeful awareness of the deep fisures now opening in the Liberal coalition. Gladstone's aloofness and lack of leadership in the preceding months had demoralised much of the rank and file. Parnell said little, and bided his time. The Liberals who had lived through the awful vicissitudes of the Irish Question since 1880 and had seen the Irish vote turned against them in the 1885 election were not only confused but bitter. There was a wild mood in the

Liberal Party, and the Conservatives hastened to exploit it. Parnell, also, was having problems of his own. As T. P. O'Connor had been elected for two constituencies, there was a vacancy at Galway. O'Shea, who had been defeated in his bid for a Liverpool seat in the election despite the support of Chamberlain and Parnell, wanted Galway. Parnell decided to support his candidature, to the shock and anger of the local Nationalists. Eventually Parnell got his way, but not after a considerable amount of public unpleasantness which was eagerly picked up in London.

For a time the Conservatives were themselves acutely divided about how to act. 'I am feverishly anxious to be out', Salisbury wrote early in January. 'Internally as well as externally our position as a Government is intolerable.' Churchill was embittered and distressed by the rejection of a proposal for the projected Queen's Speech and had to be soothed, and then he and Beach, anxious to maintain Irish goodwill, threatened resignation unless a prepared coercion bill were dropped. Carnarvon's resignation was at length accepted, but acute disagreements arose over his successor, and the matter was still undetermined when the Government fell. In the end Churchill and Beach were placated, the Queen's Speech anticipated coercive measures in vague terms but was explicitly hostile 'to any disturbance of that fundamental law' (the legislative Union), and on January 26th Beach announced to the House of Commons—which had reassembled on the 21st[1]—the Government's intention.

The actual debate that evening was on an Opposition amendment to the Queen's Speech deploring the absence of any provision in it for the agricultural workers. It was a weird, carefully staged, occasion, Members speaking of allotments and peasant proprietors while behind them loomed the stark issue of Home Rule. The Government, accepting the Amendment as a vote of confidence, was duly defeated by seventy-nine votes, but Hartington, Goschen, and Sir Henry James were among the eighteen Liberals who supported it in the lobbies, and seventy-six Liberals abstained. The Conservatives—Salisbury carefully rejecting an appeal from the Queen for a dissolution—resigned the

---

[1] Bradlaugh had been re-elected for Northampton—for the fifth time—but when Beach raised the matter Mr. Speaker Peel emphatically ruled that he was entitled to take his seat and refused to accept the decisions of the previous Parliament. On January 27th 1891 the House expunged from its records the Bradlaugh Resolution of June 22nd 1880, three days before Bradlaugh's death.

next day, and left Gladstone, by now highly excited, to form an
Administration as best he could.

The extent of the Liberal schism now became truly evident.
Hartington, James, Goschen and Bright would not serve. Dilke was,
as Gladstone curtly noted, 'unavailable'. Chamberlain was offered,
and reluctantly accepted, the Presidency of the Local Government
Board, having asked for and been denied the Colonial Office, and did
so on the understanding that he would give 'an unprejudiced examination' to Gladstone's proposals. Harcourt went to the Treasury, John
Morley, after only three years in the Commons, became Irish
Secretary, and Rosebery became Foreign Secretary at the age of
thirty-seven—an advancement which he quickly justified. But, compared with the previous Liberal Government, it was markedly under-
gunned, and lost more vital artillery when Chamberlain and George
Trevelyan resigned on March 15th.

Chamberlain's links with Churchill had grown stronger since the
Hawarden Kite, but it seems very probable that Gladstone could have
retained him if he had tried. He did not try at all, and while it is
going too far to conclude that he deliberately provoked Chamberlain's
resignation he was not displeased when that event occurred. It was to
prove a very costly misjudgement. On April 8th Gladstone introduced
his 'Bill for the Better Government of Ireland' in an atmosphere of
intense excitement and in a speech of over three and a half hours
which was one of his most superb performances. This event in itself
checked the confidence of the Conservatives and sent a ripple of
political apprehension through the ranks of the hostile Liberals.

Gladstone's proposal was to establish an Irish Parliament and
executive in Dublin which would have overall control but for certain
specific reserved subjects, and Irish representation at Westminster
would be ended. It was this proposal on which Chamberlain fastened,
and caused the Government the greatest difficulty. When Gladstone
offered to withdraw it, he laid himself open to the charge that the
Irish M.P.s would have in effect two votes. Neither on this occasion,
nor in 1893, was Gladstone able to devise a formula that satisfied his
supporters or his wavering critics in his party. But the Bill as a whole
was a remarkable tribute to Gladstone and his colleagues, particularly
Morley. The 'reserved' subjects were very considerable, and would
have made the reality of Home Rule considerably less than the
independence for which the Irish had been agitating, and the attempts

to protect the Protestant minority in the proposed Irish legislature resulted in so complicated an arrangement that it is difficult to see how it could have worked without intense difficulty and friction. The interests of Ulster were inadequately appreciated and met. But, given the situation and the shortage of time, the Bill was a very formidable achievement and received the qualified—but firm—endorsement of Parnell.

Everything now depended upon the dissident Liberals. Hartington and Salisbury had met early in April at the Turf Club at Churchill's suggestion, but there was little possibility of, or enthusiasm for, a Conservative-Liberal Unionist alliance at this stage. But the key factor was a Conservative pledge not to oppose any Liberal who voted against Home Rule—a pledge which was, with difficulty in many constituencies, scrupulously observed.

At this point a digression is necessary.

The formation of the Conservative Central Office in 1870 had been a response to the recognition of the problems created by the enlarged electorate, and also in tribute to the success of the Liberal Registration Association, established in 1861, and to which the National Union of Conservative Associations, founded in 1867, had not been an adequate answer. John Gorst had been the first Principal Agent, and his main task had been to ensure that every constituency had a candidate and that the development of local associations be actively encouraged. Gorst also maintained a list of approved candidates for submission to associations. They were not obliged to accept these recommended candidates, but the development of this practice gave the party leader —to whom the Principal Agent reported directly—an influence over the composition of the Parliamentary party which, although very limited, was much greater than ever before. A Conservative Prime Minister, with the power of patronage and honours, who particularly desired the selection of a candidate, or who indicated his preference for a particular *type* of candidate, did not have to dictate to the associations. A hint was enough.

In 1886, with Middleton in firm control, Salisbury's pledge that the Liberal Unionists should be given a clear run against the Liberals could be duly honoured in eighty-seven constituencies (out of ninety-three). Operating out of his cramped little rooms in St. Stephen's Chambers, Middleton's spider-web ran to every constituency and every association, and it was well-known that he spoke for Lord

5 'Vice Versa': the Old Chancellor of the Exchequer and the
New—Gladstone and Lord Randolph Churchill, 1886: *The Graphic*

6 The Lobby of the House of Commons, 1886: by 'Lib', *Vanity Fair*.

From left to right: Inspector Denning, Mr Milman (Clerk Assistant), Mr John Bright, Sir W. Harcourt, Mr Gosset (Deputy Serjeant), Mr Labouchere, Mr Bradlaugh, Mr Chamberlain, Mr Parnell, Mr Gladstone, Lord Randolph Churchill, Lord Hartington, Mr Chaplin, Mr G. Leveson Gower, The Hon R. Spencer,

7 H. H. Asquith: by 'Spy', *Vanity Fair*

8 Gladstone introducing the Second Home Rule Bill, 1893

Salisbury, and a courteous request that a certain candidate be favourably considered, or another be rejected, was in most instances decisive. Thus, by 1886, having started much later than the Liberals, and having neglected their organisation badly for ten years, the Conservatives were far ahead of their opponents, and had established the general principles which dominated the Conservative organisation until after the Second World War.

Thus, at this critical moment, the Conservatives possessed the essential machinery to ensure that their pledges could be honoured.

*

On May 5th the committee of the National Liberal Federation supported Gladstone—save in Birmingham, where a bloody contest was decided in Chamberlain's favour—as did most of the local associations. The extraordinary cohesive power that Gladstone still exercised in the party had never been more dramatically demonstrated, and the dissidents found themselves fighting for their political lives. The appearance of Hartington and Salisbury on the same platform in London on April 14th grievously damaged Hartington's authority among his followers, and made the outcome even more in doubt.

But on May 12th, fifty-two Liberals met at Chamberlain's house, and, not uninfluenced by a letter opposing Home Rule from John Bright, resolved to vote against the second reading. On May 15th Salisbury appeared to have wrecked the possibility of Conservative co-operation with the dissident Liberals when he delivered a vehement speech in London in which he compared the Irish with the Hottentots as incapable of self-government and put forward the Conservative alternative to Home Rule as 'Government ... honestly, consistently, and resolutely applied for twenty years'. The motives for this speech remain unclear. He was certainly expressing emotions which he had held— and expressed—for some time; it may be that he blurted out these feelings, insensitive to the trouble they would cause to the dissident Liberals; it is also possible that he was deliberately sabotaging the movement towards a Liberal government under Hartington with Conservative support.[1] In any event, the speech did not—as the Gladstonians had hoped—bring Liberal unity. Too much had happened too quickly, and the internecine bitterness was too intense.

[1] See A. B. Cooke and John Vincent: *The Governing Passion*, 81, for this interpretation.

In particular, the debates between Chamberlain and Gladstone were marked by a clear and profound antipathy, and Hartington's revulsion from Home Rule was expressed in speeches of very high quality and obvious sincerity. It is, of course, possible to see in these events a variety of personal factors, of jealousies and ambitions; but the reality was that Home Rule was one of those issues which in itself and in its implications was genuinely divisive. When it came to the final choice, many Liberals could not and would not endorse it. The formation of the Liberal Unionist Committee—which held its first meeting on May 20th—demonstrated that the rift was too wide to be bridged.

Despite a last-minute attempt by Gladstone to conciliate his critics at a party meeting at the Foreign Office on May 27th—neatly sabotaged by Beach and Churchill in an exchange in the House which left the waverers with the firm impression that Gladstone had not been straight with them—the die was cast. Early in the morning of June 8th, the debate, in which Parnell made a magnificent contribution, was ended by Gladstone in one of his greatest speeches:

> Ireland stands at your bar, expectant, hopeful, almost suppliant. Her words are the words of truth and soberness. She asks a blessed oblivion of the past, and in that oblivion our interest is deeper than ever hers. . . . So I hail the demand of Ireland for what I call a blessed oblivion of the past. She asks also a boon for the future. . . . Think, I beseech you, think well, think wisely, think not for a moment but for the years that are to come, before you reject this Bill.

Matters had gone too far for rhetoric or appeals. The packed House immediately divided, and in the subsequent Division the Bill was defeated by 341 votes to 311 amid scenes of pandemonium. Ninety-three Liberals had voted against the Bill, and both the tellers against the Bill were Liberals. As Chamberlain strode exultantly out of the Chamber Parnell called out 'There goes the man who killed Home Rule.' Ministers agreed unanimously to advise dissolution rather than to resign, and the battle was taken to the constituencies.

Although Home Rule was the dominant single issue in the General Election, elections are never fought on single issues alone, and the result can hardly be interpreted only as a massive rejection of Home Rule—except, of course, in Ulster, when there were ugly riots, principally in Belfast—and an overwhelming Conservative victory. What the election did do was to demonstrate the price which the Liberals had to pay for disunity; in 114 constituencies in England, Scotland, and Wales there were Liberal candidates in contention, and many of these contests were fought with great bitterness. In the counties, not only as a result of disillusionment with the neglect of attention to land matters after the heady visions of the previous autumn, but also as a consequence of much greater Conservative effort after the shock of 1885, the Liberal cause faltered badly.

The outstanding contribution on the Conservative side was Lord Randolph Churchill's ferocious onslaught on Gladstone in his Address to the Electors of Paddington, in which the Liberal leader was depicted as 'an old man in a hurry', and which deserves to be read in full as an example of sustained invective.[1]

The Conservatives were now beginning to reap some advantages from 'Captain' Middleton's management of party affairs, and the considerable increase in the size and membership of the Primrose League—the direct result of the combination of the Home Rule and 'Imperial' issues, and upon which the Conservative leaders sedulously played. Middleton worked quietly, almost single-handedly, and with very limited resources. His great advantage over Gorst was that he was uninterested in a political career for himself, was self-effacing, and was on very close terms with the leader. His major contribution was to bring some order into the selection of candidates and to improve the quality of those who were recommended by the party to local constituencies. He also instituted *The Constitutional Year Book*, which was published annually from 1885 until 1939, and which was an invaluable, very professional, and usually very objective compilation of facts and statistics primarily intended for candidates and the party but also generally available to the public. In this venture one can see the beginnings of the Conservative Research Department, which was not to be formally instituted until 1930. Middleton had made himself—and the development was to become much more marked in following years —virtually a one-man Central Office and Research Department, working very closely with Salisbury and the Government Whips, and beginning to provide a cohesion and organisation which had never existed before. In 1886 the party began to receive the first benefits from this important development.

[1] See Winston S. Churchill: *Lord Randolph Churchill* (1951 edition) Appendix.

The crucial feature of the Corrupt and Illegal Practices Act, 1883, was that it had made effective national organisation dependent upon voluntary and unpaid workers. The 1880 General Election had been very expensive indeed for both parties—the exact cost is impossible to estimate, but it is known that the Conservatives spent some £100,000 on fifty-five seats in the Midlands; under the new Act they would be limited to £37,000. In one constituency (Leicestershire North) the Conservatives had spent £6,306 for 3,369 votes.[1] It was evident that under the new financial restrictions the entire nature of fighting elections—excluding direct bribes the most significant expenditure was in many cases paid canvassers—had to be transformed. Thus, the voluntary party devotee who was prepared to give his own time to the service of the party between elections as well as during them suddenly became a central figure. The Conservatives recognised this at once, and the dramatic improvement in their political position was the direct result of their realisation that the day of the mass party had arrived. The extraordinary success of the Primrose League drove the point home. Salisbury keenly disliked this development, and was profoundly concerned at the real possibility that a party machine might develop which dominated Parliament and made its members 'enslaved by the caucus', but he recognised the new realities and developed them after his own manner. Thus, as the Conservative machine developed to a high point of efficiency, and the party became a mass party for the first time, a subtle but vital balance between the old and the new was created, and has endured.

Although the National Liberal Federation had stood by Gladstone, the loss of the Birmingham machine was harmful in the Midlands, and the party as a whole was in disarray. In these dismal circumstances the Liberals were fighting to retain their position rather than to win the contest.

In the event, the result was not a complete disaster for the Liberals. The Conservatives won 316 seats, the Gladstonian Liberals 191, with seventy-eight Liberal Unionists and eighty-five Parnellites (O'Shea having lost in Galway, not altogether surprisingly in view of the fact that he had voted against the Home Rule Bill).

Although the Liberal Unionists now held the balance, and Salisbury

[1] These figures were given in a talk by Mr. G. C. T. Bartley—who fell foul of Lord Randolph Churchill—to a party gathering in 1883, and are quoted in Robert Mackenzie, *British Political Parties*, 164.

went through the motions of proposing that Hartington take the Premiership in a coalition administration, he knew full well that this was a political impossibility—particularly as he had taken care to emphasise that he would not serve in a Cabinet with Chamberlain. Thus, after these formalities had been concluded, an exclusively Conservative Government was formed, with Lord Randolph—aged thirty-seven—elevated to Chancellor of the Exchequer and Leader of the House of Commons and Iddesleigh, rather unexpectedly, Foreign Secretary. Hicks Beach became Chief Secretary for Ireland, and W. H. Smith went to the War Office. The only real surprise was the elevation, on Lord Randolph's urgings, of the politically unknown Henry Matthews as Home Secretary, which proved a most unfortunate appointment. Otherwise, it was very much the mixture as before, with the veteran Lord John Manners creakingly bearing the banner of Disraelian Young England at the Duchy of Lancaster. The intellectual and political domination of Salisbury and Churchill was total.

On August 3rd the new Cabinet proceeded to Osborne to kiss hands. 'How long will your leadership last?' Rosebery asked Churchill. 'Six months'. 'And after that?' 'Westerminster Abbey!'

Gladstone wrote in his diary (December 29th) that 'It has been a year of shock and strain. I think a year of some progress; but of greater absorption in interests which, though profoundly human, are quite off the line of an old man's preparation for passing the River of Death. I have not had a chance given me of creeping from this Whirlpool, for I cannot abandon a cause which is so evidently that of my fellow-men, and in which a particular part seems to be assigned to me.'

On these contradictory but characteristic notes this narrative of the Home Rule Crisis of 1886 may be conveniently ended.

CHAPTER FOUR

CROSS-CURRENTS, 1886–1892

AUGUST 1886 found the Liberal Party, on the morrow of defeat and division, in confusion and perplexity. The loss of the Hartingtonian Whigs was perhaps tolerable, the defection of Chamberlain less so; what was most serious of all had been the rasping and bitter nature of the reproaches which the erstwhile colleagues had hurled at each other over the past months. Gladstone had described Chamberlain as a trimmer, while Morley compared the latter to 'the envious Casca'. Hartington had only narrowly survived at Rossendale, and Henry James had only just scraped through at Bury, both against Gladstonian candidates, an important factor in Hartington's refusal of Salisbury's offer.[1] Dilke was gone. The party was wholly committed to Gladstone's Irish policy, and its fortunes dependent upon it.

Home Rule, as a cause, was one which many Gladstonian Liberals regarded with actual distaste; most were indifferent to it. Although Rosebery and Harcourt—to take the most conspicuous examples—had followed Gladstone, neither was deeply committed to Home Rule, and Harcourt's dislike of the Irish in general and Parnell in particular was ill-concealed. A new generation of talented Liberals, including Edward Grey, R. B. Haldane, and H. H. Asquith, was impatient that this measure should so dominate Liberal thoughts and ambitions.

But for Gladstone, Home Rule was the only issue that kept him in public life, and in those years he thought of little else. The decline in his powers now became even more marked, and was accompanied with an increase in excitability which often clouded his judgement. He remained an astounding phenomenon, and his public meetings in the 1886 election reminded observers of the passion and frenzy of the

[1] Until 1918, newly appointed Ministers had to seek re-election. Normally they were unopposed, but it was evident that this convention would not be followed in these cases.

glories of Midlothian. Both in Parliament and in the country he was an outstanding and dominating figure, and he enjoyed an immense personal following in the Liberal Party. But it cannot seriously be denied that this amazing longevity and energy were a source of deep misfortune for the party which he had in effect created, and whose character and policies had been so notably shaped by his towering personality, sincerity, political skill, and passion. He was thus at one and the same time the Liberals' greatest asset and their most grievous liability. Until Home Rule was passed, or Gladstone passed on, the Liberals were inextricably linked to that issue. When it prospered, their cause prospered; when it was in decline, they were in decline. And in the meanwhile other projects of social reform were delayed, neglected, and impeded. On all sides, 'Ireland blocked the way'. Gladstone was enthusiastic for Home Rule, so was John Morley. The bulk of the party, seeing the terrible damage already inflicted upon it, and fearful of worse to come, rallied around Gladstone because he was Gladstone, and not because of Home Rule.

Another consequence of Gladstone's longevity and new obsession was the postponement of the question of the future leadership of the party. Hartington and Chamberlain had not wholly lost hope of a reunified Liberal Party, but their chances for the leadership had vanished in the fire and fury of the Home Rule battle. The perennial Harcourt, 'his eye fixed firmly, but by no means unerringly, on the main chance' in Winston Churchill's phrase, aroused little enthusiasm. Morley, although Gladstone's *fidus achates*, was too new. Rosebery, picked out by Gladstone himself as 'the man of the future', would have been the choice of most had he not been so young and also in the House of Lords. But the fact was that, whether consciously or not, Gladstone had not given the party an obvious and generally accepted successor. This in itself was to cause serious strains and tensions at the top, and to give the party as a whole a sense of uneasiness and insecurity for the future.

By this stage it was evident that the Home Rule issue was emotionally closely linked with the new Imperialistic fervour which was to become so evident in the later 1880s, and which had a striking public demonstration in the Silver Jubilee celebrations and the first Colonial Conference in 1887. The Jubilee was a surprising popular triumph for Queen Victoria, who had become a remote and almost mythical figure since the death of her husband more than twenty years earlier, and whose active involvement in political affairs was not widely known. The establishment of the Imperial Institute in Kensington, the Conference of the Colonial leaders, the great naval review at Spithead, and the popular excitement, troubled many Liberals, and particularly those who sympathised with the new mood and resented the political advantages going to the Conservatives and the still-expanding Primrose League. The division within the Liberal leadership over its attitude to Imperialism now became marked, and was to destroy much of its effectiveness over the next twenty years. Liberals like Harcourt, Morley, and Campbell-Bannerman shared Gladstone's suspicions of the new movement, and were implacably opposed to any further colonial commitments; others, of whom Rosebery was the most prominent, were defiantly self-styled Liberal Imperialists. The Conservatives' blatant linking of the issues of Imperialism and Home Rule, arguing with increasing confidence that to be an Imperialist Home Ruler was a contradiction in terms, also had its effect. Even at this stage there were present the divisions within the Party that were to have such fatal results in the 1890s and early 1900s.

Thus, in the short run, the Liberals were irretrievably committed to the Irish Home Rule cause. In the long run there was a fundamental division in the Party about its future course and on the attitudes it ought to adopt in changing circumstances. And, while the Liberals battled with these perplexing issues, a new political power was developing which was eventually to replace the old Liberal Party as the party of the Left. Any understanding of the rise of the Labour Party must begin with a realisation of the decline of the Liberals from 1886–1906 and the factors that caused that decline. In 1886 there was no such thing as a Labour Party. Twenty years later fifty-three Members of the House of Commons described themselves as 'Labour', of whom twenty-nine were members of the new Party.

*

For the Conservatives, 1886 had been an *annus mirabilis*. They had converted the minority of 1885 into a handsome majority. Their opponents were divided and dispirited. Although the leading Liberal Unionists refused to join the Conservative Government, and were initially cautious about their relationship with it, the political and social affinities were close, and were to become steadily closer. By 1892 the Unionist coalition was a definite political reality. For nearly twenty years after 1886 this coalition was to enjoy almost uninterrupted political supremacy.

The Unionist Alliance, although the direct result of the events of April–June 1886, was some time in developing. The leaders found difficulty in adjusting themselves to the new situation, and for the rank and file the early strains on the alliance were severe. Although it was evident to the dissident Liberals that their survival depended upon the support—or at least non-intervention—of the Conservatives in the constituencies, this did not mean Coalition in the full sense of the word. As Chamberlain wrote to Hartington:

> Of course, I would not join any coalition; it would be absurd in me, and I need not argue it. With you it is somewhat different. You might join and be perfectly consistent. But if you do you must make up your mind to cease to be, or call yourself, a Liberal. The force of circumstances will be irresistible, and you will be absorbed in the Great Constitutional Party.

Thus, at least for a period, there was no formal alliance beyond an electoral compact, and many of the dissident Liberals hoped that when the issue of Home Rule was removed or settled, unity might be restored.

The Conservatives played the game carefully so as not to offend their new allies. The Local Government Act of 1888, for example, put into effect reforms that Chamberlain had been campaigning for since the early 1870s. The 1892 Education Act, providing free education in the public elementary schools of England and Wales, the most important legislation enacted by this Government, similarly owed much to Chamberlain's influence and work. But the most significant feature of the first years of the Unionist alliance was the extent to which Chamberlain, Hartington and the Conservatives found that their views were very similar on both domestic and foreign issues. Chamberlain's imperialist attitude were gradually emerging, and he was as alarmed as any Conservative by what he considered to be the confiscatory and aggressive features of socialist and trade union attitudes. To Balfour he wrote on December 8th, 1894:

> The intermediates—the men who hold the balance of elections—are disgusted and frightened . . . at the projects of confiscation which are in the air and [which] found expression at the Trade Union Congress the other day.

Gladstone's 'Newcastle Programme' of 1891 seemed to embody all Chamberlain's fears about the new Radicalism, and this was probably the final and decisive moment in his permanent estrangement from the Liberal Party. The 'programme' contained compulsory land acquisition, universal suffrage, and measures for employers' liability. Chamberlain attacked the Newcastle Programme root and branch, and this was really the end of 'Radical Joe'. By February 1894, when he spoke at Leeds, he was emphatically estranged. The objectives, he declared in this speech, of the 'new Radical' were 'to merge the individual into the State, to reduce all to one dead level of uniformity, in which the inefficient and the thriftless and the idle are to be confounded and treated alike . . . with the honest, and the industrious, and the capable.'

But personal factors played a very important part, as the Irish Question entered a particularly virulent and bitter period. As Winston Churchill has written of Chamberlain:

The Irish were his most persistent foes.[1] They added to British politics a stream of hatred all their own and belonging to centuries from which England has happily escaped. They knew that more than any other man he had broken Mr. Gladstone and frustrated Home Rule. The malignity of their resentment was unsurpassed by anything I have ever seen in this confused world. He retorted with scorn and long, slow, patient antagonism. He made them feel they had been right to hate him.

The duels that now developed between Chamberlain and Gladstone, who sat beside each other in the House of Commons in icy proximity, were more intense and personal than even the Disraeli-Gladstone confrontations of the '60s and '70s. Chamberlain ascended to new heights of debating skill: 'He never spoke like this for us', Gladstone once remarked after a Chamberlain speech. The failure of the 1887 'Round Table' Conference and the continuation of the Irish debate

[1] And not only the Irish, i.e. Labouchere at Bradford, November 1888:
'Mr. Chamberlain had thrown over his old colleagues because the Radicals would not help him to supplant Mr. Gladstone; he had been activated by hatred and envy, declared Mr. Labouchere. Mr. Chamberlain had been called Judas. He did not approve of historical comparisons; they were seldom exact. Judas had some good about him. He betrayed his Master, but he did not afterwards stump Judaea, dine with Herod, sup with Caiaphas, sing the praises of Pilate, appear on platforms surrounded by Scribes and Pharisees, and then declare that he alone of the Apostles was a true Christian.' (*Maccoby: English Radicalism 1886–1914*, 112).

put aside the possibility of an early reconciliation. The movement away from the Gladstonian Liberals was steady. At Glasgow, on February 13th 1889, Chamberlain emphasised the nature of the division:

> In my opinion every Liberal who places the Union first of all is bound to make some sacrifices for what will be his paramount object. He is bound to make some sacrifices of extreme views. He is bound to put aside for a time some of his cherished ambitions. This is an elementary condition of all combinations whatsoever.

But the historian who omits the personal element in this dispute omits the dispute itself. Gladstone and Chamberlain saw in each other what each feared in himself, and thus assailed. Much has been made of the attraction of opposites, too little of the revulsion between similars. This, for all their differences of backgrounds and philosophies, was the essential Chamberlain–Gladstone dispute.

As a consequence of many elements, the Liberal Unionists were being propelled inexorably towards formal and complete coalition with the Conservatives. Although this did not occur until 1895, the movement towards Coalition was steady after the great Liberal split of 1886.

*

The Conservatives, after their triumph, were not in the mood for further excitements, and settled down contentedly to a period of power tempered by the practical realisation that their survival depended upon the perpetuation of the Liberal division. It was a time for cohesion and care. Salisbury's distaste for Chamberlain personally as well as politically was profound, although he appreciated the need to placate and satisfy him. Churchill, on the other hand, regarded Chamberlain as a natural ally, and saw him frequently. This was not the only factor that was placing an increasingly unbearable strain upon the relationship between Salisbury and Churchill. Churchill, although he proved an able Minister and a much better Leader of the House than many had expected, was proving an overbearing colleague, and behaved with an air of arrogance and impatience which exasperated the Cabinet and taxed Salisbury's soothing skills to their limit. When Churchill started interfering in foreign policy and making major public speeches without consultation, Salisbury had had enough. It was simply a question of when, and on what issue, Churchill would make his fatal mistake. It came in December, just before Christmas, on the matter of economies in the estimates of the War Office.

Churchill, from a position of weakness, and without calculation, made claim to virtual equality in the Cabinet with Salisbury. He grossly misjudged his man, his issue, and his occasion. He threatened to resign unless his demands over the War Office estimates were met. Salisbury in effect accepted his resignation, but carefully not in so many words. Churchill, trapped, was faced with the alternative of climbing down or actually resigning. When he, inevitably, chose the latter, and informed *The Times* of the fact, the Government tottered but did not fall. Churchill found himself in political desolation, his admirers appalled and baffled, his friends astounded and offended, and his many enemies exultantly merciless. Too late he realised the fact that his opponent had completely out-manoeuvred him, and that Salisbury was both a wily and a hard man. In retrospect, we can see that it was hardly a fair contest. 'His character', Salisbury wrote of Churchill, as if in dissection of a distant acquaintance who had aroused his dissatisfaction, 'moreover is quite untamed. Both in impulsiveness and variability, and in a tendency which can only be described by the scholastic word 'vulgaris', he presents the characteristics of extreme youth.' There was truth in this harsh estimate. Churchill had received many warnings but, in the continued exhilaration of his meteoric rise, had ignored them. Salisbury, eyeing him closely, had awaited the moment when Churchill's impetuosity and vanity would put him at his mercy, and then struck with cold efficiency.

Nonetheless, so high was Churchill's reputation and position that his crash made it appear that he must bring down Salisbury as well. But the calculations of the older man had been careful. Had he accepted battle on another issue, in other circumstances, and at another time, it might well have been different—but he had been careful not to do so.

Another offer to Hartington—this one even less serious than that of August—was made by Salisbury to step down in favour of him, but again had absolutely no chance of acceptance, a fact of which Salisbury was fully aware. But the progress towards achieving a Liberal Unionist participation in the Government succeeded when Goschen succeeded Churchill at the Treasury. Salisbury also used the occasion to resume control over foreign affairs by removing Iddesleigh; the distressed old man, who had read of his dismissal from the newspapers, collapsed and died at 10 Downing Street while making his formal farewell. Smith took Churchill's Leadership in the Commons and proved a considerable success, and Beach's failing eyesight—only temporary— gave Salisbury the opportunity of appointing Balfour to the post of Irish Secretary. Thus, the crisis passed, and Salisbury emerged from it infinitely stronger.

Churchill's extraordinary political career virtually ended at this point. Although he remained in politics, something in that febrile and tense personality was destroyed by this disaster and he was never the same man again. From 1891 until his death in 1895 he was in marked physical and mental decline. Rosebery's moving valediction on him should not be omitted:

He will be pathetically memorable, too, for the dark cloud which gradually enveloped him, and in which he passed away. He was the chief mourner at his own protracted funeral, a public pageant of gloomy years. It is a black moment when the heralds proclaim the passing of the dead, and the great officers break their staves. But it is sadder still when it is the victim's own voice that announces his decadence, when it is the victim's own hands that break the staff in public.

His career, although brief, had left its mark. 'Tory Democracy' may have been an imposture, as Rosebery argued and Salisbury certainly believed, but it had considerable and enduring effects. 'He made the people believe in us', one elderly Tory said of him, and it was not an ignoble nor an inaccurate epitaph. But Churchill had done more than coin phrases, superb though many of them were. He had restored Conservative morale at a critical moment. He had been the architect of what was to become the Unionist Alliance, another of his phrases destined to become reality. He had been the first to see the political implications of the Ulster issue, but his deep knowledge of, and genuine sympathy for, the Irish people gave him a very particular place in their affection and respect. He had been the leading spirit in the annexation of Upper Burma, and in his perception of British rule in India he had demonstrated a vision and understanding which made a profound impression upon his officials and advisers. In his brief period at the Treasury he had won new and unexpected admirers.

He leaves behind him an impression of youth, freshness, and vigour, of work unfulfilled, of promise uncompleted. For all his faults of judgement and character, Lord Randolph was a politician of the very front rank. But he was not vouchsafed time and experience, and we are left with a series of unanswered questions. To many of his contemporaries he always remained the most brilliantly equipped, fascinating, and perplexing individual in public life whom they had ever encountered. The more one examines his speeches and letters, the more one is struck by his fundamental seriousness and his acute perceptiveness. He possessed what the Welsh call 'the seeing eye'. His approach to questions was often intuitive, and often wrong, but his basic attitudes to democracy were far ahead of almost everyone in active politics in his time. He was Conservative only in name; he was in reality a rebel against his class and the structure of society, seeing the future and not fearful of it. It was this element above all others that Salisbury detected, and which was the root cause of their differences.

It is one of the persistent tragedies of life that nature endows certain individuals with outstanding intellectual qualities but denies them other essential necessities to success, while favouring others with lesser qualities but better fortune in health and personal circumstances. In the case of Lord Randolph Churchill it bestowed many qualities on a fragile frame. He was a solitary man, with a disappointing marriage, serious financial difficulties, and few personal friends. It could be argued by those who saw him, as did Lord Ripon, as 'a reckless and unprincipled mountebank', that he deserved his loneliness, and that his defects of character were bound to bring to nothing his abilities. But this is strikingly not the judgement of his most eminent contemporaries, and which included Gladstone, Rosebery, Beach, Parnell, Morley, and Asquith. They were touched by his courtesy, his moods of caressing gentleness, lack of jealousy—a quality that struck Rosebery particularly—and consideration and kindness. But to the world he showed a different face, and it is not to be wondered that so many found it repulsive and dangerous, and were joyous at his downfall.

It has been often argued that his deadly error in December 1886 was at least partly due to physical factors, and that he was already gripped by the disease that was to kill him so slowly. While this is possible, it seems much more probable that it was a political miscalculation by a young man hell-bent on power who was, not unjustifiably, intoxicated by his successes. It has happened before, and subsequently. In any event, it is not clear precisely what was the disease that destroyed him, or when he contracted it. The opinion of his medical advisers was General Paralysis of the Insane, a euphemism for syphilis, but there was no autopsy and, given the state of medical knowledge of brain conditions at the time, this verdict is not fully convincing to this commentator. Among other real possibilities of the source of his decline and death is a brain tumour, a diagnosis which the limited available evidence strongly indicates could have been the cause. But, whatever it was, the fact was that Lord Randolph Churchill, insane, died at the age of forty-five in London, in January 1895, and that it was left to his older son, whom he hardly knew and whom he somewhat despised, to revive his memory and to perpetuate his name.

Thankfully uncluttered by this turbulent and disturbing personality, the Salisbury Government braced itself to meet the burden of issues that now marched relentlessly upon it.

*

The resignation of Lord Randolph Churchill led directly, but unavailingly, to the last serious attempt to create a Liberal rapprochement. The much-heralded 'Round Table' Conference—in fact a series of meetings—held in London in January 1887 only served to demonstrate the differences and did nothing to bring the warring groups together. In Chamberlain's own words, 'All hope of reunion was at last abandoned.'

For the next six years, in Lucy's phrase, 'all Parliamentary roads led to Ireland'. We can now see that Parnell's '86' marked the peak of his power. But it did not seem so at the time, and indeed until the end of 1890 his position, and the fate of Home Rule, seemed assured. The Conservatives set out firmly to restore law and order on the one hand and, by judicious meeting of certain Irish grievances, to 'kill Home Rule by kindness' on the other.[1]

In Arthur Balfour the Unionists discovered an unexpectedly firm, sly, courageous and resourceful Chief Secretary. It became evident that behind a languid charm Balfour concealed many strong qualities, in which ambition and ruthlessness were not omitted. As Winston Churchill was to write of him many years later, with paternal and

[1] For the best account, see L. P. Curtis: *Coercion and Conciliation in Ireland 1880–1892*, Chapters XI–XV.

personal experience, 'had his life been cast amid the labyrinthine intrigues of the Italian Renaissance, he would not have required to study the works of Machiavelli'. A critical turning-point was his handling of the situation which arose in September 1887, when the police opened fire at a meeting at Mitchelstown and killed three people. The Irish and the Liberals were outraged, but Balfour emphatically supported the police and blamed the organisers of the assembly. Gladstone raised the cry of 'Remember Mitchelstown!', but the effect upon the Conservatives and the hard-pressed and demoralised Irish officials was very different. It may have been that Ireland between 1887 and 1892 required such a combination of strength and subtlety; what is without doubt was that the new Unionist Coalition did. Balfour swiftly became their hero, and the memory of Lord Randolph faded equally swiftly. As the Liberals and the Irish raged against 'Bloody Balfour' and the tumult rose, Balfour's imperturbable Parliamentary skill and Ministerial decisiveness gave new heart to the Government benches and established his position. In the Commons, with Churchill and Beach on the back benches, and W. H. Smith hardly in serious contention,[1] Balfour seized his opportunity to become the Conservative heir-apparent. The long rule of what was later derided as 'the Hotel Cecil' had begun.

The Irish Question now entered a period of extreme unpleasantness. To meet Irish obstructionism, a new Closure procedure was introduced, whereby the Speaker could accept a motion to end debate at any time from any Member and put it at once to the vote; if there were more than 200 votes in the majority voting for the proposal, the main Questions would be put immediately. This new procedure could have become—as many feared it would—a terrible weapon in the hands of any Government to curtail debate. But in Speaker Peel, one of the greatest of all Speakers, the minority's rights were firmly defended at all times, and the apprehensions of the opponents—by no means only Irish and Liberals—proved unfounded. Nonetheless, it marked a major change in the procedure and the character of the

[1] In the words of Herbert Paul: 'Mr. Smith's speeches were intelligible to careful listeners who understood the subject, and he knew how to arrange the business of the House. But as chief of a great party in a historic Assembly he left something to be desired.' (*A History of Modern England* (1906), Vol. V, 87). But, affectionately dubbed 'Old Morality' by Henry Lucy, Smith proved a popular and well-regarded leader during a period of exceptional virulence and difficulty, and the strain undoubtedly hastened his death in October 1891.

House of Commons. The 'Plan of Campaign', initiated in October 1886, incited tenants to withhold rents if the landlords refused what the tenants regarded as fair rents; the Criminal Law Amendment Act of 1887 was the Government's response, and gave it sweeping powers to 'proclaim' districts, to conduct trials of agrarian offences before courts of summary jurisdiction, and to declare specific organisations to be dangerous and liable to prosecution as such. Then, in May 1887 *The Times* initiated a series of articles on 'Parnellism and Crime', which deeply implicated the Irish leader in the Land League.

Parnell had prominently disassociated himself from the Plan of Campaign on the grounds that he would not support any actions which would alienate English opinion and harm the Liberals. *The Times* articles were designed to show that Parnell, behind a veneer of moderation, was in fact closely linked with the most violent aspects of the Irish agitation, that his movement was 'essentially a foreign conspiracy', and that the Liberals had allied themselves 'with the paid agents of an organisation whose ultimate aim is plunder and whose ultimate sanction is murder, to paralyse the House of Commons and to hand Ireland over to social and financial ruin'. The articles aroused only modest interest until, on April 18th, *The Times* published a facsimile of a letter allegedly written by Parnell, dated May 15th 1882, in which he expressed regret at his having been obliged, for political reasons, to condemn the Phoenix Park murders.

It was not know at the time, nor until a long time afterwards, that the Government was deeply involved in this calculated and well-planned attempt to destroy Parnell,[1] although many Irishmen and Liberals immediately suspected it at the time. The sensation was immense, and the charges against Parnell seemed to be confirmed by his own response. *The Times* challenged Parnell to bring an action if he dared, but Parnell merely denounced the letters as forgeries and seemed prepared to ignore the matter. In fact he was engaged in extensive and often heated discussion with the Liberal leaders about the best course to take, while *The Times* articles continued with more sensations.

F. H. O'Donnell, a popular Irish Nationalist of an eccentric manner and disposition, sued *The Times* for a reference to himself in their articles. The Attorney-General, Sir Richard Webster, appeared for

[1] See F. S. L. Lyons: 'Parnellism and Crime', *Transactions of the Royal Historical Society*, Fifth Series, Vol. 24 (1974).

the newspaper, and produced more facsimile letters allegedly written by Parnell. The Government, meanwhile, was considering how to maximise its advantage and, on the urgings of Chamberlain, initiated an investigation of the charges against Parnell; to the merited fury of the Liberals and Irish—who had wanted a Parliamentary investigation of *The Times*'s allegations—it appointed a special commission of three judges to look into the much wider and more fruitful questions of the complicity of the Land League and the Irish Parliamentary Party in agrarian and other outrages. This partisan manoeuvre was denounced in private by Churchill as 'a revolutionary tribunal for the trial of political offenders' and publicly by the Liberals and the Irish in exceedingly harsh debates. But Parnell, intent upon proving the letters published by *The Times* to be forgeries, reluctantly accepted the Commission which Morley justly categorised as 'one of the ugliest things done in the name and under the forms of law in this island during the century'.

The Government's discreditable strategem misfired. The proceedings of the Commission increasingly bored the public until on its fiftieth day, in February 1890, Richard Pigott appeared before it. After brutal cross-questioning by Sir Charles Russell it was established that this disreputable journalist had forged the letters so injudiciously accepted by *The Times*. J. L. Garvin's account of the scene should not be omitted:

> First the fatuity with which the forgeries had been accepted and paid for was disclosed. Then the lamentable Pigott with his bald head, red face, white whiskers, loose mouth, his disreputable but not unkindly lineaments, foolishly smiling—he looked like a church-warden or sidesman gone wrong—was racked and crushed in the witness-box. . . . Blackmailer, parasite, most mercenary of grubs in Grub Street, vendor of obscene books and photographs, he was hopelessly exposed.[1]

Pigott fled the country and committed suicide in Madrid; the reputation of *The Times* lay in ruins; the Government's strategy was shattered; and Parnell's prestige soared, even in England. The Liberals embraced him in ecstatic relief. The Eighty Club honoured him. Edinburgh gave him its freedom. He was warmly invited to Hawarden for discussions with Gladstone. Lord Randolph, who had so prophetic-

[1] Garvin: *Chamberlain*, III, 394-5.

ally attacked the Commission in private, now denounced it in the House of Commons with a ferocity that shocked even those who agreed with him, describing it as 'in every sense of the word an Elizabethan procedure. . . . What has been the result of this uprootal of Constitutional practices? What has been the result? Pigott! What has been the result of this mountainous parturition? A thing, a reptile, a monster. Pigott! What, with all your skill, all your cleverness, has been the result? A ghastly, bloody, rotten foetus—Pigott! Pigott!! Pigott!!! *This* is your Nemesis.'

The excitement and Liberal euphoria were deceptive and dangerous. The situation in Ireland itself continued to be bad, and the Irish Question remained highly volatile. A careful reading of Parnell's evidence to the Commission and of its Report emphasises that there was more substance to his critics' charges than the forgeries of Pigott. But the Pigott affair had other, much more fatal, consequences. It raised Parnell's position to such a height that, when the fall came, it was to be precipitous. It prompted many to disbelieve other charges which were in fact justified. And it linked the fortunes of the Liberals more than they had ever been before to the personal fortunes and strange personality of this complex man.

The period of Parnell's glory was brief indeed. In December 1889 Captain O'Shea instituted divorce proceedings against his wife, citing Parnell as co-respondent. Nearly a year elapsed between the filing of his petition and the hearing of the case, and Irish opinion, although disquieted, appeared to accept that this was another English attempt to discredit Parnell and on the same level as the allegations of *The Times*. Those who knew the facts were more apprehensive, but the general reaction was strongly supportive of Parnell. In the words of Conor Cruise O'Brien, 'the nationalist movement as a whole simply drifted towards the catastrophe, with a dumb confidence in its leader's ambiguous assurances, and a dumb expectation of another Pigott'.[1] 'One of the most marked traits in the psychology of Irish politicians', Davitt's biographer wrote, '—and perhaps the generalisation might be extended to politicians of other countries—is their capacity for imitating the ostrich whenever anything disagreeable appears on the horizon. They are inclined to make an excessive application to politics of the methods of Christian Science, and to imagine that to ignore an inconvenience is equivalent to annihilating

[1] O'Brien, op. cit., 282.

it. This was the principle on which Parnell's followers appear to have acted during the time when the O'Shea affair was in the air and had not yet been submitted to the tribunals'.[1]

But the Liberals were no better prepared. It was not until two days before the case was heard that Morley raised the matter with Parnell, received the firm assurance that he had no intention of retiring from the leadership, and assumed that Parnell would emerge from the matter unscathed. These reactions among the Irish and Liberal leaders, who were fully conversant with the facts, would be inconceivable except in the context of the Pigott affair, the extraordinary position of authority that Parnell had acquired, and their desperate wishful thinking.

It is still not clear why O'Shea intervened at this time. Considerable suspicion, then and later, fell on Chamberlain as the principal instigator. Much attention has been given to a statement by Sir Alfred Robbins, at the time the London correspondent of the *Birmingham Daily Post*, that in September 1889 he 'was asked by one on the inside of the liberal unionist "machine" whether Parnell would be politically ruined by a divorce, the then recent Dilke instance being given as a precedent, and Captain O'Shea, it was added, being willing to take proceedings'. This is very paltry stuff. Even if this was Chamberlain to whom Robbins was referring, one does not feel that Chamberlain required instruction from a journalist in the political implications of involvement in a sordid divorce case at that time. And no one could have foreseen how Parnell would handle the matter.

But there is much more compelling and serious evidence, although inconclusive, that Chamberlain was not uninvolved in O'Shea's action.[2] Chamberlain had been active in prompting the Government to set up the Special Commission, a fact which he denied in his personal account but which was subsequently revealed.[3] He had, as has been related, made use of O'Shea as an emissary in the past, had campaigned for him in Liverpool in 1885, and had supported his controversial candidature for the Galway seat in 1886. O'Shea had appeared before the Commission as a witness for *The Times* at Chamberlain's instigation, and had testified to the accuracy of Parnell's signature in the

---

[1] F. Sheehy-Skeffington: *Michael Davitt*.

[2] Although, interestingly, not from Parnell, who, although he believed that the proceedings were politically inspired, accused *The Times*.

[3] Chamberlain: *A Political Memoir*, 283, and Garvin, op. cit., III, 386–7.

Pigott letters; he had worked with Chamberlain in 1885–6 in seeking information detrimental to Parnell from the Home Office.[1] Thus, in spite of O'Shea's alleged duplicity in 1885, the evidence is overwhelming that Chamberlain worked with him closely thereafter. Why?

O'Shea took care to inform Balfour in December 1889 when he filed proceedings that Chamberlain was 'acquainted with the facts'. His counsel was the Solicitor-General, Sir Edward Clarke. Although it was quite proper for a Law Officer of the Crown at this time to accept private clients, the presence of Clarke in such a case, following Webster's appearance for *The Times*, necessarily arouses strong suspicions that the Unionists, having failed to destroy Parnell in *The Times* and the Special Commission, were making a third attempt. We now know that they were deeply involved in the first two ventures, and it is difficult to afford them the benefit of the doubt in the third. Clarke evidently relished his opportunity, and was devastatingly severe on Parnell, but he subsequently wrote that the two surviving children of Mrs. O'Shea were 'unquestionably' Parnell's,[2] a fact that demolished an important part of O'Shea's case as the deceived husband only recently aware of the true facts. It is not clear whether Clarke knew this at the time of the trial; it takes a considerable amount of credulousness to state that the thought had not crossed the mind of so experienced and politically dedicated a lawyer. There is nothing absolutely conclusive, but the number of coincidences is such that the allegations that O'Shea was driven on by factors wholly unconnected with contemporary politics become somewhat implausible.

But there were several factors that would have persuaded O'Shea to take action on his own account, of which the most compelling were financial. The belated death of Mrs. Wood in May 1889, at the age of ninety-eight, was an event of crucial significance. Mrs. Wood left all the considerable wealth to Mrs. O'Shea in such terms that it seemed not capable of claim by her husband nor within the scope of her marriage settlement. But O'Shea was not the only indignant claimant; several other relatives of Mrs. Wood were eager to contest her will, and were very ready to believe and to claim that its terms had been influenced by Mrs. O'Shea in her favour. O'Shea was by this time an embittered man politically, and was now embittered financially. We may discount the possibility that he was outraged by the realisation

---

[1] F. S. L. Lyons: *The Fall of Parnell*, 70.
[2] Clarke: *The Story of My Life*, 291–5.

of his wife's infidelity. But was he, in the eleven months between the filing of his petition and the hearing in court, engaged in blackmail? In short, was he seeking to be paid off for his silence? Mrs. O'Shea later told Henry Harrison that this was indeed the case, but that in view of the objections to Mrs. Woods's will it was not possible to meet his demands. The explanation may help to explain Parnell's confidence, and then his defiance. But it is unsatisfying by itself. One feels that other factors were involved, and that O'Shea did not act alone, nor for pecuniary reasons only. It was too convenient, too well-timed, and too well organised, to be dismissed as one of those historical events which, in the course of human affairs, occur at particular moments merely by chance. The arm of coincidence may indeed be long, but hardly as long as it was in this particular episode.

But the key factors in Parnell's downfall were his eagerness to marry Mrs. O'Shea, his aloof self-confidence, and his contempt for English courts and English opinion. Thus, when the case came to court on November 15th 1890 only one side of the case was given, O'Shea was awarded his decree nisi, and Parnell was depicted in the most severe and lamentable light. The revelations of what seemed to be a prolonged record of duplicity and tawdriness on Parnell's part provided excellent material for his enemies. More significantly, they put his colleagues and the Liberals in a difficult position which rapidly became untenable. It was this belief that they had been duped that imparted so much savagery to the political aftermath of the O'Shea divorce.

First reactions from Ireland, however, were very encouraging to Parnell, indeed so encouraging that the Irish Catholic leaders were unsure of their course and held silence. Of the leading Nationalists only Davitt urged Parnell to efface himself temporarily, at least until after he could marry Mrs. O'Shea, but with this exception there was initially no movement in Ireland to condemn Parnell nor to seek his resignation. Following the old pattern of Irish-English reaction, the abuse heaped upon Parnell in England was not likely to precipitate such a movement in Ireland, and for a brief period it seemed that Parnell might surmount even this episode as successfully as he had weathered previous storms.

But the Liberals, who had suffered so much for the Home Rule cause, were more keenly receptive to the uproar in England, and the rank-and-file, now convinced of a heavy victory in the next election, was dismayed at the prospect of fighting the rejuvenated Unionists with a discredited adulterer and deceiver at their side. This mood was very evident at the annual meeting of the National Liberal Federation on November 20th–21st at Sheffield, and the prospect of Parnell's voluntary retirement—even if only temporary—became very alluring.

Gladstone refused to condemn Parnell for his immorality, but he saw the political perils very clearly. Cardinal Manning urged him to repudiate Parnell, and, at the other extreme of the religious spectrum, the Nonconformists advised the same course. The Nonconformist influence may not have been what it once had been, but it was very raucous, and was still a very formidable political reality. Thus, it was eventually agreed on November 24th that Gladstone should write a letter to Morley which the latter would show to Parnell before the meeting of the Irish Parliamentary Party on the following day. The key passage, which stated that Gladstone's position would become 'almost a nullity' if Parnell remained was omitted from the first draft, but was in the final version. Gladstone also saw Justin McCarthy, Vice-Chairman of the Parliamentary Party on the 24th, and conveyed the same message. On the next day McCarthy found Parnell obdurate, and Parnell was re-elected Leader for the new session before he saw Morley and read Gladstone's letter. It is not clear whether this was wholly accidental, but from Parnell's attitude at this time it is difficult to believe that it would have had much influence. Parnell read it immediately after his election, and told Morley that he would not resign. Gladstone, shocked by the news, authorised the publication of his letter, which appeared on the next day. With that, the storm broke.

The Nationalists were in an agonising position. Many argued that Parnell should step down, but hated the idea of bowing to English clamour and the panic of the Liberals. Others, although alarmed by the situation, became more defiant in their support of Parnell for much the same reason. They all, as in the past, looked to Parnell for leadership and salvation. And at this point he made the rupture inevitable.

On November 26th there was an agitated and inconclusive special meeting of the Parliamentary Party at which Parnell refused a request to reconsider his position, and in which his haughty demeanour was such that Thomas Sexton commented to Tim Healy that an intelligent foreigner would have concluded that the entire Party was being tried for adultery, with Parnell as the judge. But Parnell appreciated the strength of the forces building up against him and realised he would have to act, and act quickly. Characteristically, he resolved to go on the attack. He prepared a Manifesto to the Irish people, published on November 29th, which denounced Gladstone for attempting to influence the Party's choice of leader, gave details of the Home Rule settlement which the Liberals would introduce when elected, blamed the Liberals—particularly Morley—for persuading him to attack the Land Purchase Bill, and finally claimed that Morley had proposed that Parnell or one of his colleagues should become Chief Secretary and that the Nationalists should have one of the Irish law offices in a Liberal administration.

This was a very tough counter-attack indeed. It was not an emotional outburst, but a calculated stroke, characterised by language which was obviously deliberately designed to outrage the Liberals and rally Irish sympathy. The references to 'the integrity and independence of the Irish parliamentary party having been apparently sapped and destroyed by the wirepullers of the English Liberal party' and 'the English wolves now howling for my destruction' were bad enough, but it was the final defiant claim that a postponement of Home Rule was preferable 'to a compromise of our national rights' which the Liberal connection would involve, that was bound to cause the deepest anger in the Liberal ranks.

Parnell had clearly broken confidence in his revelations of the Liberal proposals and had deliberately distorted what had actually occurred in his discussions with the Liberal leaders. His outrage at the proposals, furthermore, was in very marked contrast with his actual public conduct when he had learned of them. Finally, he had never indicated to his own colleagues this new sense of contempt for Gladstone's proposed measures.

What Parnell was in reality doing was attempting to divert attention —and particularly in Ireland—away from the divorce case and its implications to the issue of who was to choose the leader of Ireland. It was a bold stroke, but unsuccessful. After the first surge of instinctive loyalty, second thoughts came very swiftly, and the intervention of the Catholic hierarchy had already begun. The Manifesto in fact had made the Liberals' point much stronger. Parnell was now attempting to appeal to Ireland over the heads of the Parliamentary Party and the Church, and although the anger of the Liberal leaders was naturally intense, it was hardly less among the Nationalists themselves. A group in the United States engaged in fund-raising, and which included

Dillon and T. P. O'Connor, had initially supported Parnell. When they read the Manifesto and had received a highly-charged cable from Sexton and Healy declaring that unless Parnell went 'general election lost, campaigners ruined, dissolution inevitable' and that on this there was 'practical unanimity', they denounced it in a counter-manifesto issued in Chicago on November 30th. On the same day Archbishops Croke and Walsh broke their silence, Walsh adding that Parnell's Manifesto was 'an act of political suicide'. And so it proved to be.

The battle for Parnell's leadership now moved to Committee Room Fifteen in the House of Commons. The debates were prolonged and bitter, and have been often described.[1] Parnell fought for his position with skill and passion. An attempt to negotiate new terms with the Liberals on substantive points was stillborn when the Liberal leaders refused to discuss them until the leadership issue was settled. The Irish retired back to Committee Room Fifteen and the temperature rose sharply, particularly when Healy called out 'Who is to be the mistress of the Party?' and was denounced by Parnell as 'that cowardly little scoundrel who dares in an assembly of Irishmen to insult a woman.' At 4.30 on the afternoon of December 7th Justin McCarthy rose and said with dignity that 'I see no further use carrying on a discussion which must be barren of all but reproach, ill-temper, controversy, and indignity, and I will therefore suggest that all who think with me at this grave crisis should withdraw with me from this room.' Forty-four left with him, leaving Parnell with his faithful but disconsolate remnant of twenty-seven.

Parnell resolved to fight on in Ireland, but his position was now hopeless. For a time he was misled by the fervour of Dublin itself and the enthusiasm of his most dedicated admirers, but from this point an ominous silence began to seep across Ireland—the bitter silence of the sense of betrayal. The first real test was a by-election at Kilkenny, where Davitt and Healy ran the anti-Parnellite campaign, and in which, on Healy's claim, some seventy of the eighty-two Irish Nationalist M.P.s were engaged. It was a terrible election, even by Irish standards. Parnell hurled himself into the battle, and was denounced by Davitt as 'an insolent dictator'. Healy was particularly savage, and Parnell responded in kind. Davitt accused him of insanity, and was injured in a scuffle, and Parnell was pelted with mud and lime. Davitt, the former Fenian, was now the champion of the

[1] For the best account see Conor Cruise O'Brien, op. cit., 313–46.

constitutional approach, while, as his situation became more desperate, Parnell appealed to older and darker forces. The Church, discreetly, became very active in the battle, and at the end of this cruel and often squalid contest Parnell's candidate was badly beaten.

But he fought on, with failing health and feverish passion, against relentlessly increasing odds. To many who had fought at his side for so long and who now fought against him, this was a period of agony, and they would have agreed with Dillon, who wrote on December 20th: 'I long with an unspeakable longing to get out of politics and have done with the sordid misery of that life, and get to read and think and live at least for a few years before I die, but I fear it is too late now.'[1] An attempt to reach a reasonable settlement was made at Boulogne at the end of December, in which Parnell proposed that he would retire from the chairmanship of the Parliamentary Party but would remain at the head of the National League. It was a skilful manoeuvre, coupled with the proposal that O'Brien should replace him and seek new assurances from Gladstone on Liberal policies. At a second conference at Boulogne, on January 6–7th, Parnell produced a memorandum of agreement, but Dillon was now to be his replacement. Dillon would have nothing to do with it, and it was evident that Parnell's attempt to relinquish the title of leader while retaining the reality of power was wholly unacceptable.

At this point the Unionists easily held, with an increased majority, a by-election at Bassetlaw, in spite of the personal involvement of Gladstone, the first serious disappointment the Liberals had received for nearly two years; shortly afterwards the Liberals won a by-election at West Hartlepool, but only after their candidate had been compelled to strongly endorse Gladstone's repudiation of Parnell. The Liberals could not change their conditions, and Parnell himself was by now intractable. The story of the Boulogne Negotiations—continued at Calais—is a complex one, but the important result was that they failed, and that it was Parnell who broke them off. The Liberals could have been more forthcoming, but by this time their feelings about Parnell were barely rational, and their eagerness to see him gone was greater than their willingness to reach an agreement on joint policies. If this was a disastrously short-sighted approach, it was entirely understandable. Parnell, also, was under severe physical and emotional strain. After this brief lull, the battle was continued with even greater

[1] Quoted in Lyons, op. cit., 192.

ferocity, and was only ended by Parnell's death at Brighton on October 6th 1891, by which time the Irish Nationalist Party and the cause of Home Rule itself had received further terrible blows.

This extraordinary and tragic episode was of profound political importance. As has been rightly written, 'Parnell directed a movement of revolutionary inspiration from within a relatively conservative and constitutional party. This is the peculiarity that made "Parnellism" such an equivocal term and so elusive and effective a force. . . . "We created Parnell", one of the ablest members of the party was to write, "and Parnell created us. We seized very early in the movement the idea of this man with his superb silences, his historic name, his determination, his self-control, his aloofness—we seized that as the canvas of a great national hero".'[1]

Now that was gone and all discredited. The Irish movement was cruelly split and in anguished disarray. It seemed that the patient work of decades had been utterly destroyed within sight of victory. With Parnell's death, the heart seemed to go out of Ireland, as though the tensions and hopes of his leadership and the ordeal of his final agony had produced a collective exhaustion from which it would take a generation or more to recover. Among even his most bitter enemies in Ireland there were now feelings of remorse and even of guilt at their part in his awful and abrupt downfall. For fifteen years Parnell had utterly dominated the Irish Nationalist Party, and if in Ireland itself his hold had been less total he had, more than any man since Grattan, won the claim to regard himself as the one leader of the Irish people. Had he been struck down by an assassin or died before 1891, his legacy would have been assured. But he had fallen under the blows of his own people in an atmosphere of rage and betrayal, himself fighting with violence and extremity of language, cursing and reviling as he went down. His harsh denunciations of his former followers and theirs of him could not be stifled by his death, and were to poison Irish politics until time brought calmer perspectives. But it was to be a very long time.

The Liberal Party could only watch the ghastly culmination of Parnell's career with helpless dismay. The crusade element in the Home Rule movement, which had been of significant importance since 1886, now vanished, having perished in 'the stench of the Divorce Court', and at Kilkenny. The approaching election now

[1] O'Brien, op. cit., 9–10.

loomed with a grim and forbidding aspect. The confidence of the Unionists was now surging. By the beginning of 1892 it was evident to all observers that it was going to be a very close-run thing.

*

v.I.P.

The dramatically fluctuating fortunes of the Home Rule issue between 1886 and 1892 obscured other developments which, in their long-term effects, were to be of at least equal importance to the devastation of Gladstone's hopes for a large Home Rule majority.

During the early 1880s there had been little concept of 'labour' as a distinct class or problem, let alone a distinct political group. The enfranchisement of manual workers in the 1867 and 1885 Reform Acts and of agricultural workers in the 1885 Act had increased the political importance of these groups, but there had been no signs that this new voice might develop into an independent one. Disraeli had seen the potentialities of this new electorate, and Lord Randolph Churchill had calculatedly wooed it, and not without success. The Liberals, however, regarded it as their natural birthright vote, automatic to themselves, and did not work to bind it to their cause. The attitude, which was most notable at the local level, was that the duty of voting Liberal did not carry with it any privilege of involvement in the actual process of politics. From time to time a working class candidate was triumphantly flaunted, but in the main the associations preferred middle class candidates, spurning the eager Keir Hardie for the safe London barrister Sir William Wedderburn, to take but one example.

This attitude, which was very widespread, was serious enough for the future of the Liberal Party, but it was even more serious in the context of industrial and social unrest in which it was dominant.

The industrial discontent that flared up in 1886 and continued intermittently for the next three years provided indications that there was much bitterness under the surface of apparent prosperity. On 'Black Monday' (February 8th 1886) a mob smashed in windows in Pall Mall; two days later it was rumoured that a mob of 50,000 unemployed was marching from Deptford and Greenwich, looting and wrecking on the way. Although the apprehension was exaggerated, there was a new uneasiness. On November 9th there was further alarm when it was rumoured that a mob of unemployed proposed to join the Lord Mayor's Procession to call attention to their plight. In October 1887 there were further disturbances in London, including an invasion of Westminster Abbey by more than two hundred unemployed men. Between October 18th and 20th there were three days of rioting in Hyde Park, and on November 13th—'Bloody Sunday'—there was virtually a pitched battle in Trafalgar Square between an enormous crowd and some 4,000 policemen and 300 men of the Grenadier Guards with fixed bayonets; and the 1st Life Guards were called out before order was restored. And this in Jubilee Year!

The causes of this new unrest cannot be easily categorised. The slump of the seventies, the agricultural distress that drove farm-workers to the over-crowded cities, the growth of the scale of production and the consequent further weakening of the worker-master relationship, which encouraged both unskilled workers and disgruntled artisans to combine to protect themselves, were undoubtedly important contributing factors. But it is necessary to differentiate between blind inchoate striking-out of the under-privileged against exploitation and poverty, and organised labour movements. For it was in the latter that the destiny of 'labour' really lay.

The essential novelty of the 'New Unionism' that developed in the later 1880s was that men were organised in the industries that employed them rather than through their old crafts, although unions based on the latter still survived. But it is probable that the revival of collective action would not have been so speedy had there not been a remarkable demonstration of what could be achieved by these methods. This occurred in 1889.

The London Dock Strike, which lasted from August 13th to September 16th, has been seen, justifiably as one of the most important single events in the history of the British Trade Union movement. It followed successful action earlier in the year by the Sailors' and Firemen's Unions, and John Burns has claimed that a gas workers' victory also had its effect; 'they [the dockers] caught the spirit that we were trying to inform them with and when the gas workers had won their victory . . . the dockers in their turn became restless.'

The London Strike was between casual dock workers, estimated at some 90,000, and the Directors of the four dock companies in the Port of London. The employers themselves were disunited; the members of the four Boards and the owners of many hundreds of wharves on the Thames were unable to work together in harmony.

The conditions of the dock workers were grim. Mayhew has

described the daily scene at 6 a.m. when the casual labourers gathered:

> As the foremen made their appearances, so began the scuffling and
> scrambling forth of countless hands, high in the air. All were
> shouting, appealing, coaxing. The scene is one to sadden the most
> callous, with thousands of men struggling for one day's hire, the
> struggle being the fiercer from the knowledge that hundreds must
> be left to idle the day out in want.

The men's pay was 5d an hour, out of which they had to 'treat'
the contractors who hired them (a tradition not extinguished until
1921). The only union was The Tea Operatives and General Labourers
Association, formed by a worker in the dock tea warehouses, Ben
Tillett.

The strike found the Dock Companies at a low ebb. On August 7th
Tillett requested the head of the South West India Dock to pay his
men 6d an hour and 8d an hour overtime in lieu of 5d and 7d, and to
guarantee a minimum engagement of four hours for each casual
worker taken on. This would have cost £100,000 a year. No reply
came, and 2,500 casual men at the East and West India group struck;
by the 16th those at the much larger Royal Victoria and Albert Docks
came out, as did the Irish workers building Tilbury Dock.

It is possible that the strike might have failed and certainly taken a
very different course, had it not been for John Burns, who took the
leadership in the struggle. It was not an occasion for half-hearted
measures. Picketing had to become 'unpeaceful', and was so. Organised intimidation and violence were certainly practised. But Burns was
also fully aware of the importance of public support, and had a
precocious sense of public relations. He organised a daily march
through the City to the West End, an orderly, impressive, demure
daily ritual that also raised funds from sympathetic bystanders.
Other unions helped to finance the strike, and when a strike account
was opened the Lord Mayor sponsored a fund that raised £1,400 and
Australian workers contributed £24,000. The Salvation Army provided soup kitchens and cheap food depots for the strikers. The Lord
Mayor—Sir James Whitehead—persuaded Sir John Lubbock,
Sydney Buxton and Cardinal Manning to form a committee to
find a solution. Eventually, 'the dockers' tanner' was conceded.[1] 'As a

---

[1] See Colonel R. B. Oram: 'The Great Strike of 1889' (*History Today*, August
1964) for further details.

An ironical, and rather melancholy footnote may be given to this victory. In

Trade Unionist', Burns wrote in the *New Review* (October 1889), 'my own notion of the practical outcome of the Strike is that all sections of labour must organise themselves into trades unions; that all trades must federate themselves, and that in the future, prompt and concerted action must take the place of the spasmodic and isolated action of the past.'

Although it was not until 1889 that Charles Booth published his electrifying statement—weightily supported by evidence—that some 30·7 per cent of the people of London were living at, or below, the poverty line, intelligent middle class interest in the condition of the poor had established, even before Booth made his researches public, massive evidence of the grim background to the unemployed marches and the revival of trade unionism. Britain's wealth had been built, and was being perpetuated, on cheap labour, and exploited cheap labour at that. One did not have to look far for evidence of poverty and malnutrition in London, and in the great industrial cities it was overwhelming. The subsequent idyllic concepts of English country life bore no relation to the actual realities in the last decades of the nineteenth century. The fact that Englishmen visiting Ireland were so shocked by conditions there is as illustrative an example as any of how awful those conditions were. But, since the 1840s, with the increase of national self-confidence and prosperity, a tacit acceptance of these conditions on the understanding that measures for amelioration would occur from time to time had been characteristic of what had once been so articulate and vehement an element in British post-Industrial Revolution society. Now, the calm was beginning to end.

It is important to emphasise that at this time, and indeed until much later, Socialism as such had very little impact upon the new Unionism. Furthermore, it was still assumed that the answer for working class discontent lay with the Liberals. Nevertheless, the middle class interest in the subject was to have important long-term consequences, and cannot be overlooked even at this early stage.

The Fabian Society came into existence at the beginning of 1884, as a by-product of a 'utopian' group called The Fellowship of the New

November 1923, Ben Tillett, in dire financial straits, approached the Conservative Prime Minister for financial support, in return for which he offered 'to fight Communism'. £2,000—or, failing that, £1,000—was the price he requested. (See R. R. James: *Memoirs of a Conservative*.)

Life founded by Dr. Thomas Davidson of New York in 1883. The Fellowship of the New Life was both too idealistic and insufficiently Socialist for those members who left to found the Fabian Society.

The quality of the Fabian Society has always lain in the intellectual questioning and disputes of its members. Among the original members were Frank Podmore, Edward Pease, and Hubert Bland,[1] and in May 1885 George Bernard Shaw and Sidney Webb (then a clerk in the Colonial Office) joined. Shaw also persuaded the formidable Mrs. Annie Besant—disenchanted by Secularism—to join at the same time; she was to become the celebrated organiser of the Bryant and May matchgirls' strike of 1888, but in 1890 she abandoned the Fabians for Theosophy and India, where she spent the rest of her life.

The Fabians, from the outset, were essentially middle class, intellectual, London-based and London-orientated. The 'Fabian outlook' was a curious blend of English Liberal tradition—notably J. S. Mill—Continental Positivism, and a certain vague Marxism. Although some of their early Tracts had a distinctly revolutionary flavour, the Fabians approved neither of revolutionary methods nor of the Marxist Social Democratic Federation (nor its leader, H. M. Hyndman), particularly after the fiasco in the 1885 General Election when two S.D.F. candidates stood for London seats and received twenty-seven and thirty-two votes respectively. The Fabians kept aloof from the unemployment troubles of 1886–7, and indeed actively disapproved of revolution by the proletariat. 'The unhappy people', Bland wrote, 'though not without their importance in a quasi-political movement, are *not* the people to make a political revolution, or even to carry out a great reform. The revolt of the empty stomach ends at the baker's shop.'[2] If this attitude may arouse resentment both for its tone and its content, it was not a wholly unfair deduction to draw from the recent history of British working class revolutionary movements. But, as other Fabians realised, this passivity was ending.

The contribution of the Fabian Society to the history of English

---

[1] Podmore retired from the Executive in 1888 to devote himself to literary and historical work. Pease was honorary secretary 1886–9, General Secretary 1890–14 and 1919–39. Bland was perhaps the most outspoken and vigorous of the early members, antagonistic to the Liberal Party and a keen advocate from the beginning of a new independent Socialist Party. He was married to Edith Nesbit, the distinguished writer of admirable children's stories.

[2] *The Practical Socialist*, October 1886.

Socialism remains controversial. Although it was primarily a London, middle class, self-conscious, intellectual group, its influence on younger people of the same class and background was profound, and it produced a series of proposals for social reform, many of which were put into practical effect. The foundation of the London School of Economics, and the Webbs' profound and enlightened involvement in educational reform were particularly important. Men of the calibre of R. H. Tawney, R. C. K. Ensor, G. D. H. Cole, Graham Wallas, Hugh Dalton, Clement Attlee, John Strachey and Hugh Gaitskell, came from the same background as the Webbs, and although the long-term influence of the Webbs may have been slight in proportion to their astonishing literary output, the manner in which they undertook their social investigations, and many of their conclusions, gave socialist reformers invaluable guidance and ideas.

If the Fabians had been meeting and talking in a vacuum their relevance would have been negligible, but they were not. Their own movement away from Liberalism to a new political and social philosophy was also taking place among more directly involved groups. Thus, as the Liberals preached the gradualist doctrine of Peace, Retrenchment, and Reform, and were alternately exalted and cast down by the gyrations of the Irish Question, the groups on which their future depended were beginning to ponder doubts about the merits of gradualism.

It was to be a long time—indeed, a surprisingly long time—before disillusionment with the Liberal Party became widespread in the trade union and intellectual sections of the new 'labour' movement. Respect for Gladstone personally, lethargy and apathy, the Liberal tradition, the conservatism and pragmatism of British trade unions, all formed a powerful negative coalition against converting irritation and disillusionment into actual revolt. The principal characteristic of British working class movements in the century, and particularly since the 1850s, had been to work within established institutions to bring reform, and of all these institutions the Liberal Party had become the most hallowed. But now, 'Ireland blocked the way'; furthermore, the radical assumption of a succession of progressive Liberal Governments with occasional brief Conservative interludes now had to be revised.

Gladstone's Newcastle Programme of 1891 offered a great deal to labour including 'one man, one vote' and land taxes, but even at that stage there were serious doubts about whether it would be implemented

—doubts which were to be amply confirmed. The 1886 Liberal Government had ignored—to its electoral cost—the allotment issue, and its only legislative achievement on social reform was the work of a private Member, Sir John Lubbock, a persistent and single-handed reformer who achieved a great deal. His Act prevented women and children from being employed for more than twelve hours a day, an item of legislation that throws a glaring light upon the indifference of Liberal leaders to the basic social questions of the day. Of equal significance was Gladstone's appeal to the miners of Nottingham in 1892 to give preference to Home Rule over the question of the eight-hour day, and thus sacrifice their 'own views and apparent interests' to a 'wider and weightier cause'. The fact that the Liberal Party was a middle class party with working class support was accepted so long as the party's priorities approximated to those of its mass support. But Irish Home Rule, Local Option—whereby a vote by three-quarters of the ratepayers could close all public houses in a district—disputes over Imperial policy, the role of the House of Lords, and Welsh and Scottish dis-establishment, were not the dominant concerns of labour in the 1890s.

At this moment there occurred an event that clearly demonstrated these schisms. In the General Election of 1892 Keir Hardie was elected to the House of Commons for West Ham South. His arrival at Westminster, bearded, wild-eyed, and wearing a cloth cap, aroused interest, derision, and trepidation. But his life and career were of great significance since, outside Irish politics, no one remotely like him had ever reached the House of Commons before.

Hardie had been born in Lanarkshire in 1856, an illegitimate child brought up in great poverty. As he later wrote, 'I am of the unfortunate class who never knew what it was to be a child—in spirit, I mean. Even the memories of boyhood and young manhood are gloomy.' He began work at the age of eight, and for years his family lived on the brink of destitution. From the age of ten until he was twenty-three he was a coal miner, but one who was determined to educate himself. He read widely and avidly, became a Christian, and developed his own personal and idiosyncratic version of radicalism which embraced strict temperance, a severe puritanism, a mystical attitude towards human progress, and a certain personal arrogance, vanity, and love of the dramatic which not everyone found endearing. Hardie's political philosophies changed, but were always intensely personal and perplexing to those who tried to work with him. Originally he believed in the inevitable alliance between Capital and Labour, whose interests he regarded as identical, but harsh experience tempered this belief into political atheism. He became secretary of the newly formed Scottish Miners' National Federation in October 1886, and concerned himself with the militant leaders of other miners' organisations. Hardie himself became a militant, and his burgeoning doubts about the Liberal Party as the true instrument for working class reform began to increase greatly. In February 1887 the coalowners responded to a miners' strike with police, and then troops, and the miners were routed. So, also, were Hardie's dreams of a happy alliance between Capital and Labour.

Moving to a larger stage, he interested himself in international socialism, and visited London for the first time in 1887 and attended the Trade Union Congress at Swansea, where he shocked the delegates by a violent attack upon Henry Broadhurst, the very model of the safe Liberal–Labour alliance leader, and by moving for larger working class representation in Parliament with a new 'labour party'. This was widely regarded as being in execrable taste, and was universally denounced. But Hardie was still a Liberal, and probably would have continued to be so if he had been shown any encouragement. Rejected twice by Liberal associations—in both cases losing to prosperous southern barristers—he was driven towards independence. He seemed a transient phenomenon, interesting but laughable, and of little account. But in reality he was a portent of doom to the Liberal Party. He had been theirs for the asking, and they had ignored and humiliated him. For this they were to pay a very heavy price.

In 1893 the Independent Labour Party was formally founded at Bradford with the specific purpose of sending working class men to Parliament who would be independent of the major parties. Although the I.L.P. at this stage was never much more than a propaganda society with little real support, and although 'Queer Hardie' lost his seat in the 1895 General Election, the thought had been put forward that it might be necessary to establish a new political confederation which could combine the forces of the new unionism, the industrial discontent, the intellectual radicalism which could find little satisfaction in a Liberal Party obsessed by other questions, and the growing feeling that the traditional political parties could not and would not meet the new imperatives of creating a more equitable society. It was only a first and very tentative step, but, as the ancient proverb reminds us, in a long march the first step is the most important.

But despite these ominous developments, and the catastrophe which had befallen them over the fall of Parnell, there is little evidence that the Liberals felt much concern about their long-term future in 1892. As their correspondence and recorded discussions demonstrate, the Liberal leaders were troubled about tactics and their immediate prospects, and were deeply concerned by the traumatic events through which their confederation had passed since 1885. But hardly anywhere does one detect any apprehension that the structure of politics lay elsewhere than in the struggle for mastery between themselves and the Conservatives. What cries of alarm that arose were on the alienation of working class supporters by contemporary policies; that the alienation lay much deeper was hardly discerned at all. 'I am vexed to see portions of the labouring class beginning to be corrupted by the semblance of power as the other classes have been tainted and warped by its reality,' Gladstone wrote to Morley in 1892, 'and I am disgusted by finding a portion of them ready to thrust Ireland, which is so far ahead in claim, entirely into the background. Poor, poor, poor human nature'.[1] There were younger Liberals who clearly saw the perils of such attitudes, but in the vital 1890s their party held office only fleetingly, and in that interlude the opportunity was not seized.

[1] Gladstone Papers. Quoted in D. A. Hamer: *Liberal Politics in the Age of Gladstone and Rosebery*, 227.

CHAPTER FIVE

A LIBERAL INTERLUDE, 1892–1895

THE PROFESSION of politics is not a solitary exercise, and thus the observer is often baffled by those apparently inexplicable but very real moods of high exaltation or deep despair that sweep across political groupings, and for which there is no logical explanation beyond the obvious one that human associations are always very human, and consequently often very irrational. In 1892, the Conservatives, whose record since the beginning of 1887 had been disappointing in electoral and administrative terms, eagerly looked forward to the forthcoming elections and the prospect of defeat, while the Liberals were cast into the deepest gloom by that of victory. Individual Conservatives were dismayed at the prospect of losing office, individual Liberals were exultant at the prospect of gaining it, but the collective opinion was wholly contrary. The Conservatives wanted to get out, the Liberals did not want to go in. The former narrowly gained the advantage.

The overwhelming damage done to the Liberal Party by the downfall of Parnell and the lack of any real policies apart from Home Rule could not be repaired by the hasty adoption of every possible radical policy in the Newcastle Programme, nor by the lung-power of Liberal oratory. The rift between the Gladstonian Liberals and the Chamberlain–Devonshire[1] Liberal Unionists was now so substantial that the possibility of Liberal reunion could no longer be seriously discussed. There were indications that the magic of Gladstone's name was itself declining, even in the Liberal ranks, and particularly in those sections that were bored by the issue of Home Rule and were impatient for radical measures at home.

[1] In 1891 Hartington had succeeded his father as the eighth Duke of Devonshire, and had left the House of Commons after having been a Member for thirty-four years, and having been offered—each time under impossible circumstances—the Premiership on three occasions.

When the General Election came in the summer the Home Rule majority was only forty—315 to 355—and Gladstone himself was nearly defeated at Midlothian. The Liberal leadership had hoped for a majority independent of the Irish; now they were wholly dependent upon Irish votes and Irish co-operation in order to maintain themselves in office. The bitter divisions within the Irish Nationalists were demonstrated by the fact that only nine former Parnellites were returned. Gladstone was again—and for the last time—at Dalmeny with Rosebery when he learned of the final majority. One of the company ventured to suggest that it would be sufficient. 'Too small, too small', Gladstone sadly replied.

Salisbury did not resign at once, but decided to face the new Parliament, thus giving the Liberals over a month in which to regroup their forces for the new Government. They needed the time. On August 11th, a motion of no confidence moved by H. H. Asquith in a speech described by a Conservative as 'drastic, caustic, masterly,' was carried in the House of Commons by exactly forty, and the Liberals gloomily and apprehensively took office. The Queen, deeply chagrined by the prospect of Gladstone again, made the unprecedented announcement in the *Court Circular* that she had accepted Salisbury's resignation 'with great regret', and expressed in private her disgust at 'having all those great interests entrusted to the shaking hand of an old, wild and incomprehensible man of $82\frac{1}{2}$'; Gladstone for his part described the meeting between the Queen and himself as 'such as took place between Marie Antoinette and her executioner'.

The existence of the Queen's violent antipathy to Gladstone was not widely known in her lifetime, and his loyal silence on the matter was as noble as it was remarkable. But, for all her fulminations and the severe difficulties she caused him, Gladstone had a real respect for her, and to the end hoped that the relationship might be improved. The Queen, under the wise guidance of the Prince Consort, had come to recognise the perils of the blatant partisanship that had characterised the early period of her reign, and she had excellent advisers, of whom Sir Henry Ponsonby was the wisest. Her common sense, strong understanding of *realpolitik*, and devotion to her work invariably impressed those who had to deal with her. They were all, in truth, in awe of her, even Salisbury, and her influence remained strong. Now, in addition, she was more popular than at any time in her reign, and her rare public appearances produced immense crowds and enthusiasm. But although her antipathies were well concealed, in practical terms she was not unlike the House of Lords—politically quiescent when a Conservative Administration was in office, and a vigilant defender of the national interest when the Liberals were in power. Her impact on policy—particularly foreign policy—could be substantial, and her strong support of Rosebery and Cromer in the 1892–5 Government was to be of considerable significance. If she had little real power judged in normal terms, her influence was very great, and all in public affairs regarded her with respect and apprehension.

Rosebery, whose wife had died suddenly in 1890, and who had been in virtual seclusion since then, had refused to join the Government, and was only persuaded with very great difficulty to take the Foreign Office again. One of the most significant elements in persuading him was the pressure put upon him by the Royal Family. But he made it plain that he came in on his own terms. Gladstone's impatience with him for causing these difficulties was quickly fortified by alarm at Rosebery's policies. Reginald Brett recorded on September 7th of Rosebery that 'he is absolute at the F.O. He informs his colleagues of very little, and does as he pleases. If it offends them, he retires. We shall remain in Egypt, and the continuity of Lord S's policy will not be disturbed. All this is excellent.' There was some point to Harcourt's remark to Rosebery that 'without you the Government would have been simply ridiculous; now it is only impossible!'.

By now, Gladstone was a very old man. The solitary and melancholy Rosebery was aloof. John Morley and Harcourt were on bad terms. At some stage in the period of Opposition—it is not clear exactly when—Morley and Harcourt's son, Lewis (generally known by the unlovely soubriquet of 'Loulou') had come to agreement at Harcourt's New Forest home, Malwood, that Morley would support Harcourt for the leadership when Gladstone retired. The 'Malwood Compact' was showing severe signs of strain by the summer of 1892. Asquith has admirably portrayed this unlikely combination:

They belonged not only to different generations, but in all essentials, except that of actual chronology, to different centuries. Both of them were men of high and rare cultivation; on the intellectual side, Morley was what Harcourt most loathed, an *ideologue*, and Harcourt was what jarred most upon Morley, a Philistine. Harcourt, with a supposed infusion (however diluted) of Plantagenet blood; the grandson of a Georgian Archbishop; brought up with the tastes and habits of the castle in which he was born; but a natural mutineer, with a really powerful intelligence, a mordant wit, and a masculine and challenging personality, soon shook off his hereditary fetters, and seemed at one time to be in training for the post of the great Condottiers of the political world. Morley, sprung from the Lancashire middle-class, dipped but not dyed in the waters of Oxford, a youthful acolyte of Mill, had hovered for a time around the threshold of the Comtean conventicle. . . .

Political exigencies make strange stable companions, but rarely two, to all appearance, less well assorted than these. They had hardly even a prejudice in common. . . . Had they a common political faith? It is hard to say—except that, from different points of view, they were equally ardent disciples of what used then to be called the Anti-Imperialist and 'Little England' school.[1]

These clashes of personality and outlook at the top were serious enough, and were to have important and enduring consequences. But perhaps even more serious was the fact that, beyond Home Rule, the Liberals had no agreed programme and no strategy. In spite of his endorsement of the Newcastle Programme, Gladstone was not a believer in programmes but in great unifying single issues as in 1868, 1879–80, or 1885–6. A party, as he had declared in November 1885, should be 'an instrument for the attainment of great ends'. The trouble was that in the 1892 election many—if not most—Liberals had fought on those particular issues in the Newcastle Programme which had most attracted them or seemed most attractive to their constituencies. Home Rule—and Gladstone's own leadership—constituted the only unifying elements in this very heterogenous coalition, and the Liberals came to Westminster with firm but wildly differing priorities. For a time the excitement of Gladstone's last great campaign concealed this fatal deficiency, but when the Home Rule fight was lost nothing remained but a babel.

It was in justifiable low spirits and uneasiness that, on August 18th, the incoming Ministers travelled across the Solent to Osborne to receive their Seals of Office from their bleak and unsympathetic Sovereign. The ceremony took place in a cold and unbroken silence, and the party returned across the waters in a fierce storm amid

[1] Asquith: *Fifty Years of Parliament*, I, 246–7.

flashes of lightning and crashes of menacing thunder. The Queen privately recorded her impression of the new Ministers as 'rather depressed and embarrassed'. The only surprise in the Cabinet was the elevation of Asquith, at the age of forty, to be Home Secretary, but the appointment of Sir Edward Grey to be Under-Secretary of State at the Foreign Office was almost as significant. Apart from these, and Rosebery, aged forty-five, it was an ageing, dispirited, and divided Government.

All Parliamentary roads led to Ireland. The Second Home Rule Bill differed from that of 1886 in many respects, but the key difference was that the Irish would have representation at Westminster but could only vote on Irish or Imperial concerns, a compromise which had to be abandoned under pressure after the Bill was introduced, and which made matters even worse. As in the 1886 Bill, questions of trade, foreign affairs, and military control were excluded from the scope of the proposed Irish Parliament. As in 1886, and despite the clear evidence of overwhelming Ulster feeling, the special problems and position of Ulster were ignored.

The Bill occupied virtually the entire time of the House of Commons from March until September 1893. It consumed eighty-five sittings, and was piloted throughout by Gladstone himself, a phenomenal performance for a man in his eighty-third year. Chamberlain, in his most relentless and trenchant temper, still sitting on the Liberal benches, and still referring to Gladstone invariably as 'My Right Honourable Friend' was by far his most formidable opponent. 'In the present controversy', Gladstone wrote of Chamberlain to the Queen, 'he has stood very decidedly first in ability among the opponents of the present Bill in the House of Commons.' Henry Lucy reported that: 'It is only when Mr. Chamberlain steps into the arena, and Mr. Gladstone swiftly turns to face him, that benches fill, drooping heads are raised, eyes brighten, the Chamber resounds with cheers and counter-cheers, and the dry bones of the debate rattle into strenuous life'.

Lord Randolph's elder son, Winston Churchill, then aged nineteen, was a witness of Gladstone's winding up of the Second Reading, and which he recalled nearly forty years later:

Well do I remember the scene and some of its incidents. The Grand Old Man looked like a great white eagle at once fierce and splendid.

His sentences rolled forth majestically and everyone hung upon his lips and gestures, eager to cheer or deride. He was at the climax of a tremendous passage about how the Liberal Party had always carried every cause it had espoused to victory. He made a slip. 'And there is no cause,' he exclaimed (Home Rule), 'for which the Liberal Party has suffered so much or *descended so low*'. How the Tories leapt and roared their delight! But Mr. Gladstone, shaking his right hand with fingers spread claw-like, quelled the tumult and resumed, ' But we have risen again'.[1]

Faced with the implacable Unionist opposition, the Government resorted first to the Closure and then to the Guillotine procedure, and, chunk by chunk, the Bill was rammed through. When Chamberlain depicted the Irish Members as 'nominated by priests, elected by illiterates, and subsidised by the enemies of our country', Gladstone accused him of using 'habitual, coarse, and enormous exaggeration'. On July 27th the accumulated passions of a long and a hot summer exploded when Chamberlain was replying to Gladstone. 'The Prime Minister calls "black" and they say "it is good". The Prime Minister calls "white", and they say "it is better". Never since the time of Herod has there been such slavish adulation.' There was a scream of 'Judas!' from the Irish, and the House fell quickly out of control. Members jostled each other, minor scuffles broke out, the galleries hissed in disapproval, and order was not restored until the majestic figure of Mr. Speaker Peel appeared. This was, however, the final point of passion in the long debate, and was not characteristic of its general temper. It was harsh in expression, bitterly fought at every point, but dominated by the restrained passion of Gladstone and Chamberlain. And at one point there was an incident that no one who witnessed it—including the young Winston Churchill in the galleries—ever forgot.

Chamberlain's elder son, Austen, had been elected for East Worcestershire in 1892. In appearance and dress, even to the monocle, he was startlingly like his father, and his maiden speech was an ordeal of very particular difficulty in which he acquitted himself well. On the first possible public occasion Gladstone—who had been genuinely impressed—turned to Joseph Chamberlain and remarked that 'it was a speech which must have been dear and refreshing to a father's

[1] Winston S. Churchill: *My Early Life*, 34.

heart'. Churchill relates that he saw Chamberlain's normally sallow countenance go pink, he started 'as if a bullet had struck him' and then he half rose and bowed, 'then hunched himself up with lowered head. . . . It was the way the thing was done that swept aside for a moment the irreparable enmities of years'.[1]

Gladstone's last and greatest effort was in vain. The House of Lords, the constitutional undertakers, contemptuously buried the Bill on September 8th after a debate of insulting perfunctoriness by 419 votes to forty-one. It was said that 'not a dog barked'. Gladstone wanted to dissolve Parliament and fight the Lords in the country, but was overruled by his colleagues. From this point the Liberal Government was lost.

*

On paper, this was a strong and talented Government, and more cohesive than the 1880–6 Governments. Gladstone, Harcourt, Morley and Rosebery provided the ballast and experience, supported by men of the calibre of Campbell-Bannerman (War), Henry Fowler (Local Government) and Lord Spencer (Admiralty), while Asquith and Edward Grey represented the very able group of young Liberals who had entered the Commons in the 1880s. But in practice it was sorely divided. Gladstone and Morley cared deeply about Home Rule, Harcourt and Rosebery hardly at all. On foreign and, above all, colonial policy, Rosebery found himself confronted by the hostile trio of Gladstone, Harcourt and Morley, yet this combination was beset by personal antipathies. Harcourt's well-known tendency to hectoring arrogance was now more raspingly apparent than ever. Gladstone was an old man obsessed by Home Rule, who viewed all other issues with impatience. Harcourt delighted in issuing fierce memoranda and commands to his colleagues from his Treasury desk. Morley sulked in Dublin, while Rosebery locked himself up in the Foreign Office and took command of foreign policy. As an indication of the manner in which this Cabinet operated, a letter from Asquith to Rosebery (February 10th, 1893) may be quoted:

> I understand that on Monday a Bill (To 'amend the provision' for the Government of Ireland), which neither you nor I have seen, is to be introduced into the House of Commons. I send you word of

[1] Churchill, op. cit., 35.

this, as you may possibly like to be present, and hear what Her Majesty's Government have to propose.

Behind the personal differences they lay important issues, of which the most significant and divisive was over foreign—and specifically colonial—policy. Rosebery, having come in on his own terms, was determined to maintain a strong British presence in Egypt and to extend British influence in East Africa by taking over responsibility for Uganda from the ailing East Africa Company. On both points he was strongly opposed by Gladstone and Harcourt, yet on both, after sharp disputes, he gained the day. But the ill-feeling which had been generated was to prove enduring. The Queen was impressed by Rosebery's resolute handling of these matters; the anti-Imperialist section of the Liberal Party was not.

Gladstone did not have the authority to remove Rosebery, although he was sorely tempted. The titanic feat of piloting the Home Rule Bill through the Commons, only to see it arrogantly butchered by the Lords, was now followed by the refusal of his colleagues to follow his urgings for immediate dissolution. Those colleagues hoped— some none too secretly—that he would resign quietly and that there would be an agreed and orderly succession. Gladstone was indeed seeking a way out of his position, but it was to be on an issue of principle and conducted in a manner which was to make his successor's position as difficult—if not—impossible as could be contrived. It was not deliberately or calculatingly done, but no assessment of Gladstone can afford to omit that element of moral vanity in his personality, made more marked by age and disappointment.

The crisis that led to Gladstone's eventual resignation was over the issue of naval rebuilding. Concern at the relative strength of the Navy, particularly in the Mediterranean, was given dramatic emphasis by the loss of the battleship *Victoria* in June 1893. The Admiralty produced a desired and a minimum programme, and by the middle of December Spencer had agreed to the latter one. His arguments were accepted by the entire Cabinet, with the exception of the Prime Minister. Gladstone virtually cut off relations with his colleagues, and the Cabinet operated in limbo until Gladstone ended this embarrassing interlude with his resignation on March 2nd. If he had been asked to name his successor he would—the Naval Estimates notwithstanding— have recommended Spencer. He felt, with good cause, that his advice should have been sought by the Queen, but it was not. It was a heartless, brutal snub, which Gladstone felt keenly. It did not reflect well on the Queen, but for all her faults she was supremely honest. She loathed Gladstone, regarded him as unbalanced and irresponsible, and was glad to see him go at last. On March 3rd her Private Secretary called at the Foreign Office with a letter inviting Rosebery to form an Administration.

Why Rosebery? Subsequently, there were many Liberals who regretted the Queen's choice. But, at the time, there was virtually no questioning. He was the natural selection, 'the man of the future' as Gladstone had once described him. The Cabinet would not have Harcourt, and the intensive lobbying of the devoted Loulou had only served to demonstrate this fact. Most significant of all, Morley was deeply estranged and the Malwood Compact had been abrogated. All Loulou's attempts to stir up anti-Rosebery and pro-Harcourt feeling conspicuously failed. The Liberal Press came out strongly for Rosebery. It was an uncontested succession—or so it was thought.

*

Modern British politics present us with few careers and personalities of greater interest and complexity than that of Archibald Philip Primrose, fifth Earl of Rosebery. An early biographer, E. T. Raymond, has commented fairly that:

> By omitting certain sets of facts, and placing others in a strong light, he can be proved almost anything we like—a man before his age, a man behind it; a strong, far-seeing statesman, a sentimentalist bemused by his own incantations and watchwords; a patriot too pure for the vulgar commerce of politics, a politician too slippery to be trusted by men themselves not over-particular. . . . His admirers will have him all godhead. His detractors make him all clay feet.

The broad outlines of his career may be briefly summarised. He had been born in 1847, the elder son and third child of Archibald, Lord Dalmeny, and Lady Wilhelmina Stanhope, daughter of the fourth Earl Stanhope. He was educated at Eton, and then at Christ Church, Oxford, until, given the choice between relinquishing the ownership of a racehorse and remaining at Oxford, he chose the horse.

His father had died suddenly in 1851, and he succeeded his grand-
father to the Rosebery title and estates in 1868. Ten years later he
married Miss Hannah Rothschild, one of the greatest heiresses of the
day. In his twenties he became increasingly interested in politics, and
was identified with the Liberal Party from the beginning. In 1879, as
has been recorded, he sprang into national prominence when he
sponsored—and helped to finance—Gladstone's Midlothian campaigns. It would be difficult to overemphasise the importance of this
episode on Rosebery's career. In Scotland, his reputation was, and
always afterwards remained, immense. 'The first time I ever saw
Lord Rosebery was in Edinburgh when I was a student', J. M. Barrie
wrote, 'and I flung a clod of earth at him. He was a peer; those were
my politics . . . [but] during the first Midlothian campaign Mr.
Gladstone and Lord Rosebery were the father and son of the Scottish
people. Lord Rosebery rode into fame on the top of that wave, and
has kept his place in the hearts of the people, and in oleographs on their
walls, ever since.' And Margot Asquith has related:

> Whenever there was a crowd in the streets or at the station, in
> either Glasgow or Edinburgh, and I enquired what it was all about
> I always received the same reply: 'Rozbury!'.

On the public platform he had a commanding presence and
wonderful voice. As Augustine Birrell has written: 'His melodious
voice . . . his underlying strain of humour, his choice of words, never
either staled by vulgar usage or tainted with foreign idiom, and above
all his "out of the way" personality, and a certain nervousness of
manner that suggested at times the possibility of a breakdown, kept
his audience in a flutter of enjoyment and excitement. He was
certainly the most "interesting" speaker I have ever heard.'

In private he could be a fascinating companion. 'The marvel of his
conversation', John Buchan has written, 'was its form. He spoke
finished prose as compared with the slovenly patois of most of us, and
his thoughts clothed themselves naturally with witty and memorable
words'. And Winston Churchill has recorded:

> It is difficult to convey the pleasure I derived from his conversation,
> as it ranged easily and spontaneously upon all kinds of topics 'from
> grave to gay, from lively to severe'. Its peculiar quality was the
> unexpected depths or suggestive turns which revealed the size of the

subject and his own background of knowledge and reflection. At the same time he was full of fun. He made many things not only arresting, but merry. He seemed as much a master of trifles and gossip as of weighty matters. He was keenly conscious about every aspect of life. Sportsman, epicure, bookworm, literary critic, magpie collector of historical relics, appreciative owner of veritable museums of art treasures, he never needed to tear a theme to tatters. In lighter vein he flitted jauntily from flower to flower like a glittering insect, by no means unprovided with a sting. And then, in contrast, out would come his wise, matured judgements upon the great men and events of the past. But these treats were not always given.

To the public, Rosebery possessed political glamour. His wealth, particularly after his marriage to Hannah Rothschild, was considerable, and he lived in the grand style. 'There are many glass doors', Edward Grey wrote of Mentmore, the Rothschild-Rosebery palace in Buckinghamshire, 'but some are locked, and others open with difficulty—and egress and regress are more or less formal; you may *go* out or in but not *slip* out or in.' Rosebery's style, his ownership of racehorses, his intellectual interests and pursuits, combined to make him a refreshing and exciting political figure.

As has been indicated, his relationship with Gladstone had not been an easy one. It reflected both Gladstone's inadequacies in dealing with men and also Rosebery's acute sensitiveness. He refused office in 1880, in spite of much pressure: 'Lord Rosebery would accept nothing', Granville told the Queen, 'as he said it would look as if Mr. Gladstone had paid him for what he had done.' To Gladstone he wrote that if he took office 'I should feel that where I only meant personal devotion and public spirit, others would see and perhaps with reason personal ambition and public office seeking.' But a vacancy occurred at the Home Office in July 1881, and Rosebery had become a junior Minister with special, but undefined, responsibilities for Scottish affairs. This had not been a happy interlude. Rosebery's senior Minister had been Harcourt, and although the relationship between the two men had not been, at this stage, uncomfortable, Rosebery had quickly discovered that his actual responsibility for Scottish affairs was minimal. Gladstone, heavily occupied with other major problems, had insufficient time or inclination to respond sympathetically to the complaints of a junior Minister. Gladstone was also a firm believer in the values of seniority. It was unwise to have taken this attitude; Rosebery might have held only a junior position in the Government, but, although young, he was not a minor public figure. He very nearly resigned when Parnell was released from Kilmainham in April 1882, then stood beside his leader when Cavendish and Burke were assassinated.

In the autumn of 1882, when there was a Cabinet reconstruction, Rosebery was left out. Furthermore, his ambiguous position at the Home Office had preyed on his mind. With tactful handling all might have been well, but Gladstone did not handle the matter tactfully, and there was a somewhat sharp exchange of letters. In May 1883 Rosebery eagerly seized an opportunity to resign.

This episode was significant in many respects. It demonstrated the lack of real personal sympathy and understanding between Gladstone and Rosebery which was never to be fully created, and it also showed a defect in Rosebery's character which has been admirably summarised by Winston Churchill:

> In times of crisis and responsibility his active, fertile mind and imagination preyed upon him. He was bereft of sleep. He magnified trifles. He failed to separate the awkward incidents of the hour from the long swing of events, which he so clearly understood. Toughness when nothing particular was happening was not the form of fortitude in which he excelled. He was unduly attracted by the dramatic, and by the pleasure of making a fine gesture.

After telling Gladstone that he would never return to office except as a member of the Cabinet, Rosebery had ventured to Australia. This journey had had a decisive influence on his attitudes. The Empire was only just beginning to excite serious interest in Liberal political circles, but Rosebery had been, from his earliest days, a believer in the Empire. In 1874, in his first major public speech, he had drawn a picture of Britain as 'the affluent mother of giant Commonwealths and peaceful Empires that shall perpetuate the best qualities of the race', and in 1882, in his Rectorial Address at Edinburgh University he had compared the Empire to 'a sheet knit at the four corners, containing all manner of men, fitted for their separate climate and work and spheres of action, but honouring the common vessel which contains them.' Thus, in 1883 he went to Australia a supporter of Empire; he returned with a burning conviction in the future development of the colonies, and at Adelaide, on January 18th 1884, he made his famous declaration that: 'There is no need for any nation, however great, leaving the Empire, because the Empire is a Commonwealth of Nations.' On his return he described himself as a 'Liberal Imperialist', and said that 'Imperialism, sane Imperialism, as distinguished from what I might call "wild cat" Imperialism, is nothing but this—a larger patriotism.' He declared his support for the Imperial Federation League, and made a greatly applauded speech on the subject to the Trades Union Congress at Aberdeen.

Attempts to bring him back to the Government might have failed had not the death of Gordon, and the temper of public feeling against Gladstone, aroused him. He became Lord Privy Seal and First Commissioner of Works.

When he accepted Gladstone's offer of the Foreign Office in January 1886 at the age of thirty-seven, he was not particularly enthusiastic about Home Rule but was prepared to accept it as the only practical alternative to further coercion. This stand won him not only high office but enormous enthusiasm within the Gladstonian Liberal ranks, and his conduct of foreign affairs had been widely—and excessively—praised. He enunciated the doctrine of the continuity of British foreign policy, continued Salisbury's policies, and won golden opinions from all sides. When he became, in 1889, first Chairman of the new London County Council, this attracted the admiration of progressive Liberals everywhere, and particularly those at Westminster to whom Ireland obstinately barred the way to bold social reform.

And then, in November 1890, his wife died. This personal tragedy brought out a latent melancholia, and seemed to destroy what personal ambition he had ever possessed. Insomnia, which had always plagued him in moments of crisis, now became chronic. Until this disaster, Rosebery had everything. To Liberals, he was the young hero of Midlothian, the mature Minister, the radical social reformer, and one of the most arresting public speakers of the day. The Unionists respected him. He was known as a man of taste and style, civilised and alert, adept at all situations. His friends were awed by his wit and intelligence, and his brief biography of Pitt, published in 1890, had won new admirers.

But beneath this glittering surface there lay many doubts and indecisions, and a very taut and nervous personality. The death of Hannah Rosebery was a blow from which he never really recovered, and whose severity startled even those who thought they knew him best. Amateur psychologists may see in Hannah Rosebery the emotional replacement for the mother whom Rosebery had never liked and from whom he was distant, even as a child. Certainly she gave to him a strength and a confidence which he was never to recapture. Perhaps, with his fatalistic and gloomy view of life, he considered that a chapter had closed, and should not be reopened. Whatever the causes, the Rosebery after 1890 was a different man, in the sense that the latent weaknesses which were dimly evident to the more observant before then were now magnified.

But it is doubtful if any member of the Cabinet could have pulled together the Liberals in March 1894. The political circumstances of Rosebery's accession to the Premiership could not have been less inspiriting. It was, as Winston Churchill has written, 'a bleak, precarious, wasting inheritance'. The internal schisms were an added misery. Harcourt and his son did not accept their defeat; they attempted to secure conditions on foreign policy, and throughout the rest of the existence of the Government they made no attempt to conceal their contempt for the man who had destroyed their joint ambition. To say that they behaved badly is to place too charitable a judgement upon their activities during the following fifteen months.

Morley, too, was chagrined. It is difficult to explain his sudden movement away from Rosebery when the brief succession crisis was over without taking into account his intense sensitivity to small or imagined slights. Morley had come to value his position too highly. He was an intellectual who was fascinated by power, and his devotion to Gladstone had been total, almost filial. He was now emotionally overwrought, disconsolate, and affronted. He informed Rosebery that he would only be responsible for his department, and returned to Dublin, where he brooded bleakly for the rest of the life of the Government.

The Queen also oppressed Rosebery. She treated him in a different manner to that with which she had dealt with Gladstone, but with similar effect. Her letters to him were maternal but minatory. An early missive set the tone:

She does not object to Liberal measures which are not revolutionary and she does not think it possible that Lord Rosebery will destroy well tried, valued, and necessary institutions for the sole purpose of flattering useless Radicals or pandering to the pride of those whose only desire is their own self-gratification.

These were heavy burdens, and Rosebery was not the man to bear them. He began with a serious blunder when, in his first speech in the Lords as Prime Minister, he said in effect that Home Rule would have to be held in abeyance until there was an English majority that supported it. The Irish were appalled, the Unionists exultant. In the Commons that evening Labouchere seized his opportunity and carried an Amendment to the Address, by a majority of two, that practically abolished the powers of the House of Lords. It was, to say the least, an inauspicious beginning.

The first major crisis between Rosebery and Harcourt came over the latter's Budget of 1894. Harcourt's scheme—the creation of Alfred Milner, Chairman of the Board of Inland Revenue—included the introduction of a graduated death duty on property. It was a relatively modest step in itself, but its implications alarmed many, including Gladstone, who described it as 'by far the most Radical measure of my lifetime'. When Rosebery set out some of his own apprehensions in a memorandum, Harcourt retorted with a vehement onslaught, implying strongly that Rosebery was alarmed because of his own properties, and ending with the observation that 'the fate of the present Government and issue of the next Election are temporary incidents which I view with philosophic indifference.' Having delivered this highly personal philippic, Harcourt grandly agreed to the maximum being reduced from ten to eight per cent.

On Foreign Affairs, relations grew increasingly acrid as the year progressed. Again, on the main issue it was arguable that Harcourt was in the right, but, again, the manner in which he acted was intolerable. The defeat of Rosebery's proposed Anglo-Congolese Treaty in the summer of 1894 was more the result of French and German opposition than Harcourt's outbursts in the Cabinet, but the latter were not without their significance. Relations between the two men were now really bad; on one memorandum by Harcourt Rosebery minuted, 'Can *la betise humaine* further go?'.

The Cabinet did not pursue any fixed policy on any issue. Rosebery began an assault on the House of Lords that horrified the Queen—to the point that she seriously considered demanding a Dissolution—and was in effect disavowed by the Cabinet, which was indignant that it had not been consulted. Harcourt launched a personal campaign for Local Option. Morley publicly attempted to restore the Home Rule issue to its primacy. In January 1895, at Cardiff, Rosebery sounded forth on the issue of Welsh Disestablishment. The confusion was total. By-elections fell from bad to disastrous. From Gladstone, in nominal retirement, dank clouds of disapproval betokened a smouldering discontent. In the House of Commons Harcourt barely troubled to give the impression of supporting his leader, and Dilke and Labouchere seized every occasion for embarrassing the Government. This, in the circumstances, was not an especially arduous occupation. The loyal back-benchers gathered together in gloomy knots in the Lobby. Deputations to the equally bewildered Whips were fruitless. It was a hopeless, slithering, decline.

Gladstone's failure to consult his colleagues in the years of Opposition, the lack of agreed priorities, and the 'something-for-everyone' character of the Newcastle Programme, now had to be paid for. Rosebery was probably right in going for a large single issue, but not only did he not consult his colleagues but his proposals for the Lords were much too vague; the Conservatives could attack them for their imprecision, the Radicals for their moderation. Meanwhile the advocates of Welsh and Scottish disestablishment, Local Option, universal suffrage, and the rest, pressed the claims of their particular faiths upon Ministers with, in Rosebery's words, 'appeals, some of them menacing, some of them coaxing and cajoling, but all of them extremely earnest, and praying that the particular hobby of the writer shall be made the first Government Bill'.

Whatever chances Rosebery had of restoring the situation, were destroyed by the serious ill-health, aggravated by insomnia, which afflicted him from February to April 1895. On February 19th, goaded beyond endurance, he had virtually told his Cabinet to support him or let him resign, and his ultimatum had had a temporary success. But then, at a vital period in his party's fortunes he was prostrated, and whatever hope that lingered of his political recovery was lost. It was the coldest winter for more than fifty years; ice-flows were in the Thames, and there was considerable suffering, and a scourge of influenza of which Rosebery was the most conspicious victim. But influenza was hardly the only cause of Rosebery's collapse, and may be regarded as the final blow to an exhausted, lonely, and over-wrought personality.

In the January of that bitter winter, Lord Randolph Churchill was brought home to his mother's home in Grosvenor Square to die, from a tragic world tour which had had to be hurriedly curtailed. His last appearances in the House of Commons had been agonising for all, and the House had looked with sadness and pain at the spectacle of this trembling, rambling, inarticulate, and prematurely aged man. Most moving of all was the care and attention and courtesy with which Gladstone had listened to Lord Randolph's incomprehensible maunderings, and responded to them as though they had been serious contributions to debate. 'Lord Randolph stood at the Table, sad wreck of a man, attempting to read a carefully-prepared manuscript in a voice so strangely jangled that few could catch the meaning of consecutive sentences', Lucy recorded sadly. 'As soon as he rose Ministers began to move towards the door. When he had sat down he had talked the place half-empty—he at whose rising eight years ago the House filled to its utmost capacity.' Churchill's pitiable decline and death distressed Rosebery, his Eton contemporary and oldest and closest friend, very profoundly, and contributed substantially to his own melancholy.

The Conservatives in the Lords, exhilarated by the almost total popular indifference to the destruction of the Home Rule Bill, now proceeded to mutilate what progressive legislation the Government sent up to them. 'When the Conservative Party is in power', Rosebery wrote to the Queen, 'there is practically no House of Lords . . . but the moment a Liberal Government is formed, this harmless body assumes an active life, and its activity is entirely exercised in opposition to the Government. . . . It is, in fact, a permanent barrier against the Liberal party.' The Queen was not converted, describing any agitation against the Lords as 'a most revolutionary Proceeding'. The absence of public —or even party—reaction to Rosebery's attacks on the Lords encouraged the Conservatives to continue on their course. Their complete success on this occasion was to lure them into subsequent misfortune.

Thus, leaderless and disheartened, acutely divided among themselves, with the fate of their legislation at the whim of their opponents, the Rosebery Government drifted miserably towards disintegration. Campbell-Bannerman, whose rising stature was marked, eagerly sought the Speakership on the retirement of Speaker Peel—himself suddenly a shadow of his former greatness—and was distressed at

Rosebery's refusal to accept the proposal. The Parliamentary Party was becoming almost impossible to control. The Radicals were enraged by Asquith's bland attitude towards the deaths of two miners at Featherstone Colliery when troops opened fire during a bitter coal strike in 1893 which had eventually been resolved by Rosebery's mediation—his last triumph before the Premiership fell upon him. Campbell-Bannerman became locked in a prolonged, embarrassing, but eventually successful endeavour to remove the ancient and impossible Duke of Cambridge from his post of Commander-in-Chief of the Army. The full story of how the aged, spirited, and reluctant Duke was prised from his cherished post may be described with some justification as one of the more comic interludes of the time. The high point was reached when the Prince of Wales, in what Campbell-Bannerman described to Rosebery as 'in quite a casual picktooth sort of manner', told the old Duke en route to Kempton Races that the Queen wanted him to resign. The Duke stiffened. The Queen pressed him. The Duke became obdurate. His friends rallied to his cause. 'The Kaleidoscopic changes in the old Duke's humour are rapidly driving C.B. and Bigge out of their minds', the Prime Minister's private secretary succinctly reported. It was decreed that he must retire on November 1st. He issued 'a piteous letter' begging reconsideration, and then raised the issue of his pension. Another agitated series of discussions ensued, centred on the Duke's demand for an additional £2,000 a year over his Civil List income of £12,000. The Cabinet would not put such a proposal to Parliament. The Duke was defeated. He tried to revive the matter with the Unionist Government, but without success. This episode not only engrossed the attention of the Queen and the Secretary of State for War and preoccupied the Prime Minister to an excessive extent at a difficult moment, but also gave Campbell-Bannerman's successor the opportunity to pass over Sir Redvers Buller—the Liberal choice—and to appoint Lord Wolseley, now in his dotage. The post was retained, and other more vital aspects of Army Reform seriously delayed. The consequences became apparent in 1899.

A proposal to raise a statue of Oliver Cromwell at Westminster aroused wild Irish fury, and had to be abandoned. It was eventually commissioned and undertaken at Rosebery's own expense, and placed outside Westminster Hall. When his horses won the Derby in 1894 and 1895 the condemnations of outraged Nonconformity fell upon him.[1] Relations between the Prime Minister and the Leader of the House of Commons were non-existent. The Queen was deeply disappointed by the tone and style of Rosebery's speeches, and wrote to him frequently and at great length on these and other topics. Questions were asked about the bestowal of honours on certain wealthy but obscure Liberals, the first public hint of scandals to come, and which, curiously enough, really originated with Gladstone.[2] It was not surprising that Ministers anticipated the demise of the Administration with eagerness.

Despite this dispiriting situation, new Liberal reputations were being made. Asquith had fully justified his early promotion, in spite of his somewhat detached attitude towards the Featherstone deaths. From relatively humble origins he had been a moderately successful barrister but a very successful political lawyer. In May 1894 he had married the ebullient and rich Margot Tennant—his first wife having died three years earlier—and had moved into a very different circle than his previous modest existence in Hampstead. He was clearly a coming man, with a certain gravitas which made him seem older than he was, eloquent, and incisive.

On the Liberal back benches, attention was being taken of a young Welsh lawyer, in his early thirties, who had first entered the Commons for Caernarvon Boroughs at a by-election in 1890. David Lloyd George was evidently a young man of burning ambition and rare eloquence whose eyes had been on a political career from an early age. He had not been brought up in the kind of poverty that he later affected to claim, but life in the small village of Llanystumdwy provided an education hardly commensurate with that of the majority of his colleagues in the House of Commons. Elected by a majority of eighteen votes in 1890, he had increased this to 196 in 1892, and

[1] Rosebery later commented that it was interesting to note that 'although without guilt or offence I might perpetually run seconds or thirds, or even last, it became a matter of torture to many consciences if I won'. When politicians run out of political luck, everything seems to go wrong.

[2] See H. J. Hanham, *Victorian Studies*, March 1960, 'The Sale of Honours in the Late Victorian England' and the author's *Rosebery*, pp. 379–81. Although it may not have been a 'sale', the most blatant case of the use of honours was the baronetcy conferred on Captain Naylor-Leyland in June 1895. Naylor-Leyland had been Conservative M.P. for Colchester until February 1895, when he resigned so suddenly and unexpectedly that the Liberals—obviously prepared—won the seat in the by-election. Naylor-Leyland, aged thirty-one, then announced he had joined the Liberals.

particularly in the debates on Welsh Disestablishment he had given clear evidence of formidable debating skills and independence, a scourge of Ministers and disdainful of Whips. He was to survive the 1895 General Election with a majority of 194, and to escape the disaster which was to overwhelm so many Liberals and to end several promising careers.

But it was evident that the Liberals could not long survive, and their leaders had little heart for continuing their wretched existence. A chance defeat in the House of Commons on June 21st on an Opposition motion condemning the Government's handling of cordite production gave them their opportunity to resign. The occasion had certain resemblances with the celebrated defeat of the Gladstone Government in June 1885. It had been a soporific debate, in an almost deserted Chamber. There was little merit in the Opposition's case, and Campbell-Bannerman—who earlier in the evening had received much praise for his handling of the affair of the Duke of Cambridge—had spoken convincingly. But the Ministerial ranks were thin, and after the Whips had exchanged the paper giving the figures, neither believing what they read, the result was a Government minority of seven votes (125 to 132). In the words of an observer, 'Mr. Campbell-Bannerman shut up his box with a snap, and moved to report progress, thus bringing Supply, and all contentious legislation, to a close'. It also brought the Rosebery Government to its conclusion.

The decision to resign was an emotional rather than a measured decision, and was strongly opposed by the party organisers, but the spectacle of Rosebery and Harcourt in full agreement, combined with Campbell-Bannerman's insistence on resigning, carried the exhausted Cabinet without difficulty. 'There are two supreme pleasures in life', Rosebery later wrote with feeling: 'One is ideal, the other real. The ideal is when a man receives the seals of office from his Sovereign. The real pleasure comes when he hands them back.' As the Queen noted: 'To him personally it would be an immense relief if the Government were to go out as the scenes in the Cabinet must have been quite dreadful.'

The record of this ill-starred Government was far from derisory. Rosebery's foreign policy, particularly in Africa, had been aggressive and, on the whole, successful. British influence in Egypt had been consolidated, and the British presence in East Africa firmly established. A clear warning had been given to France that the British regarded the

Upper Nile as being in their sphere of influence. Rhodes's advance northwards had been tacitly approved. Vital, and long overdue, reforms had been made in the armed services—albeit not sweeping enough. Fowler's Local Government Act had been a major advance, and Harcourt's Death Duties Budget had not only opened up new and dramatic possibilities for revenue collection for future Chancellors of the Exchequer but had established a precedent for the use of property for the State which was to have immense consequences. Given the hapless circumstances of its life, the Liberal Government achieved much more than was recognised at the time.

But it entered the 1895 General Election, called immediately after Rosebery had resigned and Salisbury had resumed his interrupted occupation of the Premiership, an army defeated before the battle. Edward Marjoribanks—now Lord Tweedmouth—and a former Chief Whip wrote to Rosebery from the National Liberal Federation offices that 'I've been here all this week with really little to do except interview a few callers and struggle with innumerable demands for speakers. "You must send us Harcourt, J. Morley, Asquith or Fowler" is the cry, and as three out of the four seem determined to crow only on their own dunghills there's small chance of gratifying the criers.'

Significantly, 124 Unionists were returned unopposed, whereas only ten Liberals had uncontested elections. 'Captain' Middleton's organisation was now operating with great efficiency. Gladstone did not stand, Harcourt and Morley were among the ranks of the defeated Liberals (both returned to the Commons shortly afterwards), and the Unionist majority was 152. Rosebery wrote to Ripon that 'I expected this overthrow, and think it a great blessing to the Liberal Party'. To Gladstone he wrote that 'the firm of Rosebery and Harcourt was a fraud upon the public', and let it be publicly known that he would have no relations with Harcourt.

Thus it remained for another year, in spite of occasional, not altogether full-hearted, efforts to bring the deeply estranged leaders together. In that year the gulf between the two widened, and Rosebery thankfully seized an opportunity, provided by a speech by Gladstone on the Turkish massacres of Armenians, to resign on October 8th 1896. In his farewell speech in Edinburgh on the following evening he picked out Asquith—who was present—for particular praise, but for the next two years the Liberals were led by the uneasy partnership of Harcourt and Morley. But Rosebery, depicted as 'the veiled prophet' by the *Daily Chronicle*, retained—and perhaps even enhanced—his unique fascination for the Liberals. It was only slowly that they realised that his ambitions had been destroyed and his spirit broken by private and public misfortunes from which he was destined never to recover. He was still young, and had an immense popular following. But that inner core of resolution and self-confidence, so vital to success in politics, and so difficult to describe, had died.

One of the best portraits of Rosebery's mood is supplied by Edward Hamilton, who stayed with him at The Durdans on June 11th 1899 and recorded in his diary that he found his friend absorbed in Napoleon and Chatham and 'all the less inclined to join in the political throng and all the more minded to hold aloof. In fact he declines point blank to take up any other attitude than that which he has taken up since he retired. He will not admit that he owes anything to his colleagues, after their outrageous behaviour towards him when he was trying to lead them. No one was ever subject to greater ignominy than he was during his short reign. Moreover, public life or rather active participation in public life is, he declares, very distasteful to him; and I am sure that this is a much more genuine feeling than most people would imagine. What he likes—at least this is my belief— is to figure largely in the mind of the public and at the same time to be independent and thus not over-weighted with responsibility. And this is just what he has got though he declines to admit it. . . . He refuses to budge one inch in the direction of emerging from his shell. He declares he is a fatalist, and it is only by fate that he could possibly find himself so situated as to be forced into taking the helm again. He sincerely hoped that such a fate did not await him. . . . I am sure he is not intentionally deceiving me and others: though he may be deceiving himself, as I believe he is doing.'

Hamilton's account and conclusions are confirmed by all other sources, save the last. Rosebery was not deceiving himself; he meant every word. Unhappily, others could not or would not accept that this brilliant man, fifty years of age, had renounced politics. But he had.

Salisbury invited Chamberlain, Devonshire, Sir Henry James, Goschen, and the Marquis of Lansdowne to join his new Cabinet. All accepted, and, six months after his death, Lord Randolph Churchill's proposed Unionist Alliance of 1886 was thus formally signified, and the Liberal Interlude was concluded.

*

At this point it is necessary to take stock of the general situation as it existed in June 1895, and to turn aside from political fluctuations and fortunes.

The relative decline in British trade and industry from the 1870s onwards was significant, but should not be exaggerated. For example, British seaborne trade in the period 1880–1900 averaged £710 million a year, three times that of France and ten times that of Russia; seventy per cent of the foreign trade of China was, in effect, in British hands. Nevertheless, Britain was now third in the production of steel, her consumption of raw cotton was virtually stagnant, and save in ship-building and mercantile business, there were few exceptions to the general picture of both a real and relative slowing-up of the British economy. Agriculture, beginning to recover from the disasters of the 1870s, now suffered further blows. The Parsons turbine and the Dunlop pneumatic tyre were the only significant technological con-tributions made by Britain in this period, in sharp and painful contrast with the ingenuity and inventiveness of the rapidly ascendant Germany and the United States. Wages were increasing—by about seventy-seven per cent in real wages since 1860, a quarter of this achieved in the decade 1890–1900—but although it would be absurd to portray Britain as a poor nation, or even a nation becoming poorer, the full effects of the loss of momentum in the 1870s were being seen in the 1890s.

One effect concerned British attitudes to the outside world. The actual increase in British overseas trade from the territories acquired after 1880 was, by 1901, only 2½ per cent of the total.[1] But the economic interest in these, and prospective, acquisitions was now increasing. The new attitude has been well summarised by Dr. C. J. Lowe:

> Essentially the problem by 1900 was that with the decline in comparative industrial efficiency, the British share of world markets, though still enormous, was shrinking: hence both a determination to hold on to those still possessed and the imperialist idea of develop-ing new, closed, markets for the future.[2]

This new attitude was best expressed by Rosebery in a speech on March 1st, 1893 at the Royal Colonial Institute:

[1] J. Hobson: *Imperialism*, 35.
[2] C. J. Lowe: *The Reluctant Imperialists*, 4–5.

There is another ground on which the extension of our Empire is greatly attacked, and the attack comes from a quarter nearer home. It is said that our Empire is already large enough, and does not need extension. That would be true enough if the world were elastic, but unfortunately it is not elastic, and we are engaged at the present moment, in the language of the mining camps, in 'pegging out claims for the future'. We have to consider, not what we want, but what we shall want in the future. . . . We should, in my opinion, grossly fail in the task that has been laid upon us if we shrink from responsibilities and decline to take our share in a partition of the world which we have not forced on, but which has been forced upon us.

It was this speech in particular that Gladstone had in mind when he subsequently wrote that Rosebery had shown himself 'to be rather seriously imbued with the spirit of territorial grab, which constitutes for us one of the graver dangers of the time'. But Gladstone, in this as in so many other matters, spoke the language of an earlier era. By the 1890s the dominant tones in British Imperial discussion were those of expansion and consolidation; the controversies arose over the methods whereby British interests could be best served.

In retrospect, it may appear remarkable that the British clung doggedly to Free Trade in a world that was steadily becoming more Protectionist. But Free Trade was one of the established dogmas of Victorian Britain. The fact that the United States—as a result of the McKinley Tariff of 1890 and the Dingley Tariff of 1897—had become among the most highly protected countries in the world and that even the Dominions, notably Canada in 1879 and Australia in 1900, were moving in the same direction seemed to make the British more implacably resolved than ever to cling to a system that had, in their eyes, given them their world position and would do so in future. The Labour Party was to prove itself the most dogmatic Free Trade group of all, and was to provide in Philip Snowden in 1929–31 the last convinced Free Trade Chancellor of the Exchequer. In the 1900s onwards, the issue of Tariffs was to be one of the dominating ones in British politics. But, as the century neared its end, Free Trade still stood hallowed and revered in England alone. Germany was in effect protectionist since 1879, Russia since 1882, and France and Austria-Hungary in the same year. As the years passed, the tariff walls grew remorselessly higher against British products.

There had been a quiet revolution in British Government in the 1870s and 1880s. The creation of elective County Councils in 1887 was the most significant single development, for, as completed by the creation of district and parish councils in 1893, it based the whole of English local government upon direct popular election.

This really was a revolution. Democracy did not exist on a national scale, but it was being established in the towns and in the counties. The fact that women could vote for, and serve on, these new Councils was in itself a startling development that was to have its effect on the movement for Women's Suffrage which now began to develop seriously.

In education, the really important decisions were taken between 1870 and 1902. Few measures of Victorian Parliaments aroused fiercer opposition than W. E. Forster's Education Act of 1870, which provided elementary schools at public expense for the first time. The denominational schools had been virtually the only former institutions of this kind, and, as has been noted, the reactions in Nonconformist circles had been particularly bitter, and had brought the National Education League and Joseph Chamberlain into national prominence. But the public elementary schools were established, and in 1892 all fees for such education were abolished. The Technical Instruction Act of 1889 recognised what other countries had realised a quarter of a century before, that an industrial society depended for its very existence upon such instruction. In 1899 a single Department of Education was set up, presided over by a senior Minister. These advances paved the way for the Education Act of 1902.

The expansion of Universities and the establishment of the system of national free libraries emphasised the fact that the quality of British education was rising sharply in the latter quarter of the century. Unhappily they only served to repair the ravages of neglect and complacency. Illiteracy was destroyed, but only for future generations. It would be a very long time before the quality of the eduction in State schools approximated to the standards of the private fee-paying schools. A really full education remained the prerogative of the upper and wealthy middle classes, and the most that can be said is that the existence of the gulf was recognised, and belated steps were being taken to bridge it.

One of the most interesting developments in the 1890s was that of the 'popular' Press. The key feature of the 'new journalism' was commercialism, and its pioneer was Alfred Harmsworth, subsequently Lord Northcliffe, who made the discovery that news, or a version of it, could be sold at as great profit as any other form of merchandise. He started his first newspaper at the age of twenty-five, and it was well on the way to foundering when he offered a prize—a pound a day for life—for anyone who guessed the value of the amount of gold in the Bank of England on a given day. Circulation soared to a quarter of a million and Harmsworth moved on with his brother (later Lord Rothermere) to buy the *Evening News*, which sold at a halfpenny and showed strong signs of American newspaper influence; its editor, Kennedy Jones, had in fact studied the American Press with care. In 1896 the Harmsworths founded the *Daily Mail*, which was an immediate success, with a circulation of 543,000 within three years, a figure unapproached by any competitor.

Harmsworth was undeniably a genius, and was himself a natural journalist. Under his control the new journalism provided its readers not with news but stories. The sub-editor now became the crucial figure, re-writing reports and lacing them with his own headlines and interpretations. If Providence did not provide news, it could be manufactured, as in the notorious case in 1900 when the *Daily Mail* published the story of the massacre of the white residents of Peking; it was a pure invention, but neither the repute nor the sales of the *Daily Mail* suffered thereby, thus providing Harmsworth with another interesting lesson.

Harmsworth was the first to discover the enormous potentialities of a large and just-literate readership; he also saw that advertising was the key to really large financial success. Salisbury described the *Daily Mail* as 'written by office boys for office boys'. He was right, but office boys were developing into voters. Where Harmsworth had sowed, others reaped with him. A new figure, the newspaper magnate, entered British social life and politics. In time many of them made vast fortunes and developed megalomania in lesser or greater forms. They assumed an apparent omnipotence and inspired aversion and fear until Baldwin showed that their political influence was in fact negligible. But this was not to come until 1931.

The Harmsworth, and subsequently the Beaverbrook, Press was in business to make money. The popular press accordingly pandered to what it deemed were popular tastes, and the strident nationalism and Imperialism of the 'new journalism' in the later 1890s was not the least of the factors that drove intelligent and sensitive men into opposition of their cause, believing, probably wholly mistakenly, that the popular press was responsible for creating emotions that were in reality there, and merely being commercially exploited.

The revival of Trade Unionism in the late 1880s had been given a substantial impetus by the London Dock Strike of 1889. Concern about the legal position of the Unions increased in the 1890s; employers, alarmed by the impact of foreign competition, were beginning to combine effectively, and the Courts were upholding them. The right to picket was successfully challenged in the courts, and resulted in the Trades Union Congress resolving—by a small majority—to summon a special conference of trade unions, co-operative societies and Socialist bodies to make plans for Labour representation in Parliament in 1899. Significantly this was strongly opposed by the miners, who already had a firm grip on Liberal representation for mining areas.

In 1892 total membership of trade unions was 1,576,000; by 1900 it was 2,022,000. The most notable industrial dispute of the 1890s were the miners' strike and lock-out of 1893 and the engineers' strike of 1897. The former lasted for fifteen weeks, and included the riot at Featherstone, but in many respects the engineers' strike was more significant. After seven months the men were totally defeated. There were two lessons to be drawn from this episode. The Unions must, by fusion or federation, become larger units if they were to achieve results; and that political action was likely to be more rewarding than crude, isolated industrial protest. This had been preached for years by the Fabians; now it was realised that their answer was the correct one. Closely linked to this realisation was the new interest being shown by the Unions in the condition of life of the working classes.

These new movements coincided—and the coincidence is important —with the decline of the Liberals. From 1886 to 1895 Ireland had dominated all other issues. In 1895–6 Harcourt and Rosebery were not on speaking terms. After Rosebery retired as leader in the autumn of 1896 Harcourt took his place, only to find his position compromised and his authority fatally undermined. For all his talk and bluster, Harcourt was essentially a radical middle class London attorney, and his sympathies and comprehension of public affairs were not closely linked with nascent working class groups. The Fabians had long since been disillusioned by the Liberals; working class disillusionment was much more slow in developing, but it was in the late 1890s that those who urged separate Labour representation in Parliament began to make serious progress.

The Socialist-union conference called in 1899 met in London on February 17th–18th, 1900, and agreed to set up the Labour Representation Committee (the L.R.C.) to promote and co-ordinate plans for Labour representation in Parliament. It is perhaps possible to exaggerate the importance of this conference, but some of its decisions were crucial. In the first place, the Unions agreed to a levy—'10 shillings per annum for every 1,000 members or fraction thereof'—to finance the new party; of equal importance was an amendment proposed by Keir Hardie that the Committee's function was to establish 'a distinct Labour Group in Parliament, who shall have their own Whips and agree upon their policy, which must embrace a readiness to co-operate with any party which for the time being may be engaged in promoting legislation in the direct interest of Labour, and be equally ready to associate themselves with any party in opposing measures having an opposite tendency'; a third important decision—proposed by G. N. Barnes—was to the effect that candidates need not be working men themselves.

These decisions meant in effect that the new party was to be based very much on the pattern of the Irish Nationalist Party under Parnell. It was to have a regular source of income from the Unions; it was to act in Parliament as a separate Party, but was to co-operate with any other party which was acting in the best interests of the working classes. Dogma, in short, was to be emphatically subordinated to the requirements of practical politics.

There was at this stage no question of establishing a new party with a specific programme of reform, and there was considerable vagueness as to the exact role to be played in Parliament when, and if, it had any elected representatives. The first secretary of the L.R.C. was a young Scottish journalist, Ramsay MacDonald, who was, like Keir Hardie, an illegitimate child brought up in poverty.

The early history of Labour politics was somewhat confused, even to contemporaries. There was the Independent Labour Party, based in Scotland; the Marxist Social Democratic Federation (S.D.F.); and the Fabians. Each was represented on the L.R.C., with five members out of twelve, but were seriously at odds with each other. The S.D.F. found the Committee too tame for their brand of social reform, and quickly retired in 1900. In the 1900 General Election the L.R.C.

endorsed fifteen candidates, but could do little for them except supply leaflets and give them their blessing. Total expenditure in the election by the L.R.C. was £33. Only two of the sponsored candidates—Hardie and Richard Bell—were elected. Bell turned out to be a Liberal on every issue except when the interests of his Union—the Railway Servants—were involved. Hardie was difficult, erratic, passionate, humane and independent, whose very confusion of purpose gave him much attractiveness but with few merits as a leader, or even a guide. It was not, either in quantity or in quality, a very impressive start. Nevertheless, it was a start, and a further development in the slowly unfolding British Revolution.

*

It is desirable to examine other, more familiar, institutions in the 1890s.

The Navy was showing clear and, for those who cared to look closely, alarming signs of decrepitude. It is perhaps too harsh to say, as Professor Marder has remarked, that 'although numerically a very imposing force, it was in certain respects a drowsy, inefficient, moth-eaten organisation'.[1] The Spencer Programme of 1894–6 retained the Navy's numerical superiority, but its qualitative superiority was more questionable. The Navy had no Staff College. Excessive emphasis was placed on appearances and precise seamanship. There was ignorance of and indifference to new scientific developments. There were virtually no war plans, a fact that first became evident in the Fashoda Crisis of 1898. Gunnery was regarded with dislike and distaste. Practice firing was limited to 2,000 yards—little more than in Nelson's day—and the percentage of hits in practice, even at this range, was less than one in three. Target practices at sea were limited to one every three months. The Navy urgently required reorganisation from the top to the bottom, and it was to receive this revival under the hands of the amazing Admiral 'Jackie' Fisher. Fisher became Commander-in-Chief of the Mediterranean Fleet in 1899, was Second Sea Lord 1902–3, and First Sea Lord 1904–8. He arrived just in time. Between 1899 and 1904 the Navy Estimates had trebled, and by 1904 they stood at £37 millions. Fisher not only produced a revivified Navy but did so at less cost, which earned him the gratitude and awe of politicians no less than that of the more far-seeing officers of the Navy.

A. J. Marder: *From the Dreadnought to Scapa Flow*, Volume 1.

Fisher's reforms fall in a later period. It suffices at this stage to comment on the fact that the basis of British world policy in the nineteenth century, whether admitted or not, lay in her supremacy at sea, and that this was, for all who cared to see, a very much less impressive foundation than appeared at first glance.

The British Army was hardly in more impressive condition, but serious and partially successful attempts had been made to reform it. Edward Cardwell's tenure of the War Office in 1868–74 had removed some of the more spectacular anomalies. Small units were withdrawn from the Colonies, the War Office was centralised in London, short-service commissions were introduced, the Army equipped with the breech-loading rifle, the regimental system reorganised on a territorial basis, flogging in peacetime was abolished, and the system of 'Purchase' ended. Cardwell was less successful in other respects. The 'linked battalion' system had serious weaknesses, and the cavalry retained its privileged position; the artillery, far from being modernised, went back to muzzle-loading cannons. Until 1886 no mobilisation scheme existed at all, and no mobilisation regulations were issued until 1892. The machine-gun was not properly developed, and had not been fully introduced by the Boer War. The condition of the Ordnance Factories was described in February 1899 by the Director-General of the Ordnance as 'full of peril to the Empire'. Campbell-Bannerman's removal of the Duke of Cambridge as Commander-in-Chief in 1895 was a step forward in that it removed a considerable impediment to energetic reforms, but his replacement, Wolseley, by now a shadow of his former self, was a somewhat marginal improvement.

The British Army, like the Royal Navy, was awesome at a distance. Its competence and courage in the field were well known, and were to be seen again in the Sudan Campaign of 1897–8. In theory, 600,000 men were available for mobilisation, but in fact the practical limit for a quick mobilisation was 85,000. It was not until the Boer War that the urgent necessity for its major overhaul was fully demonstrated. But it must be emphasised that hardly anyone—if anyone—thought of the Army ever becoming involved in a major war against a comparable military power. As a young subaltern, Winston Churchill later wrote:

Nobody expected to get killed. Here and there in every regiment or battalion, half a dozen, a score, at the worst thirty or forty, would pay the forfeit. But to the great mass of those who took part in the little wars of Britain in those vanished light-hearted days, this was only a sporting element in a splendid game.

The Navy, then and always, had strong political allies; the Army, virtually none at all. The link between the politicians and the soldiers was at best tenuous; normally they operated separately, with a certain mutual contempt. For all the Cardwell and other reforms, the British Army in its essentials had advanced very little since the Crimean War. The worst abuses and weaknesses had gone, but many still remained. Compared with the vast and well-equipped European armies, the British Army was a negligible factor in power calculations. And, as the events of 1899 were to prove, it was not even prepared for the kind of minor colonial war which was its raison d'etre. 'The Government', as Wolseley complained in 1899, 'are acting without complete knowledge of what the military can do, while the military authorities on their side are equally without full knowledge of what the Government expects them to do.' From this complacency there was to be a sharp awakening.

*

The last decade of the nineteenth century saw the deaths of Parnell and Randolph Churchill, and, in May 1898, Gladstone's long life at last ended.

For more than fifty years Gladstone had astounded, angered, awed, and inspirited his countrymen. Now, a harsh fate determined that he should be stricken with one of the most acutely painful of all forms of cancer and that his extraordinary physique should resist its advance so relentlessly. At the end, as the shadows darkened over him, the fierce controversies faded. The wealthy young Conservative, the early defender of slavery and privilege, the stern but tormented Churchman and 'out and out inegalitarian' had developed slowly and painfully into the earnest and at times inspired champion of the deprived, the assailed, the weak, and the defenceless. His life had a nobility which transcended all defects, and which expunged all errors and failings. And no episode in that complex journey was more noble than the last one, so tragically drawn out, so exquisitely painful, and whose outcome was so inevitable. Let Morley describe the end:

> On the early morning of the 19th [of May], his family all kneeling around the bed on which he lay in the stupor of coming death,

without a struggle he ceased to breathe. Nature outside—wood and wide lawn and cloudless far-off sky—shone at her fairest.

*

The 1890s have been varyingly assessed by different commentators. Inevitably, each sees in this period particular facets of significance. It was undoubtedly a more exciting decade than its predecessors. It was a period of a greater relaxation in morals and in a wider and more enjoyable life[1]—demonstrated in the enormous new popularity of spectator-sports, particularly Association Football and cricket—for more people. There was a distinct relaxation of social and religious taboos and, in this respect, the increased use of contraceptives was significant. It will be recalled that in 1878 Charles Bradlaugh had been imprisoned for advocating birth control; by the 1890s the use of reasonably efficient contraceptive devices had become much more widespread in the educated and upper classes, and the marked decline in the birth rate of this minority element was one of the most interesting social phenomena of the decade. Divorce—as the Dilke and Parnell cases demonstrated—was still socially unacceptable, but opinions were changing even on this. The continuing decline in church-going, particularly in the Church of England, was very striking; although the Nonconformists lost less ground, even their records showed a noticeable reduction.

There was, in the England of the 1890s, an evident sense of change, of greater intellectual activity, and the emergence of new approaches and attitudes towards the accepted tenets of mid-Victorian England. But there were few clear indications of the directions into which these new energies and attitudes would move.

---

[1] It was in the 1890s that some manual workers began to have the long-sought advantage of the Eight-Hour day.

CHAPTER SIX

THE SOUTH AFRICAN LABYRINTH, 1895–1899

LTHOUGH SALISBURY's offer to the Liberal Unionists occasioned little remark, there was very considerable and widespread surprise at the decision of Chamberlain to go to the Colonial Office, a Department that had held a low status in the political and official hierarchy. But Chamberlain's ambitions had been centred on that backwater for several years. To his American fiancée he had written in 1888 of the South African situation that 'I mean some day to be Colonial Secretary and to deal with it', and to the same correspondent he had written that 'I am inclined to advocate a bold policy [in South Africa], fully recognizing Imperial responsibilities and duty, but then I intend that it should be the policy of the Imperial and not of the Cape Government, and should be carried out by officials taking their instructions from the former.' For the first time, therefore, London would call the tune in Imperial, and particularly South African, affairs.

The Conservatives viewed their formidable colleague without enthusiasm, and Salisbury's attitude was even more bleak than that of his colleagues. He had once described Chamberlain as 'a Sicilian bandit', and had not in reality changed his view. Lady Frances Balfour noted in November 1895 that 'I never heard him talk of any colleague as he does of him, says Chamberlain wants to go to war with every Power in the world, and has no thought but Imperialism.'

Amongst other emotions, there was a strong element of jealousy in the Conservatives' attitude to their former foe. He was, as Winston Churchill later wrote, 'incomparably the most live, sparkling, insurgent, compulsive figure in British affairs. . . . He was the man the masses knew. He it was who had solutions for social problems; who was ready to advance, sword in hand if need be, upon the foes of

Britain; and whose accents rang in the ears of all the young peoples of the Empire and lots of young people at its heart.' If this was hyperbole, it was as Chamberlain saw himself at this time. Throughout his career Chamberlain had been the principal actor upon small stages. His ambition went far beyond Birmingham sewers, radical programmes, or Home Rule. His intelligence, his vanity, and his ambition required a much more significant theatre and audience. He had now discerned where these were to be found, and he applied himself relentlessly to their conquest. He was now at the height of his powers, possessing, as Beatrice Webb wrote, 'energy and personal magnetism, in a word masculine force, to an almost superlative degree'. It was to prove to be a catastrophic combination once again.

Salisbury, whose instinct for serious politicians was usually very sound, saw this clearly. There were other things the Conservative leader knew, and feared, about Chamberlain, after long experience of him as an opponent and as an uneasy ally. He was a hard man, and had grown harder in the Home Rule disputes. His eye was always on the reality of power, and not on position. His approach had always been combative and relentless, but had become more cold and ruthless since 1885. His mind was remarkably clear. It was limited in scope, the range was not long, and the breadth was not great, but the clarity was impressive. He was a man who believed that a politician must always have a policy. It could be amended, modified, or even reversed, but at all times the politician must present himself to his following with decisive leadership. His approach had become markedly more logical and precise, and lacking in that confusion of objective and intent that characterises most politicians. He dealt with situations as they arose, and always had a policy to deal with them. He had survived the break with Gladstone, and had fought his former colleagues with fire and logic. They hated him for it, and the Conservatives did not love him for what he had done. But they had need of him, much though they feared his independent power base, his dedication to the task in hand, his implacable resolve, his popular support, and his unquenched ambition.

If many Conservatives were awed by Chamberlain, Salisbury was not. He had never trusted him nor liked him, nor even greatly respected him. Now, he trusted him less than ever. But Salisbury was ageing prematurely, tired and vague, increasingly detached from the burdens of office. His eye remained clear, and he saw more sharply than his colleagues the perils of Chamberlain's energy, ardour and inexperience in foreign affairs. He endeavoured to warn others of these dangers, but his word no longer carried the old authoritative urgency, and he had lost the mental and physical energy to press his arguments quietly yet with overwhelming effect. He was in a tragical decline, seeing all, yet helpless. Balfour, for all his cleverness and guile, did not possess Salisbury's long-term vision, his acute understanding of human nature, his experience, nor his Christian cynicism. Thus, swiftly Chamberlain became dominant, while Salisbury lamented in vain. The destiny of the Unionist Government, and much else besides, was now in the hands of this impatient, hard, and limited man.

The gulf between Salisbury and Chamberlain had always been, and would remain to the end, vast and incapable of being bridged. Salisbury was a deeply religious man, devoted to his family, and a warm encourager of lively and uninhibited disputation between his children and himself. He was an intellectual, who read much and pondered greatly. Hatfield in his lifetime was a place of accepted custom and tradition, yet of intense spirit and happiness, where he presided benignly but acutely over a family of outstanding intellect and charm, which argued incessantly at the highest level. At Highbury, Chamberlain dominated a pretentious, gloomy, and although devoted, subservient *ménage*. As Beatrice Webb noted, there was 'very *much taste*, and all very bad', and her description of the principal room as 'forlornly grand' may serve as an accurate portrait of the household. He relished good champagne, and cultivated orchids with skill, application, and success. But the food was, although grand and expensive, in quality poor. Chamberlain's family, and particularly the women, were there to comfort and applaud him, and not to contradict or dispute. Salisbury, ill-dressed and vague, was an authentic grandee; Chamberlain, immaculate and sharp, remained an authentic *arriviste*. Chamberlain was not an intellectual, nor did he have the experience, imagination or dedication to close the gulf between himself and Salisbury. Nor, did he discern any reason why he should. And so he rushed along, while the much older man viewed his progress with mounting concern and anguish, incapable of restoring the political balance.

*

Chamberlain came to the Colonial Office in July 1895 with emphatic opinions, and in his first major speech, on August 22nd, he further developed a theme much in evidence in his recent declarations that the colonies were 'undeveloped estates' that merited development. Once Chamberlain had seized on an issue, he carried it through to what he regarded as its ultimate conclusion. He had come to agree fully with Rosebery's dictum that the Empire was 'the greatest secular agency for good the world has ever seen', and that it should not simply be maintained but actually expanded. 'I and those who agree with me believe in the expansion of the Empire', he said in the Commons on March 20th, 1893, 'and we are not ashamed to confess that we have that feeling, and we are not at all troubled by accusations of Jingoism.' The Boers did not know that it was he who had been the principal impelling force that had persuaded the Gladstone Govern-ment in 1884 to send 4,000 troops into Bechuanaland to end Boer encroachments there, but there were many other indications that Chamberlain was not likely to be a friend of the Republics. A man who said that it was Britain's duty to extend her control over 'those friendly chiefs and peoples who are stretching out their hands towards us' and that 'the British race is the greatest governing race the world has ever seen' aroused justifiable concern in the Transvaal and Orange Free State.

The Colonial Office itself was fully aware of the issues now at stake in South Africa. Until the early 1890s it had been tacitly assumed in London and at Cape Town that the Cape Colony would inevitably acquire an economic domination, and that the problem of the Boer Republics would solve itself by their becoming a negligible economic, political and military factor in South Africa. The spectacular advances of Rhodes's British South Africa Company had seemed to support this assumption. Since 1889 Rhodes had acquired vast new areas of territory, and in October 1893 the Company had routed the Matabele in an ugly little war in which a small mounted force under Dr. Jameson and equipped with the revolutionary quick-firing Maxim gun had achieved an overwhelming victory. The Colonial Office stood aside, although it approved of further Cape advances, and Liberal indignation quickly faded away. 'Local Imperialism', it appeared, had all the advantages and involved no commitments or expenditure.

But by 1895 it was evident that these assumptions had proved to have been disastrously wrong. The discovery of the Witwatersrand

Gold Field in 1886 in effect trumped Rhodes's ace. His belief that the true Rand was in southern Zambesia had been falsified; it was at Johannesburg. The total revenue of the Transvaal in 1886 was £196,000; within ten years it was nearly £4 million. Thus, far from the expanding Cape Colony eventually absorbing a poor and backward farming community it now began to look as if it would be the Transvaal that would be the centre and leader of a new confederation inimicable to British and Cape Colony interests. When it seemed in October 1892 that the Transvaal might actually invade Zambesia, a Colonial Office memorandum starkly pointed out that

> . . . unless we are prepared to resist this by force, we shall have to abandon Mr. Rhodes and the British South Africa Company and the whole idea of British supremacy in the interior to a 'New Republic' which will be hostile to British capital and enterprise.[1]

If there was apprehension in London and in Cape Colony at the dramatic change in the South African situation, there was fear also in the Transvaal.

Since the discovery of the Rand, settlers had poured into the Republic, mainly from Britain and Cape Colony. There was no proper census undertaken, and it is not possible to estimate their total numbers with any precision. A census of Johannesburg in July 1896, however, revealed that of a white population of 50,907 only 6,205 were Transvaalers. The main groups of the 'Uitlanders' were the British (over 16,000) and over 15,000 from Cape Colony. It is probable that, by the mid-1890s, the number of adult Uitlander males in the Transvaal actually exceeded that of adult Boer males.

The massive infiltration represented a number of grievous political, social and economic problems for the Republic. The development of the Rand had not brought proportionate wealth for the Boers themselves; indeed, in several respects they were worse off than before. Much of the produce of the new inhabitants was brought in by the new railways; by 1890 the supply of free land—on which the Boer agrarian economy was based—had virtually stopped, and large areas were being purchased by foreigners. Outbreaks of rinderpest, plagues of locusts and a severe drought further impoverished the farming community.

The Transvaal Government was ill-equipped to handle the situation.

[1] Colonial Office Memorandum on 'The Swazi Question', October 19th, 1892. Quoted in Robinson and Gallagher: *Africa and the Victorians*, 413.

It was xenophobic, incompetent, grasping, and riddled with corruption. The formidable President Kruger was himself ageing, was surrounded with inefficient or actively dangerous colleagues, and was notably more dictatorial than ever before.

Paul Kruger had grown up with the Republic. As a child of ten he had gone with his parents on the Great Trek out of Cape Colony in 1835. In the troubled years of the Republic he had risen quickly as a conciliator and a moderator of fierce rivalries. It was he who, on the morrow of Majuba, had urged moderation on the angry Volksraad. He was a devout, and almost childlike, believer in the literal truth of the Bible. He was uncouth in speech and manner, and subject to almost uncontrollable rages when thwarted. He cared passionately for his country, and personified the Republic's motto, Unity Gives Strength, and which included the corollary that opposition and party strife were undesirable. Yet, in spite of his authority and reputation, the Presidential election of 1892 had been a very close thing. Wily and skilful himself, yet he was a poor judge of character, a defect that became more obvious with old age.

It was not surprising that foreigners, of whom he was deeply suspicious, found him politically slippery and personally repulsive. One English visitor found him sitting in a leather armchair 'in dirty-looking clothes, his hair and beard long, a big Dutch pipe in his mouth, and a huge red bandana handkerchief hanging out of the side pocket of his loose jacket'; a huge spitoon was at hand, to which he had frequent recourse, although with indifferent aim. Yet everyone of stature who had dealings with him was impressed. Rhodes, who knew a strong man when he met one, always regarded Kruger as a formidable opponent. Although unlettered and uneducated, his energy was considerable, his intelligence was keen, and his obstinacy well-established.

His contempt for, and fear of, the mercenary outsiders who had entered his country and coarsened its life was understandable. An English journalist—Flora Shaw—described Johannesburg in 1892 as 'hideous and detestable; luxury without order, sensual enjoyment without art, riches without refinement, display without dignity,' and her appraisal was echoed by many other observers.

Until it was too late, Kruger had thought that he could use these interlopers and then dispose of them; it was not until the early 1890s that he fully realised that they had come to stay and represented a real threat to the Republic.

It is necessary to look at the system under which the Transvaal was governed, for it lay at the heart of the subsequent crisis, and which was to have such profound consequences for Britain and the course of British politics.

The Volksraad consisted of between twenty-four and twenty-eight representatives, who were virtually all landed Boers. Originally a Uitlander could obtain citizenship and the full franchise for £25 after five years' residence. In 1890 the period of residence was extended to fourteen, and no Uitlander under the age of forty could vote for the Volksraad, the President, or the Commandant-General. A second Volksraad for the Uitlanders was introduced, but its powers were so circumscribed that they were vitually non-existent. There was little attempt by the Uitlanders to become full citizens of the Republic; between 1890 and 1896 only 2,087 were naturalised. This fact did not, however, inhibit them from seeking full voting rights. As early as 1887 they had begun to organise themselves into groups for this purpose, but until 1892 these efforts had been relatively feeble. But they did obtain control of the Johannesburg Sanitary Board, and it was the curt rejection of 1892 of its request for wider powers that resulted in the creation of the Transvaal National Union, which resolved to 'obtain by all constitutional means equal rights for all citizens of the Republic, and . . . the redress of all grievances'.

This was an ominous development. There is no firm evidence that the formation of the Union was encouraged or inspired from the outside, and it seems to have been an entirely local organisation. In the 1892 Presidential election it supported Joubert against Kruger— to Joubert's considerable embarrassment. But the fact was that the Union was led and dominated by British settlers from Cape Colony, and it was not long before its political potentialities were being studied eagerly and attentively in Cape Colony.

Whether regarded from the north or the south, the Transvaal was a formidable barrier to British expansion in Africa. Furthermore, there were strong indications that her nuisance value was even greater than this. The activities of W. J. Leyds—a hard, ambitious, dour Hollander almost as much disliked by the Boers as by the British—were a case in point. Leyds had become State Secretary in 1888, and had developed the lucrative system of selling 'concessions'—which were in effect monopolies—which also had a political aspect. Leyds wanted powerful capitalist influences in Europe to have a stake in the Transvaal which they would be prepared to defend. In brief, he wanted British money to be countered by French, Dutch and German money. When, in 1894, Kruger called the controversial dynamite concession 'the cornerstone of the independence of the Republic' he meant what he said. He was, in a blundering fashion, playing off the great powers. Leyds was passionately anti-British, and although his attempts to enlist strong European support for the Republic failed, these activities were an additional factor in the increasing unease and resentment with which the British viewed the situation. The Liberal Colonial Secretary, Lord Ripon, wrote to Kimberley in November 1894 that:

. . . The German inclination to take the Transvaal under their protection is a very serious thing. To have them meddling at Pretoria and Johannesburg would be fatal to our position and our influence in South Africa. . . .

Neither Kimberley nor Rosebery had to be told of this danger by the Colonial Secretary, and Kimberley—with Rosebery's full support—warned the Austrian Ambassador at the end of October 1894 that 'the maintenance of the Cape Colony was perhaps the most vital interest of Great Britain'. The British were looking at Europe as closely as they were South Africa.

The influence of Cecil Rhodes was the decisive factor in bringing a potentially critical confrontation to a head. In 1894 Rhodes began to greatly interest himself in the Uitlander cause. His motives were, as usual, very mixed. To ignore the visionary and idealistic side of his strange character is as foolish as to overlook the hard ruthlessness of the capitalistic entrepeneur. Dogged by ill-health, obsessed by visions, and haunted by the prospect that his dream of a federated South Africa under British domination would not be accomplished in his lifetime, Rhodes was a sick, eager, and impatient man.

He was in a postion of rare power and influence. His reputation extended far beyond the confines of Cape Colony, whose Premier he had been since 1890. In Britain he had powerful allies, and not least in the Liberal Party. In Cape Colony he was admired by all parties, and even in the Transvaal he was viewed with respect—and in some cases with more than respect. The young Jan Smuts was to write of him in July 1896 that, 'the Dutch set aside all considerations of blood and nationality and loved him and trusted him and served him because they believed that *he* was the man to carry out that great idea of an internally sovereign and united South Africa in which the white man would be supreme—which has been the cry of our forefathers even as it is our cry today. Here at last our Moses had appeared—and it made no difference that he was an Egyptian in blood.'

This great position, and very much more, was now to be put to ridiculous and terrible hazard.

*

In May 1894 the Transvaal Government ordered some British subjects to serve on a commando. In the subsequent spate of Uitlander protests, the leader of the Johannesburg Uitlanders, Lionel Phillips, asked the British High Commissioner at Cape Town—Sir Henry Loch—if the Uitlanders could count on his support in the event of an uprising. It was Phillips' understanding that Loch had said that he could count upon support from Cape Colony in such an eventuality. Loch then proposed to the Colonial Office that he should be authorised to use the Bechuanaland Police to support an Uitlander rising in Johannesberg, prior to the intervention of the British garrison in South Africa, which he wanted increased by 5,000 men.

Loch was not actually suggesting that a rising should be provoked; he was making contingency plans for what seemed a real possibility. But his plans were emphatically rejected by the Colonial Office, and the most severe criticism of the suggestion was written by the Permanent Under-Secretary, Sir Robert Meade. What he described as Loch's 'extremely dangerous proposal' would encourage the Uitlanders 'to make excessive demands'; it was imperative that 'every nerve should be strained to prevent such a disgrace as another S. African war'. Lord Ripon expressed his approval of Meade's attitude.

Loch was succeeded by Sir Hercules Robinson, High Commissioner 1881–9, now aged and in bad health; he was Rhodes's nominee, and had served on the board of one of Rhodes's companies. His appointment was widely criticised, not least by Chamberlain. The High Commissioner's Colonial Secretary, Sir Graham Bower, has described the difference between Loch and Robinson:

Sir Hercules was cold and calculating, very cautious and without any personal ties or personal friendships or hatreds. His first interest was to secure his safety. Sir Henry Loch was hot-headed, vain, impulsive, and with strong likes and dislikes. In the case of Sir

Hercules my difficulty generally was to get him to move at all. I spent my time with Sir Henry Loch in figuratively holding on to his coat-tails.

Before the Rosebery Government fell in June 1895 plans for a rising in Johannesberg and subsequent planned assistance from Cape Colony were well advanced. Rhodes was putting pressure on London to hand over the Bechuanaland Protectorate to the British South Africa Company, and it was essential to the plan that the township of Gaberones—on the Transvaal border—should be in Rhodes's hands. No decision had been reached by the Liberals, and Rhodes's agent in London—Dr. Rutherford Harris—put the matter before Chamberlain on August 1st. Also present at this meeting were Chamberlain's Under-Secretary, Lord Selborne, and Earl Grey. Reports of the meeting vary, although it does seem to be the case that when Harris was about to deal with the matter of why the British South Africa Company wanted Gaberones so urgently, Chamberlain swiftly changed the subject. Grey said that he subsequently saw Chamberlain alone and told him that a Uitlander rising was imminent, and that it was essential to place an armed force on the border. Grey's honesty— although not his intelligence—has never been impugned, and there is no reason to question his account, as it is confirmed by subsequent events.

Harris reported to Rhodes on August 13th:

Chamberlain will do anything to assist except hand over the administration protectorate provided he officially does not know anything of your plan. He does consider Rhodes' ingenuity resource can overcome any difficulty caused by refusal protectorate now.

Harris telegraphed further on August 20th that Chamberlain had been informed of the reason for the Company's interest in the Protectorate. On the same day Chamberlain ordered Robinson to obtain the land on which Gaberones stood from the local chief for the Company. On October 18th this acquisition was publicly announced. It is, of course, not certain that the Liberals would have proved implacable to Rhodes's persistence, but it was of real significance that Chamberlain easily and swiftly accepted the request which Rosebery and Ripon had refused. Chamberlain knew full well why Rhodes wanted Gaberones, and was from the outset a conscious but careful accomplice in the projected invasion of an independent and sovereign state. He covered his tracks well enough for contemporaries, but his active involvement in the scheme is now clear. The acquisition of Gaberones for the British South Africa Company was the key decision.

In August there had been another crisis. In order to encourage his new railway from Dalagoa Bay, Kruger raised the rates on the Cape line to Johannesburg. When Rhodes retaliated by organising supplies by ox-wagon, Kruger closed the drifts (the fording-places). Chamberlain delivered what was in effect an ultimatum to Kruger, and ordered troops to South Africa. Kruger had to climb down, and in the excitement no notice was taken of the formation of a new volunteer corps by Dr. Jameson.

Meanwhile, the organisation of the Johannesburg rising was proceeding. 'Never before', James Bryce has commented, 'was there except on the stage so open a conspiracy.' Some 3,000 rifles were smuggled in, but only half were unpacked. A ridiculous code was devised. The return of prosperity on the Rand had cooled the ardour of many of the Uitlanders. At Johannesburg, the preparations continued in an *opera bouffe* atmosphere.

There were several fatal misunderstandings. Five Uitlander leaders wrote an undated letter appealing for assistance. They were under the impression that they would summon Jameson at the proper time; Jameson considered that he was the best judge of that, and assembled less than 500 men on the border; Rhodes himself thought that he was in charge of the timing of the operation.

In London, Chamberlain continued to encourage the operation while taking care to have no personal involvement. Robinson was fully aware of what was to happen. To Bower he remarked that 'the whole thing is, I believe, sheer piracy, but I know nothing about it and have nothing to do with it'.

He was instructed by Chamberlain to proceed to Pretoria as soon as the provisional government had been declared in Johannesburg and order the immediate election of a Constituent Assembly to be elected by every adult male in the country. Chamberlain would announce his support for his action, and would also talk of a large military force being held in readiness to proceed to South Africa. Jameson would carry the British flag with him, for raising in Johannesburg. The British Cabinet was wholly unaware of the Colonial Secretary's deep involvement in this adventure; it was not until December 26th that

Chamberlain mentioned to Salisbury that a rising would occur 'in the course of the next few days'. As has been written, 'Chamberlain and Rhodes worked together to solve the Transvaal problem by a *fait accompli* with no objection from Salisbury'.[1] But there is no evidence that Salisbury realised the full implications of what his Colonial Secretary was doing.

On December 17th, when everything was—or seemed to be—ready, an utterly unexpected hitch occurred. President Cleveland sent to the United States Congress a belligerent anti-British message concerning the Venezuela boundary dispute,[2] and for the moment it appeared that there was a major international crisis. In these circumstances Meade urgently proposed postponement of the Transvaal business 'for a year or so', a letter which confirms beyond any reasonable doubt the extent of the knowledge of the Colonial Office of what was afoot. Chamberlain replied rather ambiguously, but it seems certain that his letter was interpreted by his officials to mean—and was meant to mean—that the balance of advantage lay in immediate action. One of Rhodes's agents, Rochfort Maguire, was summoned to the Colonial Office, and afterwards telegraphed to Rhodes in this sense. Although the actual telegram has not yet been discovered, there is little doubt as to what it said.

Meanwhile, the position of Dr. Jameson was not enviable. Disputes had now broken out at Johannesburg among the Uitlander leaders over the issue of raising the British flag, and this procrastination and timorousness daily reduced the chances of his success. On December 25th Jameson received telegrams counselling further delay—but nothing from Rhodes himself. Jameson thus decided to go in, and on December 29th, with 356 men, he rode into the Transvaal, having cut the telegraph lines to the Cape but, through characteristic ineptitude, *not* those to the Transvaal. He sent a telegram to Harris that 'unless I

---

[1] Lowe: *The Reluctant Imperialists*, 217.

[2] The Venezuela Dispute subsided swiftly because, although a belligerent mood certainly existed in the United States Congress, it was not echoed on Wall Street nor in the business and trading communities. But another factor was the conciliatory reaction of the British, and the impression made by Balfour's statement that 'The time will come, the time must come, when some statesman of authority will lay down the doctrine that between English-speaking people war is impossible.' It is not too fanciful to date the beginning of what Churchill was to call 'the special relationship' from the Venezuela Dispute. The concept of Britain and the United States as natural allies was slow to develop on both sides of the Atlantic, but the events of December 1895 gave it a powerful impetus.

hear definitely to the contrary shall leave tomorrow evening'. This arrived at Cape Town on Saturday 28th; Harris did not read it until the Monday, when he came into his office. By then the lines had been cut and Jameson had started his mad adventure. Much too late, Rhodes tried to stop him.

On January 2nd, after a brief fight with the Boers, within ten miles of Johannesburg, Jameson and his force were forced to surrender. By then, Robinson had repudiated him and Chamberlain had backed this repudiation. More honourably, Rhodes would not do so, thus destroying the unique position which he had created in Cape Colony with the Dutch. The Johannesburg 'rising' was a fiasco. The Jameson Raid itself marked a crucial step on the road to war between the Transvaal and Britain. Its immediate aftermath was to confirm the deep rift that had now opened in South Africa.

The Jameson Raid has many interesting points in common with the Bay of Pigs fiasco of 1961.[1] With overt encouragement from London, a highly dangerous gamble had been taken on the basis of ignorance of the strength of Uitlander feeling and power and of Boer military competence. The Colonial Office followed the policy of making the adventure possible, standing prepared to make full use of it if successful, yet without any control over how the operation was to be conducted. But the assumption that disassociation from it if it failed would be easily accomplished was swiftly proved false. International opinion was shocked by the Raid; the prestige and position of Rhodes suffered a fatal blow; the British were internationally humiliated, while the reputation of the Transvaal soared. On January 3rd the Kaiser sent Kruger a telegram of warm congratulation, and sought support from France and Russia in what would have been in effect a Three-Power guarantee of the independence of the Transvaal. Troops were ordered to proceed to Delagoa Bay for transit to Pretoria. The French and the Russians rejected the Kaiser's overtures, and the Portuguese refused to permit the troops to land. The British sent a squadron to sea that was capable of overwhelming any other Navy in the world. British dismay at the failure of Jameson was followed by indignation at the Kaiser's actions. The scene was now set for the great crisis of 1896-9.

Chamberlain's objectives in South Africa were not altered by the

[1] As Salisbury commented to Chamberlain, 'If filibustering fails it is always disreputable.' (Salisbury to Chamberlain, 30th December 1895.)

fiasco of the Jameson Raid. Indeed, they now became more implacable. On January 4th 1896, only two days after Jameson's surrender,
he instructed Robinson to press vigorously for redress of Uitlander
grievances 'as the Representative of the Paramount Power' and to use
'firm language'. The War Office, at Chamberlain's request, ordered
troops to Mafeking on the pretext of preventing further incursions of
the Jameson type. But Robinson obstinately refused to play Chamberlain's game, and countermanded the troop movements. When
Chamberlain hinted that 'large forces including cavalry and artillery'
could be dispatched to the Cape, Robinson ignored the implied offer.[1]
The High Commissioner knew that the Johannesburg Rising must
end in complete surrender and that the Colonial Secretary's hopes of
extracting something from the ruins of the Jameson venture were
illusory. 'Months afterwards', Bower has related, 'Mr. Chamberlain
reproached me with not taking a hint, and with spoiling his policy at
Pretoria'; when Bower referred to the military and international
complications of that policy, Chamberlain replied curtly, 'that was my
business, not yours'.[2] Chamberlain's only achievement was to get the
death sentences on the four leaders of the Reformers—including
Frank Rhodes—commuted and other penalties reduced.

Chamberlain's next move was to try 'to make a great coup and get
Kruger over here . . . if he will walk into my parlour it will be very
nice of him'.[3] But Kruger was only interested in the abolition of the
London Convention of 1884 and particularly the obnoxious Article
Four, which forbade the Republic to conclude treaties without
British consent. If he came to London, it would be as an aggrieved
party claiming and receiving monetary compensation and political
redress, not to discuss Uitlander reforms. A somewhat sour exchange
of letters between Leyds and Chamberlain brought this episode to an
end. It was simply a manoeuvre by Chamberlain to bring the discussion and public interest back to the alleged misfortunes of the
Uitlanders, and had no serious purpose as a discussion on the outstanding issues between London and Pretoria.[4] His final letter to
Leyds warned that the British Government 'as representing the
paramount Power in South Africa . . . cannot be blind to the danger

[1] Garvin, op. cit., III, 99.
[2] Bower's *Reminiscences*, 264 (Quoted in Marais; *The Fall of Kruger's Republic*, 106).
[3] Garvin, op. cit., 127.
[4] C.O. 537/130 (Minute of January 26th, 1896) makes this evident.

which threatens its future if legitimate causes of discontent continue to be ignored by the Government of the South African Republic'.

Against all Chamberlain's attempts to keep up heavy pressure on Kruger, the High Commissioner stood obstinately in the way. He told the Colonial Secretary bluntly that Kruger would rather face war than discuss his internal affairs and that in such an eventuality the Orange Free State and a large section of the Dutch in Cape Colony and Natal would support him.[1] A proposal by Chamberlain 'in view of possible eventualities' to strengthen the Cape Colony and Natal garrisons was also firmly resisted. Fairfield and Bower spoke the same language. Chamberlain temporarily abandoned his belligerent stance. When Bower told him that if he adopted a warlike attitude he would have to get another High Commissioner, Chamberlain replied, 'I know that.'[2]

Early in 1897 Robinson was recalled as High Commissioner. 'I would like to infuse a little more spirit into Sir H. Robinson', Chamberlain had complained, 'and I wish he would show his teeth occasionally.' A more vigorous and aggressive High Commissioner lay at hand, and with the appointment of Sir Alfred Milner the South African crisis entered a new stage.

Robinson was not the only opponent of Chamberlain's policy who was removed. Fairfield and Meade retired towards the end of 1896, and the British Agent at Pretoria was replaced by Conyngham Greene, who favoured a more aggressive policy. Graham and Wingfield, who replaced Fairfield and Meade, were also less in favour of allowing a period of calm to occur in which British relations with the Boers could be improved.

Chamberlain himself was under heavy pressure. The widespread allegations abroad that the British Government had been deeply implicated in the Raid were indignantly and vigorously denied, but now they were current in London. Some members of Rhodes's entourage—and probably encouraged by Rhodes himself—deliberately fostered them. The British South Africa Company's solicitor, Bouchier Hawksley, let it be known that he possessed incriminating documents concerning Chamberlain's personal complicity. The rumours spread swiftly, and raised, as Chamberlain's biographer has written, 'fungoid growths in the shade'.

No examination of what followed can ignore two central features of Chamberlain's character. He was a fighter, and he deeply resented

[1] Marais, 117–18.   [2] Bower, *Reminiscences*, 291.

humiliation. He now fought back at his critics at home while keeping Rhodes amenable, and adopted a determined policy to crush the Transvaal at the earliest opportunity.

The Kaiser's telegram of congratulation to Kruger had a profound effect upon British reactions to the Raid. Thus, when Jameson and his fellow officers faced the judges at Bow Street they were hailed as heroes rather than prisoners, and the Poet Laureate, the lamentable Alfred Austin, published an immensely long panegyric on the raiders in *The Times* which contained the stanza:

> There are girls in the gold-reef city,
>   There are mothers and children too!
> And they cry 'Hurry up! for pity!'
>   So what can a brave man do?
> If even we win, they'll blame us:
>   If we fail, they will howl and hiss.
> For there's many a man lives famous
>   For daring a wrong like this!

The manner in which the origins of the Raid were investigated by a Select Committee of the House of Commons was blundering but, from Chamberlain's point of view, highly successful. Its Report blamed Rhodes but acquitted Chamberlain—who was himself a member of the Committee. One of the Liberal members, Sydney Buxton, had declared that the Opposition 'would give the Government their most earnest support in endeavouring to clear the name of England of any moral stain that might attach to it', and this was indeed the principal objective of the Committee. It was significant that whereas Rosebery described the Raid as 'an Elizabethan venture', and he was only willing to 'lay a meagre and a tardy chaplet on the opulent shrine of the Colonial Secretary', Harcourt had warmly praised Chamberlain. The Committee tiptoed with elaborate caution around such potentially dangerous subjects as the 'missing telegrams', which Rhodes refused to produce, and the mysterious activities of Flora Shaw, the colonial correspondent of *The Times*, who had been closely concerned with the conspiracy and was in Chamberlain's confidence. Miss Shaw—the future Lady Lugard—handled the Committee with skill and aplomb, but it was not a particularly difficult body to handle. Bower became Robinson's scapegoat; Fairfield was cast to play the role for Chamberlain, but died before the Committee met.

The proceedings of what became cynically known as 'the Lying-In-State at Westminster' have been exhaustively examined by historians.[1] The gullibility of the Liberal members—notably Harcourt and Campbell-Bannerman—was remarkable; Labouchere proved unequal to the task of probing the truth of what had happened. It was a classic cover-up. All independent observers were outraged by the Committee's performance, and Harcourt's position never recovered in the Liberal party. In the debate on the Report on July 27th, 1897, Chamberlain vehemently defended Rhodes—with, it is alleged, copies of the 'missing telegrams' in the pocket of a pro-Rhodes M.P. in case he did not fulfil his part of the bargain. The story has never been substantiated. But this defence was, for many people, the last straw.

The effects of the Raid and its aftermath were legion. Rhodes's position in South Africa was fatally compromised; Boer self-confidence and suspicion of British ambitions were alike intensified, and preparations went forward for a more major confrontation; the Germans, sobered by the response to their challenge, began to build a Navy; in 1897 the Orange Free State joined in an offensive and defensive alliance with the Transvaal; Chamberlain nurtured revenge; South Africa was now divided into two camps. The shadows of this absurd and contemptible foray were to prove long and dark.

*

Although severely checked in South Africa, British progress elsewhere in the Continent was dramatic, and made the reverse even less endurable. Early in 1897 Sir George Goldie, on behalf of the Royal Niger Company, established British influence firmly on the Upper Niger. Lugard now began his remarkable second career in West Africa, and Nigeria was in effect established as a British possession. And then, in 1897–8, the British reconquered the Sudan. This operation had been carefully prepared by Cromer and his staff, most notably Colonel Reginald Wingate, to ensure political and public support in Britain. Milner's *England in Egypt* and the memoirs of Slatin Pasha, for ten years the prisoner of the Mahdi and his successor Abdullahi, the Khalifa, made an immense impression. The decision to act was, however, dominated by factors of European *realpolitik*

[1] See Jean van der Poel: *The Jameson Raid*; Marais, op. cit.; P. Stansky: *Ambitions and Strategies*; Woodhouse and Lockhart: *Rhodes*; Elizabeth Longford: *Jameson's Raid*.

rather than moral outrage, and particularly to check French ambitions while gratifying the Germans and the Italians, who had recently suffered a terrible defeat at Adowa at the hands of the Abyssinians. For the Anglo-Egyptian army, now transformed, the expedition was to be an act of revenge.

The task was given to General Sir Herbert Kitchener, whose irascibility in the Army was equalled by political astuteness in London, where he had the support and friendship of the Salisburys. He aroused fierce, and very contradictory, opinion, but he was ruthless, hard-working, and professional. The Sudan Campaign was essentially a matter of logistics, in which Kitchener excelled. The final stand of the Khalifa's army was at Omdurman, outside Khartoum, on September 2nd 1898, and was the most dramatic and devastating massacre in modern military annals. In a few hours, at trifling loss to the British, the Dervish army of 50,000 was slaughtered or dispersed. Although the Khalifa escaped—to be hunted down and killed a year later—his rule was destroyed in five hours. The British were not gentle victors, and their conduct—and that of Kitchener—came under strong criticism from the elder son of Lord Randolph Churchill, who had fought in the battle with the 21st Lancers, and who published a year later an account of the campaign—*The River War*—which was at once recognised as a classic of military history and was an extraordinary achievement for a young man not yet 25. But nothing could dim Kitchener's sudden fame and eminence.

The strategic importance of the reconquest of the Sudan was swiftly and dramatically emphasised. Immediately after Omdurman Kitchener received intelligence that a French officer, Captain Marchand, had reached Fashoda—some 350 miles to the south—and had raised the French flag. Grey had made it plain on March 28th 1895, that any French advance into the Nile Valley 'would be an unfriendly act and would be so viewed by England'. Salisbury was prepared to be conciliatory, but Chamberlain was emphatic.[1] The confrontation between Kitchener and Marchand brought Britain and France to the verge of war, but, once again, *force majeure* was triumphant, and the Anglo-French Convention of 1899 merely confirmed the fact. Thus, only the continued intransigence of the Boer Republics marred the general picture of British advance and

[1] All the leading Liberals supported the Government's handling of the Fashoda crisis. The protests of Lloyd George were not regarded as significant.

success in Africa, and this obstruction became increasingly intolerable.

Chamberlain had now found the instrument for his policy. Alfred Milner had been born in 1854, the only son of an English mother and a German father (whose own father had been English). On the death of his mother he came to England at the age of fifteen, and was educated at King's College, London, and Balliol College, Oxford, where he was a contemporary of Asquith and Arnold Toynbee. The latter made, at the time, the greater impression, and Milner's first public work was done in the East End of London. Milner was also subsequently impressed by Parkin's lectures on Imperial Federation, and had developed serious and intransigent views upon the destiny of Britain.

From 1884-9 he was private secretary to Goschen, and stood for Parliament as a Liberal candidate in 1885. Significantly, he never once mentioned Gladstone's name in his campaign, and was defeated after a raucous campaign; his early distaste for popular politics grew rapidly. In 1889 he went to Egypt to serve under Cromer as under-secretary for finance; in 1892 his *England in Egypt* made his name in Britain. Between 1892-7 he was Chairman of the Board of Inland Revenue, and was responsible—as has been noted—for Harcourt's Death Duties proposals of 1894. In 1897 he became, at the age of forty-three, British High Commissioner in South Africa.

Milner subsequently bore the brunt of the criticism for the sharp change in the course of British policy towards the Boer Republics that occurred after 1897. Certainly, he was from an early stage convinced that a show-down was inevitable, and he was contemptuous of what he derided as 'the no-war policy' in the British Government, and particularly the pacific attitudes of the Commander-in-Chief in South Africa, General Sir William Butler. He came to these conclusions with disturbing rapidity, and Smuts was justified in describing him as 'a proud, high-strung, impatient, ironclad man'. By the middle of 1898 the Boers were in no doubt that a formidable new figure had appeared on the scene.

John Buchan, a sincere admirer and follower, characterised what was probably Milner's principal defect—and also gives us the clue to Chamberlain's choice—when he wrote of him:

His spiritual integrity made it difficult for him, when he had studied a problem, to temporise about the solution which he thought inevitable. . . . When he had satisfied himself about a particular course—and he took long to satisfy—his mind seemed to lock down on it, and after that there was no going back.

As early as February 1898 Milner was writing with a certain exultant grimness of 'the great day of reckoning'.

But Milner was not alone in this view, and it was by no means a wholly unreasonable one. The Boers were now arming themselves rapidly; no concessions were made towards the Uitlanders or the British; Leyds was still engaged in his European activities; the Transvaal Government remained corrupt and incompetent. As one South African historian has written:

> It is only the narrowest interpretation of South African history that can seek to explain the eventful years leading to the Boer War by dwelling exclusively upon the sins of Downing Street and British Secretaries of State.[1]

Milner, like Rhodes and Chamberlain, not only saw the Uitlanders as the Achilles Heel of the Transvaal Republic, but appears to have been genuinely convinced of the justice of their cause. He had no doubt that the Kruger regime was despicable and incompetent, nor that the fundamental superiority and civilising mission of the British race in Africa must triumph. He saw the situation in clear terms. Simply to depict him as cold-bloodedly preparing for war is to over-simplify and under-estimate both the situation and Milner's character. Milner's tragedy was that he had so few doubts, and that, having locked his mind into a general situation based on his Egyptian experience, he could not appreciate the vastness of the gulf which separated that experience and those general principles with the actual situation that existed in South Africa. He went out looking for trouble, if not a *causus belli*, and he swiftly found the former.

One of the first significant episodes occurred in December 1898, when a Uitlander—Edgar—was shot dead by a constable in Johannesburg. The Boer authorities said that Edgar was resisting arrest after a street brawl; the Uitlanders said that he had been shot down in his own house. It was the kind of incident which, when it

[1] C. W. de Kiewet: *The Imperial Factor in South Africa*, 15.

occurs in an atmosphere of tension and suspicion, arouses a disproportionate amount of heat and fury.

The constable—Jones—was charged by the young State Attorney, J. C. Smuts, with culpable homicide. He was also permitted bail. The Uitlander leaders demanded a charge of murder and opposed bail. Jones was acquitted and the judge, in discharging him, uttered some appropriate words of encouragement to the police in their difficult task of keeping law and order. Smuts very properly ordered another trial—when it took place, in February, Jones was again acquitted—but tempers were now running high. An Edgar Committee was formed, and the South Africa League planned a monster meeting of protest and petitioned the British Vice-Consul. Smuts declared the meeting illegal—which it was—and after it took place on December 24th ordered the arrest of two leading officials of the League. Another meeting, which was technically legal because it was held in an enclosed space—in fact a circus building—was deliberately broken up by the police.[1]

This was exactly the situation Milner had been waiting for, to give him the opportunity of laying the Uitlanders' grievances before the British Cabinet and British public opinion. But at this point he was in England, for consultations with Chamberlain, and to his dismay, the Acting High Commissioner—General Butler—took a very different view. Butler refused to transmit the Uitlanders' petition to London and gave his opinion that the real culprits were the League and the Johannesburg rabble.

Milner took steps to ensure that future petitions would be received in a notably more sympathetic manner and began a campaign to oust Butler, whom he described in a letter to Selborne as 'out-Krugering Kruger', from his command. 'Henceforward', Smuts's biographer has written, 'he and Conyngham Greene maintained the closest possible relations with the South African League and used it as an instrument of Imperial policy'.[2] Butler's independence of attitude was to destroy his career, and his prolonged opposition to Milner was not forgotten. When his name was proposed in 1902 to command a Corps, Balfour—by then Prime Minister—wrote to the King with characteristic tartness that:

---

[1] For a markedly biased and high-flown account of the Edgar Crisis, see Garvin, III, 381–3.
[2] W. K. Hancock: *Smuts: The Sanguine Years*, 83.

General Butler is a candidate of great ability and military knowledge. Unfortunately he has never in the exercise of his military
duties been able to forget that he is a politician: while his politics
are of a kind which seriously interfere with the discharge of his
military duties. He made (as Mr. Balfour is informed) most embarrassing speeches in the course of the Egyptian Campaign: and
had practically to be recalled from S. Africa because, in spite of
warnings, he ran deliberately counter to Lord Milner's policy. A
soldier who invariably believes that the enemies of his country is
right, is seriously handicapped in the discharge of his proper
duties.[1]

1899 thus opened with a decided check for the Uitlanders and for
Milner. At a conference at Highbury he made it plain that he wanted
to 'work up to a crisis'. Chamberlain, while emphasising the importance of not precipitating matters, supported the principle. But the
Cabinet was very uneasy at the prospect of further South African
complications, and British public opinion was far from belligerent. On
board ship, returning to Cape Town, Milner wrote to Selborne, who
was becoming his closest confidant:

> *My views are absolutely unaltered*, but I have come to the conclusion
> that having stated them, it is no use trying to force them upon
> others at this stage. If I can advance matters by my own actions, as
> I still hope I may be able to do, I believe that I shall have support
> when the time comes.[2]

This was indeed true; Chamberlain had assured Milner that 'if the
situation came to danger, he would be supported through thick and
thin. He would never be let down'.[3]

On Milner's return the pace quickened. In February 1899 a protest
to the Transvaal Government by Chamberlain concerning the
dynamite concessions was curtly rejected. In March a well-organised
Uitlander petition, with over 21,000 signatures, reached Milner. This
time it was ceremoniously received, and was at once transmitted to
London. 'The condition of Your Majesty's subjects in this State', the
petition declared, 'has become well-nigh intolerable. . . . They are
still deprived of all political rights, they are denied any voice in the

---

[1] P.R.O, Cab 40, 27/28 (July 23rd, 1902).   [2] *The Milner Papers*, I, 301–2.
[3] Garvin, III, 379.

Government of the country and they are taxed far above the requirements of the country.' On April 28th Selborne cabled to Milner at
Chamberlain's 'express wish' to 'send fully your views expressed as
frankly as you consider it to be possible or advisable consistently with
your position in South Africa'. As Chamberlain's biographer has
written, 'Milner was invited virtually to address Parliament and the
country through the written word. After fourteen months of constraint
he let himself go.'[1]

The resultant explosion reached Chamberlain on May 5th—a fact
which demonstrates that it had been composed some time before—
and contained this devastating phrase:

> The spectacle of thousands of British subjects kept permanently in
> the position of helots . . . does steadily undermine the influence and
> reputation of Great Britain and the respect for the British Govern-
> ment within the Queen's Dominions. . . . I can see nothing which
> will put a stop to this mischievous propaganda but some striking
> proof of the intention of Her Majesty's Government not to be
> ousted from its position in South Africa.

The Cabinet considered this startling document on May 9th, and it
was at this meeting that Balfour began to move in the general direction
of the Chamberlain–Milner line. But other Ministers, notably Salisbury,
were becoming very uneasy. 'This country, as well as the Cabinet',
Salisbury wrote on July 18th, 'excepting perhaps Mr. Chamberlain,
were against a war.' He was to write subsequently on Milner:

> What he has done cannot be effaced. We have to act on a moral
> field prepared for us by him and his jingo supporters. And therefore
> I see before us the necessity for considerable military effort—and
> all for people whom we despise, and for territory which will bring
> no profit and no power to England.[2]

At the end of May an attempt was made, in a conference at
Bloemfontein, to solve the franchise issue. 'Milner is as sweet as
honey', Smuts noted, 'but there is something in his very intelligent
eyes that tells me that he is a very dangerous man.' Milner proposed
a five years' retrospective franchise; Kruger responded with an offer

---

[1] Garvin, op. cit., 395.
[2] Salisbury to Lansdowne, August 30th, 1899 (Newton: *Lansdowne*, 157).

of a seven years' franchise with conditions which would in no way affect the Boer supremacy. When, at one stage, Kruger cried out that 'It is my country that you want' he struck one of the few notes of realism in the conference. Nevertheless, it was unwise of Milner to break it off after only six days with the declaration that 'this Conference is absolutely at an end, and there is no obligation on either side arising out of it'. Chamberlain, who had had real hopes of a Boer climb-down, was dismayed; Milner wrote to him (June 14th) that he had probably erred, but his letter ended:

> Though I think the beginning of a war would be *very unpleasant*, owing to our scattered outposts and the fact that the thinly populated *centre* of the country is quite Dutch, I do not think the result doubtful, or the ultimate difficulty, when once we had cleared the Augean Stable, at all serious.

At this point (June 14th) the 'Helots' Dispatch was published. War began to loom ominously closer.

Neither Chamberlain nor Milner thought that it was inevitable, nor did they think it would even be necessary. Their policy was essentially one of steady pressure, with force held confidently in the background. 'The Boers', Milner wrote to Chamberlain on July 26th, 'are still bluffing and will yield further if pressure is kept up.' Neither feared war if the Boers were intransigent, but at this stage they were not working towards a war, a fact that made their policy even more perilous. If they had ever considered the military situation seriously—and neither did, save in general terms—their policies might well have been changed. For the British were in no condition to back up their threats with force.

The general condition of the British Army was not good. It consisted of 124,000 men serving abroad—of whom 73,000 were in India—and 125,000 in the home battalions. The Reserve, which had been much neglected, totalled some 90,000 men. Counting all regulars, reservists, and volunteers, there was a theoretical total of 600,000; in fact, the practical limit for a quick mobilisation was 85,000 and the standard was not high. Poor terms of service and series of easy contests against natives were an inadequate background for a war against skilled marksmen and riders in a foreign country.

In May 1899 there were in South Africa 10,300 British troops and twenty-four field guns, split between the Cape and Natal. No plan of campaign existed, and the British had virtually no maps. They had one map of Natal, 'on a scale of five miles to an inch prepared locally for educational purposes', and another to a scale of 12½ miles to the inch covering Cape Colony, Natal, the Orange Free State, but only part of the Transvaal. Even by October, when war broke out, the British forces in South Africa totalled 27,054, dispersed, which was opposed by over 35,000 mounted Boers, which were—although perhaps of not as high a quality as the victors of Majuba—still the best marksmen in the world. General Butler, for one, had no illusions about the disparity in quality as well as quantity, but his days as Commander-in-Chief were numbered, and he was recalled at the beginning of August. Nevertheless, his lack of enthusiasm for a confrontation did not help. As he subsequently wrote, 'I held the balance. There would be no war while I was there',[1] a fact that was perfectly evident to Milner. When Milner said that the Boers would not fight, Butler retorted that 'they would fight for their independence'. He considered that 40,000 troops would be insufficient for the task, and, as Milner subsequently wrote of him: 'His great merit was that he knew the size of the job.' He was one of the few who did. But his attitudes contributed to subsequent reverses. On June 22nd he was instructed by the War Office to purchase wagons and transport mules; he retorted that such action would merely increase 'the ferment which [I] am endeavouring to reduce by every means. . . . I believe war would be the greatest calamity that ever occurred in South Africa'. Butler's resignation was accepted on August 8th after a blunt meeting with Milner.

The policies of Chamberlain and Milner now began to become even closer. The publication of the 'Helots' dispatch had had a deep impact in Britain. But the new Liberal leader, Campbell-Bannerman, declared on June 17th that nothing in the South African situation justified war; more seriously, the Cabinet was now very alarmed, and Salisbury's reports to the Queen reflected this concern. On July 11th he reported:

Lord Salisbury was much impressed with the more pacific tone of the Cabinet. Some members were averse to any abatement of their indignation towards the Transvaal. But the majority of the Cabinet were impressed with the want of support such a war would seem likely to command with public opinion in the country.

[1] Butler: *Autobiography*, 414.

Even more significant was a report from Selborne to Milner on June 25th:

> The warnings Mr. Chamberlain and I gave you about the state of public opinion here have been abundantly justified. . . . The idea of war with the South African Republic is very distasteful to most people . . . we simply cannot force the pace . . . the worst service we could do the Empire would be to outrun public opinion.

Nevertheless, some deliberate pace-making in Britain was begun, and Chamberlain's speeches began to strike a more menacing note. The Cabinet increasingly came to accept his diagnosis that a policy of steady pressure with an implicit military threat would succeed in gaining the necessary concessions from Kruger. Salisbury instinctively disagreed, but his influence was waning rapidly. Indeed, in Mid-July it did seem that the Boers were backing down on the matter of the franchise, and Chamberlain authorised a statement—to Milner's dismay—that 'the crisis between Great Britain and the Transvaal may be regarded as ended'. When Milner protested that the real issue was not the franchise but 'the practical assertion of British supremacy', he was assured by Selborne that British policy was back 'on the old right track'. On August 24th Chamberlain wrote:

> It is clear that we cannot go on negotiating forever; we must try to bring matters to a head. The next step in military preparations is so important and so costly that I hesitate to incur the expense . . . so long as there seems a fair chance of a satisfactory settlement. But I dread above all the continuing whittling away of differences until we have no *causus belli* left.

Two days later, at Birmingham, he said of Kruger that 'he dribbles out reforms like water from a squeezed sponge', and went on to declare that 'the issues of peace and war are in the hands of the President. . . . Will he speak the necessary words? The sands are running down in the glass.'

They were indeed. It takes two to make a war, and by this time there was an ugly mood in Pretoria. Deneys Reitz, the son of a former President of the Orange Free State, wrote of the atmosphere in Pretoria:

> Looking back, I think that war was inevitable. I have no doubt that the British Government had made up its mind to force the issue, and

was the chief culprit, but the Transvaalers were also spoiling for a fight, and from what I saw in Pretoria during the few weeks that preceded the ultimatum, I feel sure that the Boers would in any case have insisted on a rupture.[1]

Smuts now prepared a military appraisal on the assumption that war was imminent, and which envisaged a whirlwind attack on the British in Natal and then in Cape Colony. (Fortunately for the British, the plan was not adopted.) Kruger refused to consider a suitable response on the franchise issue. On September 27th the Orange Free State publicly declared its support for the Transvaal, which meant that the Boers could put into the field at once over 50,000 mounted infantry; they had rifles and ammunition for 80,000, the total they hoped to reach by enrolling Cape Dutch volunteers. The rains had renewed the veldt grass—a vital prerequisite for campaigning. Milner advised the government not to issue an ultimatum until the expected 10,000 troops from India were on the Transvaal border. 'Personally I am still of opinion not to hurry in settling ultimatum', he wrote, 'as events of next few days may supply us with a better one than anybody can compose. Ultimatum has always been great difficulty, as unless we widen issue there is not sufficient cause for war, and if we do, we are abused for shifting our ground and extending our demands.' When Milner's papers were published, the last sentence was prudently omitted. The British belatedly ordered substantial reinforcements to South Africa under the command of General Sir Redvers Buller. But they had not arrived when the Boer Republics issued an ultimatum at the beginning of October and began hostilities almost at once.

It was, in any event, a matter of who got in his ultimatum first. As Chamberlain wrote on September 29th, if the Boers took the offensive 'the Lord will have delivered them into our hands—at least as far as diplomacy is concerned.' But the Boer ultimatum of October 9th settled the matter for most Englishmen. G. K. Chesterton has written:

> The nation seemed solid for war. . . . I saw all the public men and all the public bodies, the people in the street, my own middle class and most of my family and friends, solid in favour of something that seemed inevitable and scientific and secure. And I suddenly realised that I hated it. . . . What I hated about it was what a good many people liked about it. It was such a very cheerful war. I hated

[1] Deneys Reitz: *Commando*, 19.

its confidence, its congratulatory anticipations, its optimism of the Stock Exchange. I hated its vile assurance of victory.[1]

There were no forebodings of disaster. Chamberlain wrote to Hicks-Beach on October 7th that:

My own opinion is, as it always has been, that both Milner and the military authorities greatly exaggerate the risks and dangers of this campaign. I have never believed that the Boers would take the offensive at this stage—nor do I fear a British reverse if they do. There must be risks in all wars, but I think the risk of a successful attack on a fortified position chosen by us is a very small one. When all the reinforcements are landed my own feeling is that we shall be quite a match for the Boers even without the army corps.

In the general excitement only a few dissenting voices were heard. In the Parliament elected in 1895 the star of Lloyd George had risen very considerably, but he had demonstrated little interest in South African affairs, and was an ill-concealed admirer of Chamberlain, despite political differences. This respect was reciprocated. But Lloyd George reacted immediately to the outbreak of the war with a denunciation of the Government and of Chamberlain personally which was certainly not calculated, and which demonstrated the best part of his complex and not wholly attractive personality. In the fervent mood of the day, it took courage to point out that the British were fighting 'a little country, the total of whose population was less than Carmarthonshire—the British Empire against Carmarthonshire!'. Thus began a campaign that almost cost Lloyd George his seat in Parliament and his life, but which made him a national figure. On September 15th John Morley protested at Manchester at the possibility of war with 'this weak little Republic'.

It will bring you no glory. It will bring you no profit, but mischief, and it will be wrong. You may make thousands of women widows and thousands of children fatherless. It will be wrong. You may add a new province to your Empire. It will still be wrong.

Gladstone had been dead for a year, but his voice still lived in the land. For the moment it was a faint one, but was shortly to be heard

[1] The full extent of public enthusiasm for the war is difficult to gauge. Richard Price's *An Imperial War and the British Working Class*, emphasises the prevalence of middle class volunteers, particularly in 1900–01.

9 Gladstone on the Treasury Bench, 1893: by Phil May

10 Sir William Harcourt: by F. Carruthers Gould

11 The Earl of Rosebery, 1885: by John Everett Millais

12 John Morley: by Harry Furniss

with more insistence as the British marched confidently towards a series of military and political disasters.

But, if to many contemporaries the origins of the Boer War were complex, the issue itself seemed quite clear. 'What is now at stake', Chamberlain wrote to Salisbury, 'is the position of Great Britain in South Africa and with it the estimate formed of our power and influence in our Colonies and throughout the world.' Salisbury himself, although deeply unhappy about the situation, expressed the dilemma well when he wrote to the Queen on September 23rd:

> On the one hand we cannot abandon them [the Uitlanders] without great injustice—nor without endangering Your Majesty's authority in the whole of South Africa. On the other hand we are most earnestly anxious to avoid any rupture with the Boers, if it is possible. But they do not assist us to do so. . . .
>
> It is impossible to avoid believing that the Boers really aim at setting up a South African Republic, consisting of the Transvaal, the Orange Free State, and Your Majesty's Colony. It is impossible to account in any other manner for their rejection of our most moderate proposals. . . .

In this estimate Salisbury probably represented the majority opinion in Britain. If the Government as a whole entered the war without enthusiasm, yet it had no premonition of defeat. Elsewhere, the war was greeted with undisguised eagerness and excitement, and particularly in the Unionist Party. In one of his less happy hours Kipling denounced Kruger as 'Cruel in the shadow, crafty in the sun . . . sloven, sullen, savage, secret, uncontrolled.' Serious questioning of the justice and necessity of the war was confined to a small and derided section of the Liberal Party.

CHAPTER SEVEN

THE BOER WAR AND TARIFF REFORM, 1899–1905

THE INTELLIGENCE DIVISION of the War Office was maintained at a cost of £11,000 per annum, and two officers were responsible for the entire colonial Empire. The expenditure on Intelligence at the time by the German General Staff was some £250,000, and that of the Transvaal Republic was some £90,000. Section B of the Intelligence Division revised and issued in June 1899 a document entitled 'Military Notes on the Dutch Republics of South Africa'. It is an instructive document. After describing the Boer custom of military councils deciding daily military business in the field, it comments that:

> It is obvious, this system of leaving not only administrative details, but even strategical and tactical questions, to the decision of a large body of officers, elected by the votes of the burghers they command, must inevitably involve inefficiency and renders it improbable that a burgher force, under such conditions, will ever carry through any great enterprise requiring steadfastness of purpose, or, that in case of defeat, it would be in a position to contrive any prolonged resistance . . . although the Transvaal has spent large sums during the last three years on their military forces, they have made but little progress towards the improvement of their primitive organisation.

The document pointed out that Boer mobilisation—as the Jameson Raid had demonstrated—would be rapid; the Corps of Staats Artillery had greatly improved, although 'the standard at present reached is inferior to that of the Royal Artillery'; Joubert, the Commandant-General, was described as 'a man of vacillating purpose, and is easily influenced by those near him'. The assessment continued:

The Boers indeed today frankly own, to use their quaint expression, that 'God Almighty gave them their lives for some better purpose than to be shot at like bucks in the open', and that they consider as sheer folly that willingness to face death which English soldiers display. The real genius of the Boer is in fact to fight under cover, and this dislike to risk death seriously diminishes his military value in offensive operations or in any position the flanks of which can be turned. . . .

The Dutchman is, in fact, by race and instincts of a stolid stubborn nature, but it would be absurd to expect from untrained farmers that readiness to face death at the bidding of a superior which history emphatically teaches can only be created and fostered by discipline. . . .

It may therefore be anticipated that while the Boers will show some of their old skill in guerrilla warfare on ground favourable to such tactics, yet they will have but little chance of success if compelled to meet in the open plains of the Free State or Transvaal an adquate force of disciplined troops complete in all three arms, and it appears certain that, after serious defeat, they would be too deficient in discipline and organisation to make any further real stand. . . .

These somewhat condescending judgements were now to be put to the test.

Details of the proposed expeditionary force were sent by the War Office to the Admiralty on September 20th; ten days later the Admiralty was told to take up the required shipping. On October 7th the mobilisation order was issued and the Royal Proclamation calling out the Reserves was published. The mobilisation was efficient; ninety-nine per cent of the Reservists reported for duty, and over ninety per cent of them were fit for active service. The first Regular units embarked on October 8th, and embarkation was completed— with the exception of one cavalry regiment, delayed by horse-sickness —on November 7th.

Superficially, this was admirable. Closer inspection was less impressive. To make the force complete, staffs were taken from units which it was thought (wrongly) would not be required. It was also discovered that 'staffs of many formations, such as those of mounted infantry, ammunition columns and medical field units, did not exist'.[1]

[1] Maurice: The War in South Africa, 8–10.

One small, but not untypical, example may be given. By the end of November one battery of field artillery had lost its captain, the senior subaltern (the only one with four months' experience in field artillery), five sergeants, a corporal bombardier, 'four shoeing smiths, two trumpeters, the wheeler, six gunners and five drivers'. In December the battery commander was sent to South Africa. Ten days later the battery was mobilised; when it was brought up to strength, no member of it had ever seen the guns, which they were to operate, fired.[1]

Then, there was the case of the Royal Army Medical Corps, found to be in deplorable condition; an eminent surgeon who brought a hospital to South Africa said of the doctors in the Corps that 'you would get a few good ones, but the majority of them were shocking'.

Perhaps the same harsh judgement could be applied to the British senior officer. One British correspondent, L. S. Amery, subsequently wrote:

> All I saw during those [first] weeks left on my mind an ineffaceable impression of the incapacity of many of our senior officers, of the uselessness of most of our then army training for the purposes of modern war, especially in South African conditions, and of the urgent need of complete, revolutionary reform of the Army from top to bottom.[2]

The British Commander-in-Chief, when offered the two volumes of information on the Boer Republics prepared by the Intelligence Branch, returned them immediately with the curt statement that he 'knew everything about South Africa'. Winston Churchill, who went to South Africa as a journalist, and was to win national fame by his escape from a Boer prisoner of war camp, sailed with Buller to South Africa on the liner *Dunottar Castle*—which did not raise her speed above the normal commercial rate—and has penned this portrait:

> Buller was a characteristic British personality. He looked stolid. He said little, and what he said was obscure. He was not the kind of man who could explain things, and he never tried to do so. He usually grunted or nodded, or shook his head, in serious discussions; and shop of all kinds was sedulously excluded from his ordinary

---

[1] Ibid., footnote to pp. 11–12.
[2] L. S. Amery: *My Political Life*, I, 118.

conversation. He had shown himself a brave and skilful officer in his youth, and for nearly twenty years he had filled important administrative posts of a sedentary character in Whitehall.[1]

Churchill might have added that Buller, in addition to his taciturnity, had a notorious addiction to the bottle; as Balfour was to write on December 18th, 'for ten years he has allowed himself to go downhill'.

While the Commander-in-Chief and is staff proceeded on their leisurely and agreeable way to South Africa, matters were proceeding in an unexpected and untoward manner on the veldt.

On one point at least, the British Intelligence had been correct. Joubert was a feeble and unimaginative commander. With every advantage on his side, he engaged in desultory seiges of British garrisons in the Transvaal. Ladysmith, Mafeking and Kimberley were invested somewhat lethargically, and large Boer forces were needlessly tied to these irrelevancies. While the younger Boer commanders chafed impatiently, the British slowly gathered their forces together in Cape Colony.

Buller at once broke up his Army Corps into three divisions, and they proceeded northwards into a series of disasters. In one week in December—'Black Week'—Methuen was repulsed at Magersfontein trying to do 'a Tel-el-Kebir'; Gatacre was thrown back at Stormberg; and Buller, advancing ponderously on Ladysmith, was forced to retire at Colenso. The British forces were at every stage out-witted and out-manoeuvred by the Boer soldiers, who fought with precision and skill. Buller's nerve was broken. He recommended the abandonment of Ladysmith; the Government promptly relieved him of his command and sent out Lord Roberts, whose son had won the V.C. at Colenso but had died of his wounds.

1899 thus closed in humiliation and reverse. One bright gleam of hope was that the Empire had rallied to the Imperial cause. Canada sent 8,400 men, Australia over 16,000, and New Zealand, 6,000. Far from the Cape Colony being divided, 30,000 volunteers enlisted in the Colony on the British side. To Chamberlain in particular, these were encouraging indications of the rightness of his actions and the solidarity of Imperial unity at an hour of crisis.

But in England opinions were most sharply divided, particularly in

[1] Churchill: *My Early Life*, 228.

the Liberal Party where the dilemma of the late 1880s and 1890s was sharply revealed.

Rosebery, although he distrusted and disliked Milner—unlike Asquith—regarded the Boer ultimatum as decisive, and came out strongly in favour of the war, quoting Chatham's phrase: 'Be of one people; forget everything for the public.' In this attitude he was warmly supported by Asquith and Edward Grey and by some fifty Liberal M.P.s. At the other extreme were Harcourt, Morley, Labouchere and the young Lloyd George, quickly dubbed the 'pro-Boers', and vehemently opposed to the war. In the middle were Campbell-Bannerman, Herbert Gladstone, and some twenty Liberals who disliked the war intensely but who considered that the Boer ultimatum had given the Government no choice. The Annual Register for 1900 estimated the Liberal supporters of the Government in the House of Commons at sixty-two; the 'pro-Boers' at sixty-eight; twenty-seven who were uncertain, and the Campbell-Bannerman middle-of-the-roaders. This internecine controversy was a deep and bitter one, and whenever the war issue arose in the Commons the Parliamentary Liberal Party shivered into angry fragments. The war itself might be going badly, but the domestic political battle was proceeding very satisfactorily for the Unionists.

Then, the war itself took a dramatic change for the better in 1900. Roberts concentrated his forces and marched on Bloemfontein. At the end of February a large Boer force of 4,000 men was surrounded and forced to surrender. One by one, the beseiged towns were relieved. From this point it was a story of unbroken British success, culminating in Kruger leaving the Transvaal on September 11th and the Transvaal being formally annexed on October 25th. The war was over. Roberts returned home in triumph, Milner received a peerage, and Kitchener was left to clear up the few guerrilla commandos who had refused to surrender. It had been a war fought with very little bitterness, and marked on both sides by chivalry and respect. Prisoners were well treated; the wounded were cared for; neither side had any compunction in surrendering when surrounded and outnumbered. Each side developed a considerable respect for the other. It was, in a very real way, the last of the old-fashioned wars. The early British reverses had shocked the nation, but had been swiftly succeeded by a string of emphatic victories. In spite of much verbal abuse of Britain no other power had come to the aid of the Boers, and the other Colonies had vigorously supported the British. It seemed that the Boer problem, which had exercised British attention for two decades, had been solved in a matter of months.

It was in these highly encouraging circumstances that, in September 1900, the Cabinet decided on a new election. The Liberal position was hapless. On July 27th, for example, on a motion proposed by a prominent 'pro-Boer', Sir Wilfred Lawson, to reduce the Colonial Office Vote, Campbell-Bannerman had advised a general abstention. Grey led thirty-seven Liberals to support the Government, while over thirty Liberals supported Lawson.

The Unionists accordingly entered what the Liberals angrily called 'the Khaki Election' with every possible advantage. In terms of domestic legislation, the only real achievement had been the Work-men's Compensation Act of 1897, which gave automatic compensa-tions by employers for industrial accidents, and the election was dominated by the war and the Liberal divisions. Chamberlain was now the truly dominating figure in British politics; the Unionist party was absolutely united; the Liberal leadership was weak and not inspiriting, and the party was riven. It was not an election which the political purist could contemplate with much satisfaction. Morley declared that 'a ring of financiers . . . mostly Jewish, are really responsible for the war', and the anti-semitic campaign instigated by Lloyd George was eagerly echoed by John Burns and Keir Hardie. Burns declared that the British Army had become 'the janissary of the Jews', and he, Hardie, and eighty-one executive officers of the trade union movement signed a resolution that blamed the war not only on the capitalists and the press, but on the fact that they were 'largely Jews and foreigners'. One Unionist pamphlet exhorted:

> Electors, be up and doing. Your Children Call Upon You. They will ask you hereafter how you voted in the crisis of the Empire. Don't let your reply be 'For a Small England, a Shrunken England, a degraded England, a Submissive England'.
> No!
> To the Poll, then, to the Poll to
> Vote for the Unionist Candidate
> and for
> GREATER BRITAIN

In the circumstances, the Liberals did remarkably well. Particularly difficult was the position of those Liberals who had supported the war, but were still attacked as pro-Boers and anti-British. The pre-election Unionist majority of 130 was increased to 134, but very significantly, this was eighteen smaller than the majority of 1895. A new Unionist M.P., Winston Churchill, who had been elected for Oldham, wrote to Rosebery—who had not taken an active part in the election—that 'I think this election, fought by the Liberals as a soldier's battle, without plan or leaders or enthusiasm, has shown so far the strength, not the weakness, of Liberalism in the country'.[1] But the Liberal dissensions increased after the election, until it seemed that the party was hell-bent on self-destruction. The gulf between men of the stamp of Rosebery, Grey, Asquith and Haldane on the one hand and Morley, Harcourt and the rising young Lloyd George on the other, was so wide that it seemed impossible ever to bridge.

In 1902 Salisbury at last retired, and was succeeded as Prime Minister by Arthur Balfour. It was a wholly unchallenged succession, dutifully endorsed by a special Party meeting. But no one doubted who was the strongest man, with the greatest personal following, in the Unionist ranks. It was Chamberlain's hour.

But the Boer War now entered a long and dismal period for the British. The Boer commandos, led by men of the calibre of Smuts, Botha, and De Wet, harried the British lines. The only answer was to increase the British forces and denude the countryside of succour for the Boers. The deliberate burning of farms as an act of war seems to have begun in April 1900, and *The Times* reported (April 27th) that a column left Bloemfontein 'with definite instructions to render untenable the farms of men, who, having surrendered, were found to be still in league with the enemy, or were making use of British magnanimity as a means to save their property'. As early as March 11th Roberts had complained about the continued Boer abuse of the white flag. In May Botha protested about the burning of farmhouses. In June Roberts issued a proclamation that farmhouses in the vicinity of damaged railway lines would be destroyed in reprisal. In August it was announced that any building that had harboured the enemy would be razed to the ground. Meanwhile, Botha was also destroying farmhouses with the object of intimidating Boers who were contemplating surrender or had done so. These punitive measures had the

---

[1] But the Liberals did not contest 143 seats, another indication of their disunity and low morale.

same result. The smoke rose into the air and the victims had to search desperately for succour. 'The Devil is walking up and down this land and people have gone mad', Lionel Curtis, a strong admirer of Milner, wrote in October 1900. 'We are doing things that 100 years ago Wellington would have none of and which a year ago we should have said was impossible.'[1]

The British and the majority of the Boers were now in a very real quandary. In March, when the war seemed virtually over, Roberts had issued a proclamation permitting Boers who laid down their arms and took an oath of neutrality to return to their farms. Many thousands availed themselves of these terms. Now, it appeared, the war was not over at all.

The first indication of serious trouble occurred on September 3rd, when Roberts reported that a British officer had to look after a party of Boers, with women and children, who had come to him for help. On September 22nd an order was issued to establish refugee camps in Pretoria and Bloemfontein 'for burghers who voluntarily surrender'. Botha, considerably alarmed by the attraction of this offer, intensified his measures of intimidation, while at the same time issuing a number of allegations against the British which, although thinly based on fact, had a considerable impact abroad.

By November, farm-burning by the British had become virtually indiscriminate. In effect, it was impossible to draw any distinction between farms; every one was potential—if not an actual—source of supply for a Boer commando living off the land. Behind the protests of the Boers there lay a genuine military apprehension. The trickle of refugees became a torrent. On December 21st Kitchener drew the attention of officers to the fact that an experiment of moving all women and children to camps had reduced the morale of the men on commando.

Early in 1901, there was a brave but abortive attempt by the Boers to invade Cape Colony; the Dutch in the Colony would not support them. On March 8th–15th there was a meeting between Kitchener and Botha at Middelburg which achieved nothing. Kitchener proposed that farmhouses and their occupants should be put outside the scope of military operations, but Botha refused in terms so callous that repelled even so favourable an observer of the Boer conditions as Miss Emily Hobhouse, who subsequently wrote:

[1] *With Milner in South Africa.*

From the date of the Middelburg Conference the Boers washed their hands, as it were, more completely of the families of surrendered burghers, and, regarding them as English subjects, sent them into the English lines.

From the one side or the other it was clear that the Boer women with their little ones must suffer. They were between the devil and the deep sea.[1]

The Boers themselves were in no position to look after their own refugees, and conditions in their camps were unspeakable. The flood of Boer refugees now descended on the British, in a pitiable condition. They brought with them diphtheria, typhoid and a virulent strain of measles which was particularly lethal to children. They were also badly under-nourished, and their open life on the veldt left them easy victims to infection. The British were already badly short of medical supplies for their own troops, who were ravaged by enteric and dysentery; up to the end of May 1902 the British lost 13,750 dead and 66,500 invalided from disease. The medical facilities—bad at the outset—had completely broken down. This background shows why it was that the death-rate in the 'concentration' camps was so appalling. The number of deaths in the camps totalled some 4,000 women and 16,000 children. It was not surprising that world, and British, opinion was outraged.

On June 14th, 1901, Campbell-Bannerman, shocked by Miss Hobhouse's reports, declared that:

A phrase often used is that 'war is war', but when one comes to ask about it one is told that no war is going on, that it is not war. When is a war not a war? When it is carried on by methods of barbarism in South Africa.

This brought the Liberal schisms to a head, and led to the formation by the Liberal Imperialists of the Liberal League, led by Rosebery, Asquith, Haldane and Grey. On December 15th, at Chesterfield, Rosebery advised the party to abandon 'the fly-blown phylacteries of obsolete policies' and 'clean the slate'. Campbell-Bannerman reacted sharply, and began to demonstrate real signs of political leadership. The controversy in Britain now reached new heights of bitterness and passion. If the Jameson Raid had been her Bay of Pigs, the Boer War

[1] Emily Hobhouse: *The Brunt of the War and Where It Fell*, 102.

was her Vietnam. The circumstances under which Lloyd George narrowly escaped with his life from the Birmingham Riot of December 18th, 1901 have been often described, but they deserve repetition. No one was in any doubt, from the tone of the Unionist press in Birmingham, that Lloyd George's increasingly personal assaults on Chamberlain's competence and integrity—and particularly upon his brother's association with a company which had prospered greatly from Government contracts—represented an outrage to which the citizens of the city should respond. A well-armed mob of over thirty thousand persons surrounded the Town Hall, many of them surged into the meeting, the windows were smashed, the platform received a blizzard of missiles, and Lloyd George only escaped disguised as a policeman. The episode—strongly reminiscent of the Aston Park Riot of 1885 directed against Lord Randolph Churchill and Sir Stafford Northcote—was significant in that Chamberlain could easily have prevented it, but did not; that it established Lloyd George's reputation for physical courage, which his detractors have subsequently sought to deride; and that it made his national reputation. Mob brutality in Britain, particularly when it is obviously carefully planned, has a devastatingly counter-productive effect. The incident also demonstrated that Chamberlain had learned nothing about the true nature of British politics. In one night of brutality, in which two people were killed and over forty seriously injured, he had made Lloyd George's name a household word.

'Joe's war' ended in May 1902 on a sour and disagreeable note. It had cost the British 5,774 killed, 22,829 wounded, and over 16,000 dead from disease. The Boer losses are not known, although it is estimated that they lost some 4,000 killed in action. It had cost Britain £222 million.

Although the Boers had lost, the terms of surrender were generous. They included a money grant of £3 million to rebuild and restock farms, an act that did much to reduce the bitter feelings left by the last two years of the war. Abroad, the war had brought Britain nothing but obloquy outside the Empire, and her isolation in Europe had been painfully evident. It was this realisation that created the climate of opinion in which the new Foreign Secretary, Lord Lansdowne, started to reshape British foreign policy with the settlement of outstanding differences, particularly with France. The drastic overhaul of the British Army, so long overdue, was put in hand.

The loss of the glitter of victory was one factor that affected the Unionist fortunes. The end of the war, furthermore, although it did not result in Liberal reunion, at least removed the most crucial abrasive element in the party's internal affairs.

The first turning-point came in 1902, with the Education Act. The Act of 1870 had created a dual system with two sets of schools, one wholly provided and maintained by religious authorities, and the other by elected school boards. The 1902 Act, the work of Balfour and a rising civil servant, Robert Morant, swept away the boards, and made the new local authorities wholly responsible; it also required the religious-supported schools to provide their facilities free of charge to the authorities. These proposals aroused intense opposition. As they also strengthened the position of the Church of England Schools and restored them to equality with Nonconformist ones, the fury of the latter was intense, and was concentrated particularly upon Chamberlain. Many Nonconformists refused to pay the new Education Rate, and in Wales there was a successful capture of county councils; these then refused to levy any education rates until they had complete control of the money, and forced the Government to pass legislation giving it powers to by-pass the local authorities. This was a very significant increase in the powers of the central government, and confirmed the purpose of the 1902 Act to give the new Board of Education control over the policy of national education.

The 1902 Education Act can now be seen as a logical development of previous Acts, a legislative action of far-reaching effects, and a substantial step forward in the provision of national State education. At the time, it aroused intense passions, and the Liberals found themselves united for the first time in six years. This was a considerable check for the Unionists, but far worse was to come.

*

It is never difficult—in retrospect, particularly—to trace the processes of Chamberlain's thought. In the 1880s he had followed Lord Randolph about the country lauding Free Trade when Churchill was temporarily toying with 'Fair Trade', and the experience had made him question the essential validity of the case for Free Trade. There was now additional evidence. British exports to the Empire actually declined between 1883 and 1892, and the value of imported goods into Britain had risen sharply, by nearly £100 million, while foreign imports into the Empire countries rose. For a nation that depended upon trade for its existence, these figures were ominous. But economic factors were not the only ones. By 1902 Chamberlain's political position had slipped, and he was frustrated by his failure in South Africa and by his inability to persuade Hicks-Beach to introduce a modest Old Age Pension scheme. He was, accordingly, looking for a new national issue.

In 1897 Queen Victoria had her second—the Diamond—Jubilee. It marked the high point of national enthusiasm for the Empire, and was both in popular and political terms a spectacular occasion. Rudyard Kipling, the most sensitive, prolific, and influential writer in England since Dickens, had become, as H. G. Wells later wrote, 'almost a national symbol. He got hold of us wonderfully, he filled us with tinkling and haunting quotations. . . . He helped to broaden my geographical sense immensely, and he provided phrases for just that desire for discipline and devotion and organised effort the Socialism of our times failed to express.' Kipling was much more than the Jingo poetaster that many—including Max Beerbohm—have portrayed him. If he exalted the cause of Empire he also warned against its perils and, having been brought up in India, saw clearly the moral pitfalls of Imperialism. He also understood, as no other contemporary writer did, the difficulties and strains under which the servants of the Empire lived, and he was their spokesman and their champion. His contempt for flag-waving politicians was best expressed in a famous passage in *Stalky and Co.*, but is to be seen often elsewhere in his writings. Immensely popular, almost a national institution, derided by the anti-imperialists, his influence on popular attitudes in the 1890s was immense.

During the Jubilee the experiment of 1887 of the Colonial Conference of Colonial Prime Ministers had been repeated. Chamberlain presided, and it was attended by the Prime Ministers of Canada, Newfoundland, New South Wales, Victoria, South Australia, West Australia, Queensland, Tasmania, New Zealand, Cape Colony and Natal. Chamberlain proposed closer federation and a 'Council of the Empire' which he hoped might develop into 'that Federal Council to which we must always look forward as our ultimate ideal'. He also proposed 'an Imperial Zollverrein'. Both proposals were in effect, turned down flat. But Chamberlain was not disposed to abandon his plan so easily. In 1902, making use of the presence of Colonial Prime

Ministers at the Coronation of King Edward VII, another Colonial Conference had been held. It was notable for two reasons. The idea of 'Imperial Defence' was unenthusiastically received and, in effect, rejected in spite of cogent arguments by Chamberlain. But the Prime Ministers did agree to accepting the principle of Imperial Preference in general terms. This move forward was to have decisive importance on Chamberlain's outlook.

In the 1902 Budget Hicks-Beach introduced a registration duty on imported grain, corn, flour, and meal, emphasising that this was not to be regarded as a Protectionist measure. Chamberlain persuaded the Cabinet to respond favourably to a request by the Canadian Government for preference. In November 1902 the matter was discussed in the Cabinet. Chamberlain concluded that it had agreed that the tax would be maintained, and that the preferential remission for countries of the Empire would be increased. This was not the interpretation of the new Chancellor of the Exchequer, Ritchie, who proceeded to repeal the duties in his 1903 Budget. Until December 1916 no Cabinet Minutes were taken or distributed to Ministers, and the only record of Cabinet proceedings was a confidential letter to the Sovereign by the Prime Minister. This inefficient arrangement was bound to lead to misunderstandings, and this was to prove one of the most celebrated.

On May 15th 1903, at Birmingham, Chamberlain delivered one of the most sensational speeches in modern British politics. He called it 'A Demand for Enquiry', but it was in fact a trenchant and provocative exposition of the case for Imperial Preference and Tariff Reform, arguing that the key to Empire was commerce, coupled with a critical analysis of the deficiencies of Free Trade. He also spoke warily of 'sacrifices', referring to the inevitability of higher prices for imported food. To make the sensation even more complete, Balfour on the same day explicitly relegated Imperial Preference to 'a hypothetical future'.

Politics leaped into intense life. The Liberals sprang together, and Asquith started a tour of speeches in which he hammered away at Chamberlain's proposals. 'To dispute Free Trade, after fifty years' experience of it, is like disputing the law of gravitation', Campbell-Bannerman declared, thus characteristically putting his finger on the fatal defect in Chamberlain's approach. He was disputing not a policy, but a religion—and without advance notice. Ironically, in this matter he was right, but in the manner of his heresy he doomed it to failure. The Protectionist issue was to divide and haunt the Unionists for nearly thirty years, and was to be to them what Home Rule had been for the Liberals. The Unionists reacted in dismay, and split into Tariff Reformers and Free Traders; one of the most vigorous of the latter was the young Winston Churchill, ambitious, impatient, and already highly discontented at his lack of advancement, and whose progression to the Liberal party was now accelerated.

Balfour attempted to hold the Cabinet together. Compromise solutions were created, but could not bridge the deep fissure opened in the Cabinet. Balfour proposed retaliatory measures against high tariff countries, with no food taxes. In September he issued a pamphlet of considerable skill but which satisfied neither side. It had already become virtually a theological dispute.

On September 9th Chamberlain offered Balfour his resignation on the understanding that his son, Austen, would enter the Cabinet, so that he could propagate his cause. On September 14th Balfour in effect dismissed Ritchie and Lord Balfour of Burleigh, two prominent and intransigent Free Traders. On the following day the Free Trade Duke of Devonshire and Lord George Hamilton resigned, but under Balfour's urgings the former withdrew his resignation when he was privately told of Chamberlain's resignation. It seemed that Balfour had achieved a remarkable coup by shedding the extremists of both sides and retaining the Duke. Hartington—as his contemporaries still called him—was now an old man, and no longer particularly active in politics, but he aroused respect and confidence to a quite remarkable extent. For two weeks the political world breathlessly awaited his decision. Loud and angry accusations were made by both sides against Balfour's tactics, and the Free Traders put intense pressure upon the Duke. Persuaded that his honour was at stake, and somewhat confused, he resigned on October 6th and Balfour's elaborate scheme collapsed in ruins.

Many historians have been baffled by Balfour's tactics during this crisis, and have pondered upon his strategy. To this commentator, the strategy seems clear enough—it was to preserve the unity of the Unionist party, and to avoid a catastrophic split on the scale of 1846. If he had declared himself for one side or the other he would, as he saw the situation, become 'another Peel'. Furthermore, it was a vital part of his policy to keep the Unionists in office. He had a genuine, if very exaggerated, fear of the domestic social policies of the Liberals and their new Labour allies. He was fearful about the possibility of

the return of Home Rule as a major issue. He also was determined to
make permanent his reforms in Defence matters, to the point when a
Liberal Government would find it very difficult, if not impossible, to
reverse them. For this he needed time.

This was the strategy. From it the tactics flowed, but here he came
up against problems of personality which he could not surmount, and
he grievously underestimated the passions which lay behind the issues
of Free Trade and Protection. Balfour was not a passionate man, and
he failed to make allowances for the burning convictions, which in
some instances amounted to frenzy, that these issues aroused. At the
time, and by many historians subsequently, he has been depicted as
fatally weak and indecisive. Now, with a clearer perspective, we can
see this his strategy had its merits, and that his tactics were coherent
and intelligent. And, if nothing else, he bought his Government two
more years of office, in which many of his most cherished reforms were
established permanently.

Chamberlain now embarked upon the last great campaign of his
career. A Tariff Reform League was founded to raise subscriptions and
finance the campaign; a Tariff Commission supplied facts and
figures; although seventy, Chamberlain himself was in his most
vigorous form. But as his campaign developed it became less concentrated on Imperial Preference and more insistent on the advantages
of Protection. Chamberlain captured the Liberal Unionist organisation, and had large and enthusiastic support in the Unionist Party.
The debate raged throughout 1904 and 1905, to the agonised embarrassment of the Government and the increasing advantage of the
Liberals.

Misfortunes now descended upon the Government in a cataract.
An attempt to deal with labour problems in South Africa by bringing
in some 50,000 Chinese coolies to work in the mines for three years
resulted in outraged protests from the Liberal and Labour parties. The
conditions under which the Chinese lived and worked were unspeakable, and the Government's lack of interest in the subject
appalled middle class philanthropists and trade unionists alike. The
attitude of regarding human labour as a commodity seemed to expose
a particularly odious aspect of the Tory mentality, and 'Chinese
slavery' was a potent factor in the further decline of the Unionists in
1904–5. George Wyndham, the talented Irish Secretary, was virtually
forced out of office by the Ulster Conservatives as a result of the

activities of his Permanent Under-Secretary, Sir Anthony McDonnell, a Catholic Home Ruler. A Licensing Bill in 1904 further demonstrated the Government's ill-fortune. It was an honest attempt to deal with drunkenness by improving the licensing system; with considerable skill this was portrayed as another attempt by the Tories to assist the brewers. 'The Licensing Bill', Lloyd George declared 'is a party bribe for gross political corruption—an act which Tammany Hall could not exceed.'

The fundamental problem of Balfour's leadership was not his alleged timorousness and irresolution, but that it revealed just how profoundly Conservative a man he was. In certain areas—education was the most notable example—he was far ahead of most of his contemporaries in understanding and enlightened courage, but in others he was wholly insensitive. His refusal to accept Keir Hardie's proposals for the use of public money in creating jobs for the unemployed was a case in point, and the Unemployed Workmen Act of 1905 was a feeble palliative. His brother, Gerald, was once described by Maud du Puy as 'really the most conservative man that I have ever met. Believes the higher set of people, the House of Lords, etc., set a good example to the lower classes of people—and ever so much more stuff that I had read of but never met anyone that believed it'.[1] Balfour, for all his charm and real ability, also had certain ineradicable prejudices and fears. It was said of him by Ramsay MacDonald that 'he saw life from afar', and certainly he had little understanding of, and no sympathy with, proposals for substantial social reform. He was, like Salisbury, a vehement believer in the *status quo*, while fully admitting the need for certain changes which were necessary for the national good and for the maintenance of that *status quo*. But no further. New ideas and radical proposals were alien to him and to his concept of what the Conservative Party was, and was not. The division between the Cecils and Lord Randolph had had a strong ideological as well as personal content. Now, as the 'Imperial' issue was becoming actually harmful to the Unionists, Balfour's hostility to social reform became a major liability.

This attitude was now put to the test.

Until 1901 it had been assumed that the Trade Union Act of 1871 afforded absolute protection to union funds, and that a union could not be sued for damages as a result of industrial action. In 1901 the

[1] Gwen Raverat: *Period Piece*, 22.

Taff Vale Railway Company sued the Amalgamated Society of Railway Servants. The High Court found for the Company; the judgement was reversed in the Court of Appeal, but was upheld in the House of Lords.

This was a thunderbolt to the Unions. In a fatal moment for his Government and party, Balfour refused to entertain the unionists' proposal for remedial legislation, and they turned elsewhere. Their previous relative lack of interest in the Labour Representation Committee was now transformed, and L.R.C. membership rose dramatically from 376,000 in 1901 to 861,000 in 1903. Furthermore, in 1903 the unions increased its contribution from 10 shillings per thousand members to almost £5; a fund for the payment of future Labour M.P.s was established; and it was resolved that its candidates must 'strictly abstain from identifying themselves with or promoting the interests of any section of the Liberal or Conservative parties'. In fact, MacDonald and Herbert Gladstone—the Liberal Chief Whip— came together to make an electoral compact, whereby the majority of L.R.C. candidates would not have to face Liberal opposition. This was a secret compact, but one of great importance both for the Liberals and for the new party, and represented a form of united front against the Unionists. By 1905 the L.R.C. had fifty candidates in the field, of whom only eighteen would face Liberal opposition. In ten double-member seats one Liberal and one L.R.C. candidate fought side by side. The L.R.C. candidates, furthermore, fought on the Liberal policies.

This development made the electoral position of the Unionists more precarious than ever. Their internal difficulties became steadily worse. On November 3rd 1905, Chamberlain described Balfour's Parliamentary tactics of evading debates on Free Trade as 'humiliating' and demanded a dissolution. On November 14th he in effect captured the National Union. With the Central Office in decline since Middleton's retirement, this was a significant pointer.

But the fundamental point about party organisations in both parties was that they had no say or involvement in the formulation of policy. Thus, the capture of the National Union by the Tariff Reformers in 1905 reflected the new balance in the party, and made the position of the dwindling band of Free Fooders even more precarious, but the impetus and organisation had come from above. The Union, in short, was *used*—the rank and file did not spontaneously reach the conclusion that Tariff Reform should be the dominant policy of the party. A. L. Lowell described the situation in *The Government of England*, which was published at this time:

> The Whips may be said to constitute the only regular party organisation in the House of Commons, unless we include under that description the two front benches. The very fact, indeed, that the ministry and the leaders of the Opposition furnish in themselves the real party machinery of the House, avoids the need of any other. The ministers prepared and carry out the programme of the party in power, while a small coterie of leaders on the other side devise the plans for opposing them . . . in neither of the great parties is there anything resembling a general caucus for the discussion and determination of party policy. Sometimes a great meeting of the adherents of the party in Parliament is called at one of the political clubs or elsewhere, when the leaders address their followers. But it is held to exhort not to consult.[1]

If this was true of the situation in Parliament, it was even more evident in the country. The developing central, regional and local organisations were essentially to provide the voluntary support necessary in the post-Corrupt Practices Act situation—to raise money, to develop enthusiasm for the Cause, and to give a flattering sense of participation in great affairs. But their place was certainly not to concern themselves with issues of strategy or policy, which were reserved to the awesome and sapient leaders in Parliament, who would tell the armies what to do. Until the Labour Party came along, with very different attitudes and practices, which gave some people new ideas, this relationship was accepted and hardly challenged. There were occasional grumblings, but little more.

*

Subsequently, the Balfour Government was viewed in a more generous light than it was at the time. The Education Act of 1902, the Irish Land Purchase Act of 1903, the Licensing Act of 1904, the Anglo-Japanese Treaty of 1902, the Entente with France in 1904, and the creation of the Committee of Imperial Defence in the same year, were major achievements. Much of the credit for the *entente cordiale* with France went to the King, and certainly a triumphantly successful

[1] Quoted in Robert Mackenzie: *British Political Parties*, 71.

State Visit to Paris and the King's known fondness for France were no disadvantages in securing popular support for the new departure, but the driving force was that of Balfour, and he was entitled to remark later to Lansdowne of the King that 'So far as I can remember, during the years which you and I were his Ministers, he never made an important suggestion of any sort as to large questions of policy.' King Edward passed into legend as The Peacemaker, Arthur Balfour went down to political eclipse.

The reform of the Army had been put in hand, and the tremendous Selborne-Fisher naval programme, beginning in 1902, covered the entire field of naval activity—personnel training, redeployment of reserves, gunnery training, battle tactics, naval training and the development of the 'all big-gun ship', the *Dreadnought*, launched in February 1906. These latter advances were to be imperilled by the Liberal Government in the first two years of its existence, but the effect of the Selborne-Fisher programme was to transform the Navy.

But it was the establishment of the Committee of Imperial Defence, presided over by the Prime Minister, that was the most important development of all. 'But for Balfour's far-seeing initiative in 1904', Lord Hankey has written, 'our defensive preparations could not conceivably have been brought to the pitch that was attained in 1914.'[1] It was somewhat ironical that Salisbury had been virtually forced out of the Foreign Office in 1900, to be replaced by Lansdowne, because of Salisbury's entrenched hostility to an Anglo-German rapprochment. The attempts of Lansdowne and Chamberlain to achieve this had been curtly rebuffed, and the realisation that the Germans were now serious about naval equality and regarded themselves as a putative world power led to new assessments about future dangers. The *entente* with France was not an anti-German move, but it fitted very closely with the strategy now being urged on Ministers by a new generation of Froeign Office officials alarmed by the increasing power of Germany and its belligerence. The brutal tone of German warnings to France in the 1905 Morocco Crisis gave their arguments additional force.

Balfour's problems when he assumed the Premiership were many. His party had been in office for seven years and had gone through the perils and anxieties of a major war, whose cost, coinciding with a temporary slump, caused poor economic conditions. His attempt to

[1] Hankey: *The Supreme Command*, I, 45.

keep the party together over Tariff Reform were perhaps too ingenious, but it is difficult to see how the split could have been averted, and Balfour ensured that it did not—as seemed probable at one stage—bring the Government down in 1903. Balfour himself was deficient neither in courage nor dexterity. Abused by his opponents and constantly criticised by both extreme elements in his own party, he maintained an imperturbable calm. He did not kindle warm emotions, and he was himself somewhat cold-blooded and aloof. He did not excel at the demagogic arts. He was, by background and inclination, far removed from the problems that beset the vast majority of the people. He was a 'politician's politician', who aroused admiration and respect, yet who could not stem the tides sweeping against his party and his government. Perhaps no single man could have. The marvel was that he withstood them for so long and achieved so much. As Austen Chamberlain has commented:

> Balfour's courage never failed; he maintained consistently the line he had marked out for himself and he accomplished . . . by his own force of will . . . great reforms which, however criticised at the moment, have stood the test of time and still dominate the scene. . . . It is not easy to find a parallel to such an achievement in so short a time and amidst such difficulties.[1]

At this point Ministers were further embarrassed by the public eruption of a classic dispute between the Viceroy of India, Lord Curzon, and the Commander-in-Chief, Lord Kitchener. Curzon was a man of so many mixed aspects that, despite several biographies and analyses, it is difficult to give a clear portrait of him. It is to Winston Churchill that we owe the best portrait:

> The contradictory qualities which dwell in the characters of so many individuals can rarely have found more vivid contrasts than in George Curzon. The world thought him pompous in manner and in mind. But this widespread and deep impression, arising from the experience and report of so many good judges, was immediately destroyed by the Curzon one met in a small circle of intimate friends and equals—or those whom he treated as equals. . . . Helpful with comfort and sympathy on every occasion of sickness or sorrow in his wide circle, unpopular with most of those who served him, the

[1] Austen Chamberlain: *Down The Years*, 206–7.

master of scathing rebukes for subordinates, he seemed to sow gratitude and resentment along his path with evenly lavish hands. Bespangled with every quality that could dazzle and attract, he never found himself with a following. Majestic in speech, appearance, and demeanour, he never led. He often domineered; but at the centre he never dominated.[1]

His Viceroyalty attracted very varying estimates, both then and subsequently. It was his conviction that the real leader must be a master of detail, and he despised the view that 'it is supposed to be a mark of efficiency and even greatness to get your work done for you by other people. I frankly disagree. I say that if you want a thing done in a certain way, the only manner in which to be sure that it is done is to do it yourself.'[2] No Viceroy ever worked harder, and his achievements were considerable. But he made enemies, and the most formidable was Kitchener, who had close political contacts in London, notably with Lady Salisbury. It was a brutal clash of opposing personalities, and Kitchener won. Curzon returned to England an embittered man, and the Liberals made much capital over the defeat of a civilian administrator by a military clique. There was more to it than that, but the charge had a certain validity.

*

It is always perilous to fix dividing-lines in the study of history. Nevertheless, the nineteenth century did end with a satisfying neatness in many respects. Gladstone died in 1898, Queen Victoria in 1901, and Salisbury in 1903; Harcourt died in 1904; Chamberlain was totally incapacitated by a stroke in 1906, and although he lived until 1914 his career ended completely with his stroke; the Duke of Devonshire died in 1908. Most modern historians of the period have regarded Chamberlain with coolness, while conceding his enormous influence and importance. Although it would be unfair to blame him wholly for the great Liberal break-up of 1886, Chamberlain's political mind was such that it is difficult to believe that his influence in the Liberal Party would have been benignant, or that he would have been a comfortable colleague. As Rosebery once wrote in another context, 'independence in a great orator on the Treasury Bench is a rocket of

---

[1] Churchill: *Great Contemporaries*.
[2] Kenneth Rose: *Lord Curzon and His Circle*, 26–7.

which one cannot predict the course'. Chamberlain's defection from the Liberals had delivered that party a temporarily crippling blow and he was, in the 1890s and early 1900s, their most implacable foe. But it is doubtful if he damaged the Liberals to the same extent that he did the Conservatives. The Jameson Raid and the Boer War did much harm to the cause of Imperialism; the Tariff Reform pronouncement of 1903, and the subsequent campaign, smashed the Conservatives for more than a decade. The sudden removal of this powerful, determined, single-minded man from politics in 1906 was accordingly an event of great importance.

Salisbury's last years had been clouded by private grief, ill-health and sombre forebodings. He lamented the South African War, and his failure to avert it. The death of his wife in 1899 had been a blow from which he never recovered, but even before this disaster it had been evident that he was worn out and in melancholy physical decline. He had been seventy-two when he had thankfully retired in 1902, and his death followed not long after, on August 22nd 1903, in his beloved Hatfield, surrounded by his family, and with one of his sons reading the prayers. Complex in so many things, doubtful of so much, his Faith had always been serene and assured. It would be wrong to depict him as the last relic of a fading age. He possessed certain aspects of political character which are timeless. He is one of those rare public figures of whom one can say with real confidence that he could have succeeded at any time and in any circumstances.

It is of Salisbury, more than any other modern politician, that the historian invokes Boswell's celebrated tribute to Samuel Johnson:

> His superiority over other learned men consisted chiefly in what might be called the art of thinking, the art of using his mind; a certain continual power of seizing the useful substance of all that he knew, and exhibiting it in a clear and forcible manner; so that knowledge, which we often see to be no better than lumber in men of dull understanding, was, in him, true evident, and actual wisdom.

Yet, for all that we know of him, he remains mysterious and elusive —a wise and percipient man, yet wedded emphatically and without apology to an older order. A conciliator in foreign affairs, highly cautious, yet with a streak of recklessness. An intellectual, yet with a sharp understanding of the value of exploitation in immediate human relationships. Gentle, yet remorseless when occasion demanded. Tolerant, and yet with certain immovable prejudices. Forgiving, and yet often unpitying. Idealistic, yet cynical. Kind, yet also cruel. All in all, the most formidably equipped politician for all seasons that England had produced since Robert Cecil, first Earl of Salisbury, had made his family's eminence and fame.

Other giants of late-Victorian politics, notably Parnell and Lord Randolph Churchill, who might have been expected to be active in politics in the 1900s, had died in their middle forties, and others, like Rosebery and Dilke, although still in public life, were out of the front line for ever. The future lay with a new generation. Some, like Asquith, Grey, Curzon, the Irish leader John Redmond, Lloyd George, Austen Chamberlain, and Edward Carson, had begun their political careers before 1900. Others, such as Bonar Law, Winston Churchill, Ramsay MacDonald, Arthur Henderson and F. E. Smith, entered Parliament in the years 1900–6. There were some exceptions. Arthur Balfour's remarkable career had only reached its half-way stage when he became Prime Minister in 1902; John Morley was in active politics until 1914; Campbell-Bannerman lived until 1908. But Morley was no longer the force he had once been; Campbell-Bannerman's hour came too late; and Balfour's position never really recovered from the holocaust of 1906.

The outstanding feature of British politics from 1903 to 1914 was to be the absolute superiority of the Liberal Party. From the opening of the Free Trade battle in 1903 the Liberals were no longer in decline, and no longer wearily resigned to decades of futile and debilitating Opposition. The vaunted Conservative organisation had crumbled. Middleton had lost interest in his work after the death of Salisbury, and his successors—a Captain Wells, who lasted briefly, and a Colonel Haig—were failures. Admittedly, they could hardly have operated in a worse period, and the blame cast upon them for the 1906 débâcle is obviously harshly unfair. But the fact that Middleton's once superb machine had declined so quickly and so catastrophically added another ingredient in the Unionist misfortunes. And for this, also, Balfour must bear a large part of the censure, as the Central Office was under his personal and direct control.

The Liberals now possessed a marked superiority of talent. Asquith was clearly the coming man. Born in 1852 in relatively humble circumstances, he had had the benefit of a Balliol education during the early part of that College's golden period. He had gone into law, but was not notably successful. In 1886 he entered Parliament for East Fife at the age of thirty-three, and swiftly made a good impression. Asquith had about him, from the beginning, a massive intellectual quality and steadiness of purpose that was impressive and even daunting. At the Home Office in the hapless Gladstone–Rosebery Government he had made an excellent impression, although, viewed from this distance, he appears to have been somewhat unimaginative and conventional. But his brisk no-nonsense competence and skill in debate stood out conspicuously in that Government, and when Rosebery resigned from the Liberal leadership in October 1896, he picked out Asquith as the future leader of Liberalism. His marriage to Margot Tennant had brought him into more glittering circles, and by the end of the 1890s references to the fact that Margot was 'ruining' him were not infrequent; certainly this was the opinion of Haldane, formerly one of Asquith's closest friends and himself a politician of much promise. 'London Society', Haldane wrote tartly many years later, 'came, however, to have a great attraction for him, and he grew by degrees diverted from the sterner outlook on life which he and I for long shared. . . . From the beginning he meant to be Prime Minister, sooner or later.'[1] But too much should not be made of these charges; it is possible that, by 1915, his will had been sapped by years of good living and intellectual complacency. But Asquith's physical strength and resilience were considerable, even in 1915, and there were no indications of decline in the first ten years after his marriage.

When Harcourt had retired at the end of 1898, taking Morley with him, there was a real possibility that Asquith might succeed him, and if Campbell-Bannerman had not been interested in the leadership it seems probable that he would have done so. But Asquith was extremely reluctant to oppose Campbell-Bannerman, and 'C-B' took the leadership. But it had been a significant indication of Asquith's position in the party that his name had been canvassed so seriously.

It was unquestionably a lucky escape. Within a few months the South African cauldron began to bubble ominously. Asquith, a close friend and admirer of Milner and Rosebery, supported the Government. In 1901 he was one of the vice-presidents of the Liberal League, which was in effect if not in title opposed to Campbell-Bannerman's interpretation of the Liberal future. But it was noticeable that in this

[1] Haldane: *Autobiography*, 103.

unhappy period of the history of the Liberal Party, Asquith was cautious. While maintaining his position, he did not give the hierarchy much cause for antagonism, and when the Free Trade storm broke in 1903 he was first in the field to give sound proof of his Liberal bona fides. His biographers ascribe much of this to good fortune; but it is noticeable that Asquith had a habit of being in the right place at the right time. He was a formidable politician.

Asquith did not possess an original mind, and he had moreover a certain degree of intellectual priggishness, with a capacity for supercilious dismissal of men who did not come up to the Balliol standard; politics being what it is, there were not many who could aspire to such a level of excellence. With the great majority of his colleagues—particularly Lloyd George and Winston Churchill—he was contemptuous of 'socialism'. His attitudes were conservative, he had no interest in working class attitudes and aspirations, he believed in the rule of the elite. He was not a man who was sensitive to new movements which might imperil his fundamental philosophies. His admiration for Rosebery and Balfour was significant, and was based not only on intellectual respect. Yet he was always ready to respond to arguments whose implications were radical and even modestly revolutionary. The secret of his quality lay in his availability to a good case. Once persuaded, he would put the full strength of his intellectual and political power behind it. His intellect was powerful and fair, and was seen at its best in the reconciliation of differences and in pin-pointing the crucial features in a complicated dispute. He was a professional politician in a very exceptional way. As Gilbert Murray has written:

> Asquith made a sharp difference between business and the rest of life, and, during the times when I knew him best, he treated politics strictly as business. He worked at them, made his decisions, dismissed them and did not want to talk about them afterwards. Nearly all politicians like talking politics; Asquith preferred literature or history or simple amusement or at least something that was not 'shop'.

Behind Campbell-Bannerman, Asquith, Grey, Morley, and Haldane there were younger men of outstanding promise. Lloyd George was already a major figure as a result of the vehemence of his opposition to the Boer War and his unremitting pursuit of Chamberlain; Reginald McKenna, Lewis Harcourt, Winston Churchill—who finally left the

Unionists in 1904—and Charles Masterman were evidence of the talent available for the future. In contrast, the Conservatives looked out of date and lack-lustre. It was a remarkable reversal of fortunes.

*

What was the condition of England in the early 1900s?

Her industrial stagnation was now recognised, and was giving cause for concern. The rate of increase of the population was slackening considerably. The population was 41·15 million in 1900 and rose to 45·65 in 1913, but this net increase was more the result of a lower death-rate. In 1900 the male expectation of life was forty-six and for a woman fifty; only 14·8 per cent of the population was over fifty. By 1910 the life expectation had risen to fifty-two for a man and fifty-five for a woman, the proportion of the population over fifty had risen to 16·1 per cent.

The causes of the industrial stagnation were many, but the central one was that a nation depending upon its exporting capacity must inevitably suffer from a situation whereby every major purchasing country was raising protective tariff barriers. The figures themselves told the story. The British proportion of world trade in manufactured goods fell from 22·8 per cent in the early 1880s to 10·2 per cent by the early 1890s. There was then a recovery, but never to the previous level. The increase in the volume and cost of imports was maintained without a corresponding increase in exports. The first Census of Production in 1907 revealed that roughly a quarter of the goods consumed were imported. Comparing 1890 with 1901, the value of exports in these years rose by some £19·6 million, whereas that of imports rose by £107·699 million.[1]

One very significant factor was that, in the 1880s and 1890s, the British had done particularly well with the export of machinery; but, as these were principally to her main competitors, the British were in effect creating the industrial competition which was now challenging them.

It was becoming one of the cardinal tenets of industrialists and Unionist politicians that the increased activity of the Trade Unions

[1] W. Page: *Commerce and Industry: Tables of Statistics for the British From 1815*, 71–2. The actual figures were:

  Exports: £328,252,000 in 1890; £347,864,000 in 1901.
  Imports: £420,692,000 in 1890; £528,391,000 in 1901.

was in itself impairing industrial development. There was something in this, but the root causes of the trouble lay far deeper. Although the average unemployment figure in the years 1901–10 was 6 per cent—which was actually higher than the average in the previous decade (5·2 per cent)—the slumps were far less drastic, and in the years 1911–13 unemployment fell to figures of 3·1, 2·3, and 2·6 respectively. Of considerably greater importance were the figures of man-hours lost by strike. In 1901 they totalled 4·13 million; in 1911 they were 10·16 million; in 1912 they reached 40·89 million. Although the figure fell to a 'norm' figure of 9·8 million in 1913, this was still more than twice the 1901 figure.

But we should go deeper than statistics. The condition of the people should have been a cause for great concern. One of the shocks of the Boer War had been the revelation of the lamentable physical condition of the working class, seen in the young men who had volunteered for service. The great majority were rejected on physical grounds, particularly in the big cities. In Manchester, for example, 12,000 men volunteered and 8,000 were rejected immediately; eventually 1,200 (ten per cent) were accepted, and this at a time when the Army standards had been reduced to the lowest level since the Napoleonic Wars. In 1901 Seebohm Rowntree published a study of the city of York under the stark title of *Poverty*. It will be remembered that Charles Booth in 1889 had produced for London a figure of 30·7 per cent living at or below the poverty line; Rowntree's studies in York produced a figure of 27·84 per cent. It was significant of the changed temper in British life, and the effects of mass-circulation newspapers, that these statistics created a far greater sensation than Booth's study had done. Overcrowding in the cities, bad housing, totally inadequate sanitation, employers' exploitation and low wages presented a series of problems, none of which had been adequately understood, let alone solved by 1914, or even by 1939.

The wealth of the nation still lay in very few hands. That wealth was increasingly being used for grandeur and pleasure, and in this marked tendency the influence of the hedonistic King Edward VII was not beneficial. The ostentatiousness of the New Wealth was its most lamentable feature, and the social historian becomes bemused and impatient by the records of vast slaughters of pheasant, grouse, and deer, the gargantuan meals, the lengthy country-house weekends, and the lavish competition between the great hostesses in London. The

New Wealth was flaunted, and the contrast between the circumstances of the favoured few and the miserable many became more glaringly obvious than at any time since the Regency. This was not the least of the factors that made Salisbury, himself rich but frugal, despair of the new age. To the favoured, it was a glittering, enthralling, period. Others viewed it differently. This was the social background to the decline in productivity, the unrest of the working classes, and the increasing inclination to resort to industrial action and even violence. The revolution of the have-nots against the haves had not yet fully developed, but there was clear evidence of new forces in British society. Apprehension at these developments explains much of the reactions of the Conservatives in these years, and was to give to party politics a degree of bitterness unparalleled even at the height of the Home Rule struggle. In fact, the Liberals were equally baffled and alarmed. After the Conservative defeat of 1906, Balfour wrote that:

> What has occurred has nothing whatever to do with any of the things we have been squabbling over the last few years. Campbell-Bannerman is a mere cork, dancing on a torrent which he cannot control, and what is going on here is a faint echo of the same movement which has produced massacres in St. Petersburg, riots in Vienna and socialist processions in Berlin.

But the have-nots, in addition to their other deprivations, did not have the vote—or at least, not many of them. In 1900 the adult population of Britain totalled 22·675 million; the electorate was under 6·75 million. Only 58 per cent of the adult male population had the vote, and this was to be the situation until the General Election of 1918.

But interest in politics was still very great. In the 1900 election 74·6 per cent of the electorate voted; in 1906 the figure was 82·6 per cent, and in the first of the two elections of 1910 it rose to the figure of 86·6 per cent. The opinion of many commentators that popular interest in politics was less than in the 1870s and 1880s seems to be decisively belied by these figures. The passions that party politics evoked in the years 1900–14 also casts serious doubt on this generalisation. Furthermore, at no stage, even in 1911, did the politics of discontent take really serious extra-Parliamentary forms; indeed, had Balfour had a more acute realisation of his country he would have realised that the advent of Labour M.P.s in 1906 was a reassuring sign, and not one of incipient revolution. If there was to be a revolution, it was going to be a constitutional and Parliamentary one.

The Boer War did not mark the end of Imperialism, but it certainly marked the end of a period in which it had been the political preroga-tive of the Conservatives. The debates, often harsh and strident, and always divisive, within the Liberal Party had given it a much better claim to represent a public opinion that believed in the Empire but had become disenchanted with foreign adventures while grievous social problems remained unresolved at home. The Liberal Imperialists —who now had a dominant position in the party—had contributed a great deal, and had learned a great deal. The party, except on its extreme fringes, was no longer hostile or unsympathetic to Imperial responsibilities nor to the concept of Empire itself. To a remarkable extent, the Liberals had now accepted the Rosebery formula of the 1880s of 'a sane Imperialism' which would have been unthinkable in 1895. But the Liberal Imperialists had learned that blind devotion to the cause of Empire no longer existed. The Boer War had indeed been, in Kipling's words, 'No end of a lesson'. If it had been swift, sure, and triumphant, the political consequences in Britain might have been transitory. As it was, the revelations of arrogance and incompetence left a lasting impression upon Englishmen who had been victims of those same attitudes in their domestic affairs. The Boer War led to drastic and long overdue reforms in the British Army—although not drastic enough. But it also struck at certain casual assumptions in domestic politics, which now had to be revised. In the new attitude towards Empire, the Liberals—unwittingly, perhaps—were the principal beneficiaries.

In 1900 J. A. Hobson had published his celebrated diatribe on Imperialism which, in the long run, had an impact upon intellectuals comparable to that of Seeley in the opposite direction in 1883. Politicians, however, survive or disappear in the short run. The appeal of the Liberals in 1905 lay in the fact that they were emphatically for the Empire, but opposed to its more dangerous—and expensive— excesses. Thus, they had blundered upon the key for popular support in this confused and complex period.

In South Africa, Milner had endeavoured to make annexation work, with the assistance of a new generation of young men—derided as 'the Milner kindergarten'—from Oxford, who included Leo Amery, Philip Kerr (later Lord Lothian), John Buchan, and Lionel Curtis. But

Milnerism was fatally discredited and Milner himself left South Africa in 1905, having refused an offer to succeed Curzon as Viceroy of India. For the last three years as High Commissioner his methods had aroused increasingly virulent criticism in the Liberal and Labour ranks, particularly over 'Chinese slavery', and he had incurred the formidable and unremitting hostility of Campbell-Bannerman.

One major consequence of the war had been to expose Britain's isolation in Europe. The Anglo-Japanese alliance of 1902 had done nothing to change this situation, but it was to have substantial results. It was the first formal recognition of equality in modern history between a European great power and a non-European one. Without this alliance, it is highly improbable that the Japanese would have embarked upon their successful war with Russia—described by Balfour as 'not an unmixed curse'—and thus helped to precipitate the abortive Russian revolution of 1905. From the British point of view, the object of the alliance was to restrain Russian ambitions in the Far East, and as such was highly successful. But it also committed them to support for Japanese ambitions, particularly in Korea, and thus marked a very significant move away from the policy of avoiding formal international commitments that had been dominant since 1878.

The Anglo-French Entente of 1904 was, in essentials, a successful attempt to settle a number of matters which had caused friction between the two countries abroad, particularly in Africa. At the time there was no intention that this should draw Britain into closer involvement with France on a *European* basis, but it was a shift in policy which was to have vast consequences. Europe was slowly dividing itself into two camps; the British had taken the first step towards taking sides, in involving herself in European entanglements against which Rosebery in particular had constantly urged. It was significant that Rosebery was the only leading British politician to attack the Entente; in public, he said that it was more likely to lead to war than to peace; in private he said that it would lead 'straight to war'.

*

Balfour's last flickering hope of evading disaster had been the continuance of Liberal dissensions. For a brief moment in November 1905 it seemed as if he had calculated correctly. Rosebery had demanded, and had not received, specific assurances about the abandonment of Home Rule from Campbell-Bannerman. But here there had been a serious misunderstanding; Asquith had been privy to, and had approved, the Liberal leader's guarded declaration, and was amazed and incensed when Rosebery denounced Campbell-Bannerman at Bodmin on November 25th. This had been the last of several misunderstandings in the Liberal League. But this was by no means the only factor in Balfour's calculations. On November 25th he had circulated to the Cabinet a memorandum arguing for resignation—rather than dissolution—early in December. His eyes were more on Chamberlain, who on November 3rd had derided his Parliamentary tactics as 'humiliating' and had declared that he would 'rather be part of a powerful minority than a member of an impotent majority', than on Rosebery. But the Bodmin speech, and the subsequent turmoil, provided an apparent flicker of hope to the stricken Ministry. It was to prove illusory.

On December 4th Balfour resigned, and Campbell-Bannerman was requested by the King to form an Administration. Grey, Asquith and Haldane had agreed in September, while staying at Grey's hunting-lodge at Relugas, not to take office unless Campbell-Bannerman went to the Lords. C-B, fortified by his wife, refused, and the 'Relugas Compact' quickly disintegrated. Significantly, it was Asquith who first urged its dissolution. He became Chancellor of the Exchequer, Haldane Secretary of State for War, and Grey Foreign Secretary. Lloyd George became President of the Board of Trade. Winston Churchill, whose rising reputation was further enhanced by the publication during the election campaign of his superb biography of his father, became Under-Secretary for the Colonies, and thus—as the Colonial Secretary was Lord Elgin—chief spokesman for the Department in the House of Commons. Morley went to the India Office. By December 11th the main offices had been filled and the new Ministers found their way to Buckingham Palace, with considerable difficulty, in a thick and impenetrable fog; after over an hour groping in the Mall and around the uncompleted Victoria Memorial they reached their destination. The first Liberal Government for over a decade was in office.

Of all the leading Liberals, only Rosebery was excluded, and he had, in effect, excluded himself. He was offered the post of Ambassador in Washington, but refused, and he forbade his elder son to accept Campbell-Bannerman's invitation to second the motion for the Address in the new Parliament. It was not long before he found other

13 A. J. Balfour: by Phil May

14 Andrew Bonar Law: by 'Spy', *Vanity Fair*

15 Joseph Chamberlain in 1901: by 'Spy', *Vanity Fair*

16 Winston Churchill: by 'Spy', *Vanity Fair*

17 F. E. Smith: by 'Spy', *Vanity Fair*

reasons for disassociating himself from the Liberal Party whose leader he had been. He was fifty-six, and still a magnetic political figure, but his period in the wilderness had baffled friends and alienated moderates; by now he was politically déconsideré and knew it. The personal magnetism which he exercised had not dimmed in his ten years of political solitariness. 'I sometimes think,' Edward Grey wrote, 'that the reason why Rosebery attracts so much attention is that the genius in him lifts him up so that he is conspicuous in the crowd, a head taller than it. . . . It's as if God dangled him amongst us by an invisible thread.' In 1902, at Glasgow, 32,000 people applied for tickets to hear him deliver a Rectorial Address; over 5,000 were present in the hall to hear him. As Churchill has written of Rosebery's numerous adherents and admirers: 'At first they said "He will come". Then for years "If only he would come". And finally, long after he had renounced politics for ever, "If only he would come back".' Now, even that hope had disappeared.

The new Government was immensely strong, and was generally welcomed. *The Times*, deeply irritated by the unfortunate turn of events, merely announced that 'Sir Henry Campbell-Bannerman has succeeded in forming his Ministry'. Parliament was promptly dissolved.

The Prime Minister's performance in the election was somewhat cursory. He made only two major speeches, at the Albert Hall on December 21st, and in Liverpool on January 9th, and spent the whole of the campaign in Scotland, contenting himself with one printed address to his constituents, by whom he was returned unopposed. In neither did he produce any specific proposals, and concentrated upon criticising his predecessors. These were, however, effectively delivered. A vague reference to making the land 'less of a pleasure-ground for the rich and more of a treasure-house for the nation' sounded good, and there was one passage in the Albert Hall speech—otherwise unexciting and almost inaudible—which was extensively quoted:

The Government has executed what one might call a moonlight flitting. It has run away, not in the broad day of summer, not even in the twilight of October, but in the midnight of December.

We were told—told emphatically and abundantly—that the method of their going would be a masterpiece of tactical skill.

Tactics! Tactics! Ladies and gentlemen, the country is tired of their tactics. It would have been better for them if they had had less of tactics and more of reality.

But they have lived for some years on nothing but tactics. And now they have died of tactics.

It was left to other Liberals—notably Asquith—to spell out the detailed programme dealing with education, drink, trade union reforms, and old age pensions. The Unionist reaction was purely defensive. Balfour spoke scathingly of 'the long catalogue of revolutionary change' proposed by the Liberals, and Chamberlain, after castigating the 'essentially Home Rule and Little Englander Government' devoted his energies to Tariff Reform and Birmingham. 'Captain' Middleton, the awesome 'Skipper' of the Unionist machine, had retired, and had proved to be irreplaceable. Operating quietly, and with considerable acumen, he had been the hidden force in the Salisbury supremacy, and after Salisbury's retirement and death his zest for politics had faded. His rival, Schnadhorst, had never approached Middleton's power, nor his grasp of national and local politics, and Schnadhorst, too, proved to be irreplaceable by the Liberals. Archibald Salridge was still dominant in Liverpool, but only there. Operating out of tiny rooms in St. Stephen's Chambers, with few facilities in staff or finance, Middleton had done more than any other single individual to bring coherence and cohesion into the Unionist coalition, and had shown the way for future central party organisation. But it was to be many years before the lessons that he had quietly imparted were to be fully appreciated.

Looking back, and recalling the schisms in the Unionist ranks and the long list of their by-election disasters since 1903, a Liberal victory seems inevitable. It did not seem so at the time. There were surprisingly few in the Unionist ranks who fully appreciated the magnitude of the disenchantment of the electorate with the Balfour Government.[1] On the other side, many years of Opposition, of false dawns, of hopes shattered, and imminent victories torn away, had left the Liberals hardly daring to hope that their hour of opportunity had come. When Winston Churchill went to see Morley after the latter's appointment as Secretary of State for India, he found him despondent:

'Here I am,' he said, 'in a gilded pagoda.' He was gloomy about the

[1] See, for example, Winterton: *Orders of the Day.*

forthcoming election. He had too long experience of defeat to nourish a sanguine hope. He spoke of the innate strength of the Conservative hold upon England.

Even among those who were confident of victory, there were few who had any premonition of the enormous scale and sweep of the Liberal triumph. On the second day of the results Balfour himself lost his seat in Manchester, and after that it was an avalanche. Brodrick, Lyttelton, Gerald Balfour, Walter Long and Bonar Law were among the Ministerial casualties. Except in Birmingham, where Chamberlain's hold was complete, the Unionists crumbled. 377 Liberals were elected, with a further 24 'Lib-Labs'; the Irish totalled 83, and the new Labour Party had 29 M.P.s; the Conservatives were scythed down to 132, with 25 Liberal Unionists. In total Irish and Labour M.P.s, the Government could count on a majority of 356, a figure unequalled since 1832. Even if all other parties combined against them—a highly unlikely event—the Liberals and Lib-Labs had a majority of 132.

In the astonishment at this landslide, some highly significant facts were overlooked at the time. The vagaries of the British electoral system have rarely been demonstrated with greater emphasis than in 1905. The Unionists received 43·6 per cent of the popular vote, and returned 157 M.P.s: the Liberals received 49 per cent, and had 401 M.P.s. In terms of seats won, the Liberals and their allies had won a total, unimaginable victory; but the proportion of votes showed the extent to which Morley had been right—in spite of everything that had happened since 1900, Britain was still a very Conservative country. Another very significant aspect of the result was that, in the Unionist ranks, the 'Free Fooders' did badly; of the 157 elected, 109 were Chamberlain supporters, 32 can be classified as 'Balfourians', and only 11 were self-styled Free Fooders. Chamberlain, in purely party terms, had won the battle. His immediate supporters were exultant, and, with Balfour out of Parliament, believed that his hour had come. But the strain had been too great. Chamberlain was now over seventy. In 1902 he had been seriously injured in a cab accident in London. He had lived a full life in defiance of the advice of his doctors, one of his more admirable aphorisms being that more people died from taking exercise than from any other cause. Within months of the election he suffered a stroke (July 17th 1906) which incapacitated him totally. There was to be no recovery, no return. He lingered on until the eve of the Great War, in 1914, but his extraordinary career effectively ended in 1906.

But in the Liberal and Labour exhilaration, there was no premonition that this was to be the last General Election in which the Liberals had more Members of Parliament than the Unionists, nor that in less than five years the triumphant majority of 1906 was to be cut down to exact parity. No notice was taken of a significant remark by Balfour on January 15th at Nottingham, to the effect that it was the duty of all to ensure that 'the great Unionist Party should still control, whether in power or whether in Opposition, the destinies of this great Empire'.

Even a swift glance at the political situation should have provided the cause of Balfour's statement. In the Commons the Government had a majority of 356; in the House of Lords the Unionists had a majority of 391. The exultant Liberals were shortly to learn the bitter truth of Rosebery's warnings of 1894.

CHAPTER EIGHT

THE TRIBULATIONS OF THE LIBERALS, 1906-1910

THE EXULTANT Liberal Ministry opened the first Session of the new Parliament with a fanfare of projected legislation, of which the most important were an Education Bill to remedy the Nonconformist grievances of the 1902 Act, a Trade Disputes Bill to reverse the Taff Vale Judgement, and a Plural Voting Bill to prevent the owners of several property qualifications from voting more than once.

This was a very talented Government—perhaps the most talented of any modern Administration—and it entered office confidently. The first and real surprise was Campbell-Bannerman himself. Indolent, affable, and easy-going, he had always commanded a certain respect, but had never been regarded as a probable Prime Minister. He had emerged from the party disputes over the Boer War with heightened authority, but he never could be described as a widely popular figure in the country nor as a dominant Parliamentarian. Balfour dismissed him as 'a mere cork', but it was quickly evident that it was Balfour, and not Campbell-Bannerman, who was out of touch with realities. When Balfour returned to the House of Commons as Member for the City of London on March 12th, he delivered one of those clever debating speeches which in previous Parliaments had delighted his supporters and humiliated his foes. This time, and before this new Parliament, it was ill-received, and was contemptuously dismissed by a speech by Campbell-Bannerman which lasted barely four minutes, and which opened with the devastating words: 'The right hon. gentleman is like the Bourbons. He has learned nothing. He comes back to this new House of Commons with the same airy graces, the same subtle dialectics, and the same light and frivolous way of dealing with great questions. He little knows the temper of the new House of Commons if he thinks those methods will prevail here'; and he ended: 'I say, enough of this foolery. . . . Move your amendments and let us get to business.' The speech did not destroy Balfour, but it made Campbell-Bannerman. As a result of the lingering death of his wife, followed by his own decline which resulted in his death two years later, his appearances in the House became very few, but his authority was unchallenged.

Balfour was far from finished, and it was on the Education Bill that he showed his hand. He and Lansdowne, the Unionist leader in the Lords, had agreed, as Balfour had written to him on April 13th, that 'the two Houses shall not work as two separate armies, but shall co-operate in a common plan of campaign'. He now made it plain in public that the Lords were going to deal with the Bill in detail. 'The real discussion of this question', he declared, 'is not now in this House . . . the real discussion must be elsewhere.' The bluntness and nakedness of this statement startled even some of the Unionists. It was the first shot in a struggle that was to bring the Unionists substantial short-term advantages, and which was eventually to rebound disastrously against them and their chosen instrument of obstruction, the House of Lords.

The mood of the Unionist minority was aggressive. Its excited reactions to a most untypical maiden speech by F. E. Smith, a brilliant, arrogant, and tragically flawed man, was evidence of their violent temper.

Smith's speech contained one particular thrust that established his position, when he provoked Lloyd George into an angry denial that he had claimed that the Unionists would introduce slavery on the hills of Wales. Smith continued:

> The Rt. Hon. gentleman would no doubt be extremely anxious to forget it but, anticipating a temporary loss of memory, I have in my hand the *Manchester Guardian* of January 11, 1906, which contains a report of his speech. The Rt. Hon. gentleman said: 'What would they say to introducing Chinamen at one shilling a day in the Welsh quarries? Slavery on the hills of Wales! Heaven forgive me for the suggestion!'
>
> I have no means of judging how Heaven will deal with persons who think it decent to make such suggestions.

When he rose to speak, F. E. Smith was unknown. When he sat

down his reputation was made. The reports of his triumph spread rapidly through the demoralized Unionists throughout the country. There was rarely a debut like it before; certainly never one since.

The Conservative Party does not show up to advantage in Opposition. Regarding itself as the natural governing party, it views years in Opposition as unnatural interludes in the real purpose of this confederation. In Opposition, the Conservatives are not choosy about their weapons or their tactics. By deliberately fostering these attitudes, Balfour was also creating the passions that were to cost him the Unionist leadership.

Balfour, having thrown down the gauntlet on the Education Bill, then prepared the amendments which the House of Lords was to make to it. It was this kind of tactic that made Lloyd George retort to the claim that the Lords were 'the watchdog of the Constitution', by claiming that they were 'Mr. Balfour's Poodle'. The Lords duly mutilated the Bill, and the Government passed, by a majority of 416 to 107, a motion disagreeing with the amendments *en bloc*. The Lords promptly passed a motion insisting on the amendments. Private attempts at compromise were unsuccessful, and the Government had to abandon the Bill. Campbell-Bannerman wanted to dissolve on the cry of 'the Peers against the People', but the perils of such a course were many and considerable. The Lords, advised by Balfour, were very careful to accept the Trade Disputes Bill, but they threw out the Plural Voting Bill on Second Reading after a cursory debate of barely one and a half hours.

In the 1907 session the effects on Liberal morale of these unexpected setbacks were evident. A feeble Education Bill was introduced, was cursed by both sides, and was ignominiously withdrawn. An Irish Devolution Bill was hailed with contempt by the Irish and derision from the Unionists; it, too, was hastily withdrawn. A Licensing Bill was announced, but Ministers became increasingly apprehensive about taking on a fight with the Lords on the subject of temperance reform, an issue dear to Liberal hearts but never very close to the hearts of the British electorate. Faced with this impasse, the Government decided, not without dissensions, to pass a resolution declaring that the will of the Commons must prevail. It was a heated debate which lasted three days, in which Lloyd George and Churchill thundered at the Tories, Churchill describing the Lords as 'a one-sided, hereditary, unprized, unrepresentative, irresponsible absentee'.

But resolutions, however fierce, had no legal or constitutional effect, and the Unionist leaders were untroubled.

Ensor was representative of Liberal opinion when he wrote of this performance:

> In the light of post-war democracy no student can avoid asking, how practical men like Balfour and Lansdowne—the former of high and latter of flexible intelligence—could be so short-sighted . . . scarcely distinguishing in their minds between the Constitution and the dominance of their own order, they felt justified in using any resource of the former, however unfairly one-sided it might otherwise have appeared, in order to crush the challenge to the latter.[1]

Thus Ensor, and others, have regarded Balfour's tactics in a *class* sense. But this was only partially true. Politics is about power; deprived of it, one uses what weapons are available to harass and embarrass one's opponents. All the Unionists had after 1906, apart from obstruction in the Commons, was the House of Lords, until the nation could be brought back to Conservatism. These tactics had worked admirably in 1893–5, and, for the two years of Campbell-Bannerman's Premiership it worked well again. Ideology was important, but in fact Balfour and Lansdowne were playing party politics. Until too late, they did not realise how dangerous the new game was.

Old, tired, but defiant, Campbell-Bannerman would have dissolved Parliament at once and fought the Lords, but neither his Party nor his colleagues wanted another election so soon, having savoured office after a decade of impotence. Subsequently, the predicament of the Government was greatly complicated by the rapid decline of the Prime Minister. The death of his beloved wife had been a devastating blow, and may have contributed to his first heart attack in October 1906. In June 1907 he suffered another, and in November a third. Most of his colleagues viewed his probable departure with apprehension, convinced, as Haldane wrote, that 'C.B. is the only person who can hold this motley crew together'. But on February 12th 1908 he presided over his last Cabinet and made his final appearance in the House of Commons; on the following day he had another heart attack, and it was obvious to those close to him that the end was approaching.

Not all Liberals viewed the prospect of Asquith, the natural successor, with much enthusiasm, but Campbell-Bannerman dictated a

---

[1] R. C. K Ensor, op. cit., 387–8.

letter which was read to the Cabinet and which put the succession beyond doubt. But the Prime Minister did not resign, and the Cabinet —and particularly Asquith—became uneasy and restive. In fact, the cause lay less with C-B than with the King, who did not wish to cut short his holiday at Biarritz. Thus, it was not until April 3rd that the dying Prime Minister was permitted to resign, and Asquith was summoned to Biarritz to kiss hands upon his appointment. Campbell-Bannerman died, still in 10 Downing Street, on April 22nd. He fully deserved Lloyd George's tribute that 'he was a big figure, and got bigger as he advanced'. But it was also the case that for nearly a year— a vital year for the Government—he was a lonely, sad, and ailing man.

But Campbell-Bannerman's brief Premiership was not devoid of achievement. The most considerable was the granting of self-government to the Transvaal, in which Churchill and Smuts were deeply involved. It was bitterly opposed by the Unionists, and described by Balfour as 'the most reckless experiment ever tried in the development of a great colonial policy', warning that the Boers would make 'every preparation, constitutionally, quietly, without external interference, for a new war'. Churchill, in one of a series of remarkable speeches as junior Minister at the Colonial Office that marked him out for rapid promotion, appealed in vain for the Opposition to make self-government 'the gift of England' rather than that of a Party. The Unionists, inflamed by Liberal attempts to censure Milner, and by what Chamberlain described as Churchill's 'insulting protection' of him, were irreconcilable. Fortunately, their virulent opposition had little effect on the Boer leaders—notably Botha and Smuts—who were highly impressed by British magnanimity and understanding. The intervention of South Africa in both world wars on the British side— and particularly in 1939—stemmed directly from this reaction. Campbell-Bannerman's denunciation of 'methods of barbarism' paid handsome dividends for British long-term interests.

This was very much a personal triumph for Campbell-Bannerman, and it was followed by the grant of self-government to the Orange Free State. These generous acts led directly to the creation, in 1908, of the Union of South Africa, made by the elected representatives of Cape Colony, the Transvaal, Natal and the Orange Free State, and ratified by the British Parliament. No one contributed more to this result than the Prime Minister of Cape Colony—Dr. Jameson. In politics, time often brings strange reverses; this may be regarded as one of the strangest of all.

Subsequently, with the advantages of hindsight, we can look on this settlement with something less than the enthusiasm with which liberals everywhere hailed it at the time and for a long time afterwards. It was very much self-government for the whites in South Africa; it was impossible to foresee the evil long-term consequences of such an arrangement. But one must be fair. Politicians can only legislate for the present and for the foreseeable future; it is only long afterwards that the full effects of their actions can be adequately gauged. Judged by the standards, and the conditions, of the time it was a notable achievement.

But at home, the Lords were now in full cry. Land Reform was the main object of the 1907 Session, and four Bills were introduced, one for England, one for Ireland, and two for Scotland. The English and Irish Bills were brutally mutilated by the Lords and the Scottish pair were contemptuously thrown out.

It was perhaps surprising that any legislation got through at all. Lloyd George, at the Board of Trade, was showing just how able a Minister he was. The Merchant Shipping Act of 1906 confined pilots' licences to British subjects, restricted the employment of foreign seamen, provided better food, accommodation and terms of service in British ships, and compelled foreign ships to conform to British standards if they used British ports. The Patents Act of 1907 was another excellent and practical measure, although, by compelling patentees to work their patents in Britain within three years, it, too, was somewhat protectionist in tone. Other measures that escaped the Lords' veto provided free medical inspections and meals for elementary school children, another modest, but in its implication very progressive, advance in social reform.

Lloyd George was also responsible for taking (for the first time) a Census of Production, and for settling a major railway dispute in 1907 that imperilled the nation with a General Strike. He also created the Port of London Authority, that gave London a single central authority to administer the vast tangle of small companies and docks.

Haldane, meanwhile, was being highly—although less obviously—active at the War Office. His most important acts were the creation of a General Staff on the German pattern, and the establishment of an Expeditionary Force of six infantry divisions and one cavalry division, with artillery, transport, medical and all other logistic elements ready for rapid mobilisation and movement overseas, with suitable reserves ready. A Territorial Force—merging the Old Yeomanry and Volunteers—was also created, consisting of fourteen Divisions and fourteen mounted brigades, with their own transport, medical and other services.

In this work Haldane of course did not act alone. The Royal Commission that had investigated the lessons of the Boer War provided much valuable material; the Committee of Imperial Defence rather lost its strategic value under the Liberals, but was of considerable use in making contingency plans and undertaking specific studies, and the compilation of the War Book was one particularly significant aspect of its work. Haldane has perhaps been overpraised but it can be said of him that he provided exactly the right personal encouragement for reforms, and had clear enough ideas of what was necessary. In August 1914, twenty infantry divisions and one cavalry division, with full equipment, were mobilised swiftly and efficiently and dispatched to France. Its quality was outstanding. And this was accomplished at the same time as economies were achieved in the cost of the Army.

One controversy that gradually became more acrimonious during these years concerned conscription. The voices advocating it included that of Lord Roberts, and Haldane's opposition to it contributed to the subsequent charges that he had not properly prepared the nation for war. There was no question of a Liberal Government introducing conscription, and the Unionists had been highly embarrassed by Roberts's campaign. But in denouncing it, Haldane was able to divert Liberal attention away from the implications of his own policies. Few of Haldane's colleagues were greatly interested in military affairs, and he was given a remarkably free hand, as was Grey in the Foreign Office. In both cases there was actual deception by these Ministers of the Cabinet and the Liberal Party.

The first, and most significant, deception occurred following the Franco-German Morocco Crisis, when Grey had authorised Anglo-French military conversations in January 1906. Campbell-Bannerman, Asquith and Haldane were also consulted; the rest of the Cabinet was not, and there was to be a memorable explosion in 1911 when the Cabinet first heard of the action. Although these conversations did not bind either side, they were a truly momentous step away from isolationism. The failure to consult the Cabinet has had many ingenious explanations; the real reason was that pacifism was still strong both in it and in the Liberal Party, as the events of August 1st-3rd 1914 were to prove, and as the virulent opposition of Lloyd George and Churchill to the expanded Naval Estimates in 1908 emphasised.

Haldane was not anti-German, a fact that was to end his political career. Grey, however, had become increasingly persuaded by his Foreign Office advisers of the reality of German ambitions and by the threat posed to France. Sir Eyre Crowe's famous 'Memorandum on the present State of British Relations with France and Germany' (January 1st 1907) spelt this out very clearly. German actions—and particularly the expansion of the German Navy—did much to convince other sceptical Ministers, notably Churchill and Lloyd George, that a real threat existed. Little was attempted to resolve the increasing tension between the two nations, and British policy— unknown to the majority of the Cabinet—increasingly assumed a hostile Germany. On August 31st 1907, Britain moved even further away from isolationism by signing the Anglo-Russian Convention, the decisive step towards the Triple Entente. This was deeply repugnant to the left wing of the Liberal Party and the Labour Party, to whom association with the Tsarist autocracy had a profound symbolic meaning. The Liberal Party swallowed it, but with evident un-happiness. Had it known of the Anglo-French military commitment the alarm and disillusionment would have been formidable indeed. It is still difficult to gauge whether Grey's secretiveness—learned from Rosebery—was in the long-term national interest.

*

Meanwhile, the Government was enduring harassing fire from another, and quite unexpected, source. In 1903, chagrined by years of futile polite agitation, a group of feminist extremists founded the Women's Social and Political Union at Manchester. Its founder, head, and driving spirit was Mrs. Emmeline Pankhurst. In 1907 the extremists formed the Women's Freedom League.

Their first victim was the mild Grey, who supported women's suffrage, but who had one of his meetings rudely interrupted in the 1905 Election Campaign. Churchill, more understandably, suffered similar harassment. This was just the beginning. Everywhere, it was the Liberals who suffered, on the grounds that they were the Govern-ment Party. At times the lives of Ministers were even in danger, and public attitudes veered sharply between admiration and sympathy for women imprisoned for their political ideals and made to endure forcible feeding when they went on hunger strike, to outrage when houses were burned down and physical violence was attempted on leading politicians.

Perhaps the violence and hysteria of the Suffragette movement were symptomatic of the fever that ran through the country during this time, and which made 'the Edwardian Age' so much less placid to contemporaries than to subsequent observers. It was particularly hard that Liberals, like Grey and Lloyd George, who favoured women's suffrage were also objects of abuse and attack. Every Liberal candidate was exposed to the danger of his meetings being broken up by screaming women, and it was understandable that in these violent circumstances Liberal sympathy for the cause of female suffrage dimmed sharply. Some Liberals—notably Asquith and Churchill—were actively opposed to the idea, and ensured that every attempt to pass a Suffrage Bill went down to defeat.[1] Throughout these years, the Suffragettes provided an additional, and fierce, distraction for Ministers, which aided neither their cause nor the process of Government. Of greater significance politically was the fact that the Liberals abandoned franchise reform as a possible initiative, partly because of the issue of women's suffrage and also because it would inevitably bring up the fact that the Irish Nationalists were grossly over-represented.

*

When Asquith succeeded the dying Campbell-Bannerman in April 1908—kissing hands in the incongruous surroundings of the Hotel du Palais at Biarritz, and tactfully averting a characteristic proposal by the King that the members of the new Cabinet should accept their Seals of Office in the Hotel Crillon in Paris—he made only a few changes in his Government, of which the most important were the elevation of Winston Churchill to the Cabinet as President of the Board of Trade and the promotion of Lloyd George to the Exchequer.

---

[1] The debates on the issue were characterised by observations which read oddly today, but which were widely applauded (or at least accepted) at the time. Among the most vehement opponents of women's suffrage was F. E. Smith, who put forward to the House of Commons the asinine proposition that 'I venture to say that the total sum of human happiness, knowledge and achievement, would remain unaltered if . . . Sappho had never sung, Joan of Arc had never fought, Siddons had never played, and if George Eliot had never written'.

Most unfortunately, he did not remove John Burns from the Local Government Board. Burns, who had started in the early Labour movement, had rapidly proved himself an entrenched conservative. He was responsible for poor-law, municipal government, housing, town-planning, and public health. For the following nine years this Department was an oasis of reaction in a generally progressive Government.[1]

By this stage the Liberal situation had become very serious indeed. Few measures of real significance had been passed without the personal blessing of Balfour and Lansdowne. As Roy Jenkins has commented:

> For three years the smallest Opposition within living memory had effectively decided what could, and what could not, be passed through Parliament. In the language of the day, the cup was full, and the sands were exhaustively ploughed.[2]

If Asquith's inheritance was a bleak one, he was admirably qualified to lead a brilliantly talented but somewhat confused Government. He was to prove, in the best sense of the word, an opportunist, giving his Ministers remarkable latitude and his full support when he agreed with their case. 'When the need required it,' Churchill later wrote, 'his mind opened and shut smoothly and exactly, like the breech of a gun.'

His cool deliberation was at once put to severe test. His situation was far from encouraging. The record of the Government in by-elections was confirming the success of Balfour's tactics. Exasperated by the lack of progress, the Independent Labour Party put up its own candidate—a strange young man called Victor Grayson—at a by-election in the Colne Valley; Grayson, describing himself as a 'clean Socialist', won in a three-sided contest in a seat held by the Liberals. This was an unpleasant jolt both to the Liberals and the leaders of the Labour Party in the Commons. Fortunately, perhaps, Grayson was not a very influential or able man, was addicted to alcohol and exciting society, and disappeared in very mysterious and unexplained circumstances after he lost his seat in the 1910 election.

But Grayson did represent a growing impatience in the Labour

---

[1] It would be sad to omit the famous story that when Burns was invited by Campbell-Bannerman to join the Government he cried out, 'Well done, Sir 'enry! That's the most popular thing you've done yet'. (See, *inter alia*, Hugh Dalton: *Call Back Yesterday*, 147.)

[2] Roy Jenkins: *Mr. Balfour's Poodle* (1954).

Movement with the slowness of the arrival of the Promised Land; it aroused all the feelings against the MacDonald–Gladstone Pact—the feeling that, as four members of the Independent Labour Party Council declared in a pamphlet published in 1910 under the title *Let Us Reform the Labour Party*, 'Labour must fight for Socialism and its own Land against BOTH the Capitalist parties IMPARTIALLY'. In 1908 the Liberals lost no less than eight by-elections, and Winston Churchill was defeated at North-West Manchester, when seeking re-election on his appointment to the Board of Trade.[1] If this went on, the great Liberal Dawn of 1906 would turn out to be bleak indeed.

But deliverance was to come from the Opposition. Up to this point, the Lords had not dared to mangle Money Bills, and it was evident to Ministers that the Government's only serious hope of passing major social legislation was to incorporate it in Finance Bills. Lloyd George, in framing his first Budget, had to raise substantial new revenue for Old Age Pensions and the increased naval expenditure which he and Churchill had opposed so vehemently that Asquith had written in his diary at one stage that 'there are moments when I am disposed summarily to cashier them both'. It is extremely doubtful if Lloyd George framed the Budget deliberately to confront the Lords. Few thought that the Lords would be mad enough to reject a Money Bill, and those Ministers who thought it possible welcomed the prospect.

The Budget required the raising of £16 million. To do this, Lloyd George increased Death Duties on estates over £5,000, and income tax—from 1s. to 1s. 2d. in the £—and introduced a super-tax of 6d. in the £ on the amount by which all incomes of £5,000 or more exceeded £3,000. There were heavier taxes on tobacco and spirits, and the liquor licence duties were increased. The only concession was the introduction of children's allowances. The really dramatic innovation, however, were the Land Taxes—a duty of twenty per cent on the unearned increment of land values, to be paid whenever land changed hands, and also a duty of ½d. in the £ on the capital value of undeveloped land and minerals. This meant, of course, a complete valuation of the land of Britain. It is not surprising that many Ministers regarded this as very strong meat to swallow. In the picturesque phrase of John Burns, his Cabinet colleagues deliberated upon this alarming document 'like nineteen rag-pickers round a 'eap of muck'. But it went through the Cabinet after a series of tussles.

[1] He was almost immediately returned for Dundee.

The reactions of the Unionists were immediate and intense. Rosebery called it 'inquisitorial, tyrannical and Socialistic'; Sir Edward Carson described it as 'the beginning of the end of all rights of property'; Balfour condemned it as 'vindictive, inequitable, based on no principle, and injurious to the productive capacity of the country'. From Highbury, the stricken Joseph Chamberlain echoed these assaults.

A Budget Protest League was formed, and it was at once evident that the Government was in for a fight. Its supporters, restive and dispirited for so long, gleefully took up the battle for 'the People's Budget', described by Lloyd George as 'a war Budget—for raising money to wage implacable warfare against poverty and squalidness'. In the Commons, the Unionists waged a marathon battle against the Bill, forcing the Government to employ the 'kangaroo' closure, and occupying virtually the entire time of the House. In the country, the Liberals took up the Unionists' challenge with gusto, and Churchill became President of the Budget League, and he and Lloyd George went on the stump to great effect—to such effect indeed that the King joined in the protests at the violence of their language. The Budget Protest League began to wither in the face of this counter-assault, and Unionists themselves were becoming uneasy about the effect on public opinion of the squealings of the landed and moneyed classes.

This was exactly the kind of situation in which Lloyd George thrived, and in a speech in Limehouse, in July, he raised the issue of the class war in language not heard from a leading politician since Chamberlain had assailed Salisbury in 1883 as the representative of a class 'that toils not, neither does it spin'. The fire and eloquence of Churchill, however, were a considerable surprise, and incensed the Unionists far more, and not least because they strongly questioned his sincerity. In fact, Churchill had become enraptured by the issue of social reform,[1] and was proving a remarkably successful Minister. His speeches on the Budget further enhanced his reputation with the

[1] It was of Churchill that Charles Masterman wrote to his wife in February 1908 that 'He is full of the poor whom he has just discovered. He thinks he is called by Providence—to do something for them. . . I challenged him once on his exposition of his desire to do something for the people. "You can't deny you enjoy it all immensely—the speeches and crowds, and the sense of increasing power." "Of course I do," he said. "Though shalt not muzzle the ox when he treadth out the corn. That shall be my plea at the day of judgement".'

Liberals, and led to a corresponding further decline in his relationship with the Opposition.

There remained the House of Lords. Joseph Chamberlain, from his sick-bed, urged the Lords to reject the Bill—a curious final intervention, and one that added to his unenviable record for destroying parties. The Liberal leaders—at least Churchill and Lloyd George—viewed the prospect of the Lords mangling or rejecting the Bill with enthusiasm. Lloyd George rose to the occasion with a speech at Newcastle-upon-Tyne on October 10th in which he accused the Lords being about to initiate a revolution 'which the people will direct', and describing the Lords as '500 men, ordinary men chosen accidentally from among the unemployed'; the people, he prophesied, would ask also who made 10,000 people owners of the soil 'and the rest of us trespassers in the land of our birth'. Other ugly questions would be asked as well, he said, and added:

> The answers are charged with peril for the order of things the Peers represent; but they are fraught with rare and refreshing fruit for the parched lips of the multitude who have been treading the dusty road along which the people have marched through the dark ages which are now emerging into the light.

On November 10th 1909, the Unionists decided to kill the Budget. It was as much an emotional as a political decision. Lloyd George may not have framed the Budget to precipitate a head-on clash with the Lords, but his subsequent speeches had succeeded in provoking them mightily. At the end of November the Lords threw out the Finance Bill by 350 to 75. 'Liberty', Lloyd George thundered, and with good cause, 'owes as much to the foolhardiness of its foes as it does to the sapience and wisdom of its friends. . . . At last the cause between the Peers and the People has been set down for trial in the grand assize of the people, and the verdict will come soon.'

Parliament was promptly dissolved after the Liberals had passed a resolution condemning the action of the Lords. The great Constitutional Struggle of 1910–11 had begun.

*

In spite of many achievements in most difficult circumstances, it would be to understate the case to say that the first three years of the Liberal Government had been a considerable disappointment to its supporters. Its two major popular successes had been the Trade Disputes Act of 1906 and the Old Age Pensions Act of 1909. The latter gave a non-contributory pension of five shillings a week to persons over seventy and seven shillings and sixpence to married couples, provided that income from other sources did not exceed ten shillings a week. This very modest grant[1] aroused at the time intense enthusiasm, and it was indeed a very significant step, described by Rosebery—now firmly in spirit if not in fact in the Conservative camp—as 'so prodigal of expenditure that it was likely to undermine the whole fabric of the Empire'.

One other notable advance had occurred. The Morley-Minto Reforms in India made the legislative councils, hitherto nominated, at least partially elective, and increased their scope. Indians were also to be allowed to become members of executive councils. These changes did not alter the reality of the situation in India, but they marked the first tentative steps in the direction of the Chelmsford Reforms of 1919–20 to the granting of Dominion Status in 1935. This new phase was agreed at the fifth Colonial Conference in 1907, which also marked the failure of plans for Imperial Preference when Canada and the Transvaal insisted that each member must have the right to determine its own fiscal system.

There had been other achievements. Churchill, at the Board of Trade, had become an ardent believer in social reform—albeit with an important qualification. 'He desired in Britain', as Charles Masterman commented rather sharply, 'a state of things where a benign upper class dispensed benefits to an industrious, *bien-pensant* and grateful working class.' Churchill's social reform phase was not to last very long, but while it lasted it had excellent practical results. The establishment of Labour Exchanges and the protection of certain 'sweated' trades in the Trade Boards Act of 1909 were notable acts of social improvement, and the Coal Mines Act of 1908 had established a statutory eight-hour day in the mines; this was the first occasion on which the working hours of adult males was limited by statute, and it was a significant portent.

Churchill had demonstrated considerable ability at the Colonial Office, and enhanced that reputation at the Board of Trade. His freshness, youth and exhilaration, combined with an insatiable hunger for work, genuinely impressed all who worked with him. 'More than

[1] Its cost in the first financial year was £6 million.

any man of his time', the Liberal journalist and commentator, A. G. Gardiner, wrote of him in 1908, 'he approaches an issue without mental reserves and obscure motives and restraints. You see all the processes of his mind. He does not "hum and ha". He is not paralysed by the fear of consequences, nor afraid to contemplate great changes. He is out for adventure. He follows politics as he would follow the hounds.' But, already, he had acquired formidable opponents. The Unionists regarded him as a turncoat; not all Liberals were wholly convinced of his full dedication to radical policies. As Asquith's daughter later wrote: 'It was not in principle or theory that he differed from the rank and file of his party. It was the soil from which he had sprung, his personal background, context and experience which made him seem a foreign body among them, and as such, at times (unjustly) suspect.' His handling of the 1911 railway strike was to heighten many of these suspicions.

The claim of the Liberals that they were 'the fathers of the Welfare State'—a claim ceaselessly and wearyingly reiterated in later years by Liberal orators—has some basis in fact. But it was a cautious reforming Government of the nineteenth century Liberal pattern, in which individual Ministers dealt with problems as they arose or which particularly interested them. There was no driving force towards reform, and no central planning or direction. If Burns, at the Local Government Board, had been more energetic, competent and imaginative—or had been replaced by someone who was—the social record of the Government would have been considerably more impressive; but the mere fact that Burns remained in this office until his resignation over the intervention in the war in August 1914 emphasises the character of the Asquith Government. It tinkered—often very effectively—with social problems on the classic nineteenth century pattern; at no point did it deal with fundamental social problems; at root, it was emphatically a Free Trade and Laissez-Faire Government. It moved slowly and carefully, under a leader whose conservatism was deeply ingrained, who distrusted enthusiasm, who dealt with matters as they arose, and who was a master of political judo. By these tactics he held his government together and, on the whole, dominated it; but domination is not always the same as leadership. The vital feature of the Welfare State—massive State intervention in the life of the individual—was conspicuously absent in the pre-1914 Liberal Government, and no assaults on Socialism were more trenchant and swingeing than those delivered by Lloyd George and Churchill. In its approach, if not in some of its measures, this was a Government of which Mr. Gladstone would have been proud.

*

The enormity of what the Lords had done in rejecting the Finance Bill can hardly be over-emphasised. They had left the Government with no choice other than that between resignation and dissolution. The Legislature had refused Supply to the Government, and it simply could not go on. The Unionists' retort was that Lloyd George had himself broken the conventions of the constitution by 'tacking' legislation—such as the Land Valuation Bill—onto the Finance Bill. This, it was riposted, was necessary as a result of the performance of the Lords since 1906. 'We all know', Balfour had said on June 24th 1907, 'that the power of the House of Lords . . . is still further limited by the fact that it cannot touch Money Bills, which if it could deal with, no doubt it could bring the whole executive government of the country to a standstill'. This was precisely what had occurred, and Balfour had been to a large extent responsible for the situation.

In spite of the emotive cry of 'the Peers against the People', the Liberals fought the General Election of January 1910 under several disadvantages. Asquith described the issues as being 'the absolute control of the Commons over finance, the maintenance of Free Trade, and the effective limitation and curtailment of the legislative powers of the House of Lords'. In effect, the election was to be over the Budget of 1909; compared with 1905, it was a somewhat slender and un-exciting platform, and Asquith's performance was noticeably lacking in vigour; Lloyd George characteristically added some much-needed colour.

Asquith fought the campaign under one disability which was not known at the time. He opened with a speech at the Albert Hall with the declaration that 'We shall not assume office and we shall not hold office unless we can secure the safeguards which experience shows us to be necessary for the legislative utility and honour of the party of progress.' This was interpreted widely to mean that Asquith had secured the agreement of the King to redress the Liberal disadvantage in the Lords by the creation of a mass of new Peers.

In fact, the matter had been raised with the King, who had made it absolutely plain that he would not agree to such a creation without another General Election. This was made clear again to Asquith by Lord Knollys on December 15th—five days after the Albert Hall speech—in a letter to Asquith's secretary. This was of course a very real personal and political intervention by the Sovereign, but was accepted by the Prime Minister. Unfortunately, the matter was not made completely clear, and from the outset there was an imprecision and vagueness in the relationship between the Sovereign and the Prime Minister which was to bedevil the whole of the constitutional crisis of 1909–11.

Although the Unionists did not maintain their momentum of 1907–9 in by-elections—indeed, they lost all the seats they had won in the previous three years—they won 116 seats and became the majority party in England. Scotland and Wales redressed the balance, but the Liberals' overall advantage had gone. With 275 seats to the Unionists' 273, they now needed the 40 Labour and 82 Irish Nationalist votes to have a working majority. This, in the long run, was the real significance of the election result.

Ministers were now in a profound quandary about which course to follow. Asquith was pestered with unsolicited suggestions. Some Ministers wished to deal with the Lords' power of legislative veto once and for all. Others urged resignation. Others—notably Grey—were for reforming the Lords. Another problem was that the Irish had disliked the liquor taxation in the Budget and had even voted against the second reading. It was to the credit of Ministers that they opposed making any concessions to the Irish on this issue, desperately though they needed their votes. But each side was fully aware of the fact that a new relationship had opened between the Government and the Irish.

The major problem, however, was the matter of the King's 'guarantee' to create Peers. The clear implication given by Asquith in the Albert Hall speech had been that such a guarantee had been given. On February 21st he had to tell the Commons the facts. 'I tell the House quite frankly', he said, 'that I have received no such guarantee and that I have asked for no such guarantee.' The shock to the Liberal rank and file was palpable, and morale slumped. So bad was the situation that some Ministers considered the possibility of immediate resignation, but Asquith stood firm. It was as well that he did. At this point it seemed that, in spite of the election result, Balfour's tactics had played off with brilliant success, and that the Liberals were in a condition of paralysis and despair.

After much discussion and dissension, the Cabinet resolved to proceed by passing resolutions in the Commons which declared (a) that the Lords could not in future amend or reject a Money Bill (the Speaker to determine whether a Bill was, or was not, a Money Bill); (b) that if a Bill were rejected by the Lords it would become law provided that not less than two years elapsed between the introduction in the Commons and its third reading there; and (c) that the maximum duration of Parliaments should be reduced from seven years to five. After the passage of the Resolutions, a Parliament Bill containing their provisions was formally introduced on April 14th. On April 28th the Lords, accepting the decision of the electorate, passed the Finance Bill without a division.

Ministers had resolved that if the Lords rejected the Parliament Bill, steps would be taken—by the exercise of the Royal Prerogative if necessary—to ensure that it was given statutory effect. If that failed, the Government would resign or advise a Dissolution, with the clear implication that the King, in granting the Dissolution, would give assurances that in the event of a Liberal victory he could create sufficient Peers to pass the Bill through the Lords. This was the situation at the end of April when Parliament adjourned for the Easter Recess and the Prime Minister went off on a cruise on the Admiralty Yacht *Enchantress* with Churchill and his young wife as companions.

At this point a major distraction occurred. King Edward VII died suddenly and unexpectedly on the evening of May 6th after a brief illness. No one was prepared for this development. The new King, behind an impressive facade, was ill-equipped for the responsibilities now suddenly cast upon him. 'His planned education', as one of his official biographers has emphasised, 'ended just where and when it should seriously have begun. He was (until he had painfully taken his own education in hand late in life) below the educational and perhaps intellectual standard of the ordinary public school-educated country squire'.[1] King George's interest in intellectual matters was not only non-existent, but was actively hostile. Unlike his father, his tastes were modest and frugal, and although possessed of a formidable temper his preference was for a simple, ordered life. His wife, a lady of great beauty and presence, was austere and shy, and fully shared the King's attitudes. But if King George V was a man of limited intellect,

[1] John Gore: *King George V, A Personal Memoir*, 247–8.

he possessed great application and dedication, which were to give him a shrewdness and wisdom which earned him great and merited respect from his Ministers.

But in 1910 it was evident that he was hopelessly ill-prepared to deal with a complex, bitter, and perilous constitutional crisis. As Asquith subsequently wrote of the King he was 'with all his fine and engaging qualities, without political experience. We were nearing the verge of a crisis almost without example in our constitutional history. What was the right thing to do? This was the question which absorbed my thoughts as we made our way, with two fast escorting cruisers, through the Bay of Biscay, until we landed at Plymouth on the evening of Monday, May 9th.'

What, indeed, was to be done? There were very real humane considerations about confronting the inexperienced King, grieved by the loss of his father, with a major crisis of this complexity. Garvin, in *The Observer*, urged 'The Truce of God', a phrase that caught the popular feeling. This was the background—emotional and political— to the attempt to settle the crisis by negotiation which occupied nearly five months, and which postponed consideration of the most difficult problem of all—whether a guarantee by one Monarch, however reluctantly and cautiously given, was binding upon his successor.

The Constitutional Conference eventually broke down on one point, but it was politically crucial. The Unionists insisted that all constitutional legislation, if rejected twice by the Lords, should be submitted to a national referendum. Lansdowne, the most vigorous advocate of this point, had Home Rule firmly in mind; so had the Liberals, now dependent upon the Irish vote. On almost every other point agreement was reached; the Lords could not reject Money Bills, and if other measures could not gain the support of both Houses two years running the matter would be settled by a Joint Sitting, with the Lords' representation scaled down so that a Liberal Government with a majority of fifty could get its legislation through—after a time. But Lansdowne's intransigence on the constitutional legislation was complete, and it caused the conference to fail.

It is instructive to note how far the party leaders—with the exception of Lansdowne—had got away from their supporters. The rank and file were not consulted at all, and a proposal by Lloyd George—warmly supported by Churchill—for a Coalition made surprising progress before Balfour was told by Akers-Douglas, a former Chief Whip, that the Unionist Party would not tolerate it. This was a curious return to the theme of 'Efficiency' which had been argued by Rosebery seven years earlier, and it was significant that it now attracted Lloyd George and Churchill. The chimera of the great Centre Party was certainly not new, and had been eagerly canvassed by Chamberlain and Lord Randolph in the late 1880s. But that at a time of intense political warfare the most belligerent members of the Cabinet should be advocates of a new alliance was curious indeed.

But all this was unreal. Even if the Constitutional Conference had been successful, it is difficult to see how the Unionist or the Liberal rank and file could have accepted it. The Liberals had just risked all on the issue of the Peers against the People, and the Unionists were adamant on Home Rule. Both Balfour and Asquith made real efforts to reach a solution, but it was perhaps just as well for Asquith that, by the end of the first week in November, both the formal Constitutional Conference and the Coalition proposal had completely dissolved. After 'a rather intimate talk' with Balfour, Asquith reported to his wife that the Unionist leader was 'very pessimistic about the future, and evidently sees nothing for himself but chagrin and a possible private life'. Balfour, at least, was now grimly aware of the position into which he had led the Unionists.

The Cabinet met on November 10th and resolved to go to the country again. It was now essential for Asquith to extract a positive statement from the King, concerning the creation of Peers after the election, that he understood King Edward VII to have conceded. It was a delicate business, and it is difficult to avoid the conclusion that Asquith bungled it when he saw the King on November 11th. The King thought that he would not be asked to commit himself until *after* the election, and he agreed to this with much relief. Clearly, something had been missing in Asquith's presentation of his request, and it is probable that his manner was not well suited to handling the King, who favoured clarity and directness. 'Unaccustomed as he was to ambiguous phraseology', Sir Harold Nicolson has written, 'he was totally unable to interpret Mr. Asquith's enigmas.'[1]

Four days later, on November 15th, the King was accordingly dismayed to learn from Knollys—who saw Asquith on the 14th—that Asquith wanted the guarantee *before* the election. 'What he *now* advocates', Knollys reported, 'is that you should give guarantees *at*

[1] Nicolson: *King George V*, 130.

once for the next Parliament.' The King's other private secretary, Bigge, accordingly telegraphed to Asquith:

His Majesty regrets that it would be impossible for him to give contingent guarantees and he reminds Mr. Asquith of his promise not to seek for any during the present Parliament.

This created another crisis—one between the Sovereign and the Cabinet. It was resolved by the compromise proposal put forward by the Cabinet that although the King should give the undertaking, it should not be made public until the Cabinet thought it necessary.[1]

And there was now another crisis—between the King's two private secretaries, Knollys and Bigge. Of the two, Bigge was the closer to the King, having served him for several years; but Knollys, as King Edward's confidant and adviser, had the far greater political experience. Knollys was in spirit a Liberal, and he thought the Lords 'mad' to reject the Budget. He now advised the King to accept the Cabinet's compromise proposal; Bigge, on the other hand, strongly urged him to reject it in a series of vigorous memoranda. 'Is this straight?' he demanded. 'Is it English? Is it not moreover childish?' On November 16th the King travelled up to London with the determination to refuse the Cabinet's proposal and to send for Balfour. At this point Knollys told him a straight lie; Balfour would not, he said, take office and form an administration if invited to do so by the King. As Knollys told him a straight lie; Balfour would not, he said, take office Government, and had told Knollys positively in this sense. The King was unaware of this until 1913, after Knollys had retired. By his action, Knollys saved the King from an act which would have imperilled the political position of the Monarchy, but it says something for the King's common sense that he considered Knolly's information decisive. It is not surprising that when Balfour discovered Knollys's role he was incensed, a fact which in itself reveals the passions now aroused. Balfour was not normally a man who permitted public controversy to cloud private life; Knollys, henceforth, was an exception.

Thus, on the afternoon of November 16th, the King, with deep repugnance, gave his assent. But it remained, as the King wrote, 'a secret understanding that in the event of the Government being returned with a majority at the General Election, I should use my Prerogative to make Peers if asked for. I disliked having to do this very

[1] See Nicolson, op. cit., 136, for the text of the Minute.

much, but agreed that this was the only alternative to the Cabinet resigning, which at this moment would be disastrous'.[1] Thus, the way was cleared for the second general election in a year—and the second, moreover, in which the electorate and the majority of men in public life were unaware of the secret understanding between Sovereign and Prime Minister.

It was not surprising that public interest in the second election of 1910 was considerably lower than it had been in the first. Nevertheless a remarkable 81·1 per cent of the electorate voted—as opposed to 86·6 per cent in the first election—which demonstrated the fact that politics still occupied a commanding interest in the life of the country. The campaign itself was not devoid of interest and even excitement. Lloyd George in particular was in fine fettle; he declared that 'an aristocracy is like cheese; the older it is the higher it becomes'. When the Unionists alleged that the Liberals and Irish were being supported by American funds after Redmond had toured North America (it was, in the circumstances, somewhat tactless of the Canadian Prime Minister, Laurier, to make a handsome personal contribution) Lloyd George maliciously enquired 'since when has the British aristocracy despised American dollars? They have underpinned many a tottering noble house'. Churchill's cousin, the Duke of Marlborough, who had married Consuelo Vanderbilt and was spending part of the Vanderbilt fortune in restoring Blenheim to its former grandeur, was among those who considered this thrust to be uncomfortably close to the mark. Churchill may have thought so, too.

The campaign also further weakened Balfour's position as leader. With considerable tactical neatness the Liberals argued that if the Unionists believed in a Referendum for Home Rule they should accept one for Tariff Reform. Balfour was caught by this tactical stratagem, and appeared to give his blessing to the idea. The fury of the Tariff Reformers—by now a substantial majority of the Parliamentary party—was considerable, although not public. Balfour was now regarded as a renegade by both extremes and ineffectual by the moderates. His languid leadership grated increasingly on a party avid for office, which wanted action and not philosophical discourses. The fact that he was admired by the Prime Minister in particular was regarded as a positive disadvantage; the Unionists wanted a fighting leader, who would more accurately reflect their detestation of the

---

[1] Nicolson, op. cit., 129.

Liberals. Already, the opposition to his leadership was gathering momentum, and Leo Maxse—the Tariff Reform editor of the *National Review*—coined the phrase 'Balfour Must Go', swiftly adapted to 'B.M.G.'. There were renewed jibes at 'the Hotel Cecil', and it was evident that what Garvin described as 'the Byzantine theory of Unionist leadership—the theory of speechless loyalty to a hereditary succession' was in jeopardy.

The results of the election were a deep disappointment to all parties. Over fifty seats changed hands, but in net terms the Liberals lost three seats and the Unionists one, while the Irish Nationalists and Labour each gained two. The second election of 1910 had been a virtual replica of the first.

*

At the beginning of the new Parliament, Joseph Chamberlain made his last visit to the House of Commons to be formally sworn in. Arthur Lee helped Austen Chamberlain to carry him into the Chamber, having waited until the last Member had left. 'For a few moments he sat, piteously but proudly motionless, whilst his eye slowly surveyed the empty benches and galleries, and then he indistinctly repeated the Oath after the Clerk. To sign the Roll was for him a physical impossibility, but Austen guided his hand sufficiently to make a shaky cross, and then after another poignant pause we carried him out again. As he passed the Chair the Speaker leaned over to touch his helpless hand, and the tragic ceremony was over'.[1]

*

Asquith went into the post-election situation hoping and believing that it would not be necessary to ask the King to implement his secret guarantee. There were some Ministers—notably Churchill, now at the Home Office—who actively wanted the creation. He wanted the Parliament Bill pushed through swiftly and, if progress were delayed, 'we should clink the coronets in their scabbards'. Asquith favoured less heroic stances. Birrell spoke of 'the sudden emergence of a certainty' after the second 1910 election, and so it appeared to all except a substantial portion of the Unionist Party.

The difference between the attitudes of Balfour and Lansdowne again became important. Balfour accepted the verdict of the electorate,

[1] Clark, op. cit., 113.

and assured Knollys (January 10th 1911) that the Opposition would not publicly question the Government on the King's participation. But, on January 29th, Lansdowne saw the King—with Asquith's very reluctant approval—and gained the distinct impression that the King loathed the prospect of the mass creation, and that at least some Ministers were equally unhappy. This gave Lansdowne fresh hope that the 'guarantee' was in fact nothing but a gigantic bluff.

The idea of throwing out the Parliament Bill—an issue on which two General Elections had been held within a year—now began to be seriously canvassed among the Unionist Peers, supported by some Unionist M.P.s, including Austen Chamberlain and F. E. Smith. This was not a rational, nor a deeply-considered step. It was symptomatic of the degree to which many Unionists had lost their sense of political balance. It was not long before a distinct and eventually bitter cleavage developed in the Unionist party between those who knew that the game was up and those who did not.

As an initial tactic, the Unionists took an uncharacteristic interest in House of Lords Reform—on their own terms. As Asquith caustically commented:

> The motive for this feverish exhibition of destructive and constructive ardour is not far to seek. The Tory Party were determined at all hazards not to face another General Election with the incubus of the House of Lords on their back. There must be something to put in its place, something—it did not matter for the moment very much what—but something which could be called a Second Chamber, with a coat, however thin, of democratic varnish.

These endeavours came to an abrupt conclusion when Morley pointed out that the Parliament Bill would apply equally to any new constitution of the Lords as to the old. Lansdowne's reforms were not greatly mourned by either side. Haldane described the debate as 'sombre acquiescence punctuated every now and then by cries of pain'. Meanwhile, at the beginning of March, the Parliament Bill had passed the Commons by a majority of 368 to 273 on second reading. Throughout the early summer it progressed through the Commons. It reached the Lords late in June.

Even the Coronation of King George V and a summer of quite exceptional heat did not push the political battle into the background, and Lloyd George was booed, when entering Westminster Abbey, from the stand reserved for Members of Parliament and their families. The national rejoicings were also marred by a major seamen's strike, and other indications of serious industrial unrest. The sweltering heat of London—the temperature remained in the 90's for weeks, and 100 degrees was recorded on one occasion at Greenwich—no doubt also played its part in what followed.

A kind of madness now gripped the Unionist extremists. The Parliament Bill was massacred in Committee by the Lords, and the Government now determined—very belatedly—to play its trump card, the threat to make a mass creation of Peers. But passions were now at such a pitch that many Unionists simply would not believe the validity of the threat, even when told of it by Balfour on July 7th. The division between those who would 'die in the last ditch' against the Government and the 'hedgers' now became public and acute.

The King, in mid-July, accepted the advice of the Cabinet that the anticipated eventuality had arisen. He did, however, stipulate that the Lords should be given one last chance, and be at least given an opportunity of reconsidering their position. Asquith agreed. Balfour and Lansdowne were told of the position by Lloyd George on July 18th, and, more formally, by letter by Asquith on the 20th. Even Lansdowne realised that the situation was not recoverable. On July 21st he summoned a meeting of 200 Unionist Peers at Lansdowne House, and argued that, in view of the King's guarantee, it was no longer possible 'to offer effectual resistance'. But, like many political generals before and since, he was unable to call the troops back. Some, like Curzon, changed their position, but most of the 'ditchers' were irreconcilable. Under the titular leadership of the eighty-seven-year-old but still lively Earl of Halsbury, they resolved to fight.

In this crisis, Balfour offered no effective leadership. His private contempt for the ditchers was profound; he was, furthermore, heartily sick of the whole business. He published a letter of support for Curzon which further enraged the ditchers. When, on July 24th, they howled Asquith down in the House of Commons when he rose to explain the Government's action of the Lords' Amendments, the demonstration was as much against Balfour as against the Prime Minister. From that moment his leadership was doomed. It was a disagreeable episode, described by Churchill as 'a squalid, frigid, organised attempt to insult the Prime Minister', but characteristic of that torrid summer.

The Constitutional Crisis, amidst stifling heat and in circumstances of high drama, moved towards its close. Relations between the hedgers and ditchers deteriorated further. One 'die-hard' newspaper wrote of the Peers who had voted for the Bill or who had abstained that 'no honest man will take any of them by the hand again, their friends will disown them, their clubs will expel them, and alike in politics and social life they will be made to feel the bitter shame they have brought upon us all'. On July 25th the supporters of Lord Halsbury gave a dinner at the Hotel Cecil, at which Austen Chamberlain referred to 'this revolution, nurtured in lies, promoted by fraud, and only to be achieved by violence', in which the Prime Minister had 'tricked the Opposition, entrapped the Crown and deceived the people'. The Government unenthusiastically prepared its list of five hundred Peers, and, when the Parliament Bill returned to the Lords on August 9th, Morley stated bluntly that if the Lords did not accept it, rejection would be followed by 'a large and prompt creation of peers'.

Although, even at this point, there were those Unionists who could not grasp the reality of the threat, Curzon's efforts, supported by the King, began to make a distinct impression. After a debate in the Lords, on August 9th–10th, of great passion and tension, and in suffocating heat, the Lords passed the Parliament Bill by 131 votes to 114. The King thanked God for deliverance from 'a humiliation which I should never have survived'. His estimate of politicians, never high, had not been raised by his experiences. As his official biographer has written, 'King George remained convinced thereafter that in this, the first political crisis of his reign, he had not been accorded either the confidence or the consideration to which he was entitled.'[1] The list of Liberal Peers was put aside.

*

The Constitutional Crisis of 1909–11 was, of course, the culmination of the battle opened by Balfour in the Education Bill of 1906. The unscrupulous tactic of using the Unionist majority in the Lords to humiliate and negate the Liberal majority had worked with brilliant success up to the rejection of the Budget. Even that action had its credit side for the Unionists, as it forced an election on the Government considerably earlier than it had wanted. It also made the Government look weak and pusillanimous, and to some extent undermined its position as the great reforming party. It now seems clear that Campbell-

[1] Nicolson, op. cit., 139.

Bannerman's desire to dissolve early in 1907 was soundly based, as was Gladstone's in 1893. If the challenge had been taken up earlier, the Liberals might have been spared much. The policy of 'filling the cup', of forcing the Lords to extremes, eventually succeeded, but not before the Liberals had suffered severely themselves. In 1906 they had had the greatest majority of modern politics; by early in 1910 this superiority had been swept away, never, as it happened, to be restored, Most seriously of all, the Constitutional Crisis had absorbed the attention of Ministers for two years, and held up other legislation. It was, all in all, a tragic irrelevancy.

Asquith's own leadership is open to criticism. Until forced by events, and by the extremism of his opponents, he was anxious to negotiate a settlement which would have left the situation basically unchanged. This was characteristic. Asquith was constitutionalist, a gradualist, a believer in established institutions, responsive to enlightened proposals for social reform, but essentially cautious and moderate. He tended to assume in his opponents the same basic philosophy, but Balfour's reasonableness when he fully grasped the enormity of the implications of his strategy was unrepresentative of the fierce mood of the Unionist Party, determined as it was to claw down the Liberals by virtually any means. At no point does Asquith appear to have grasped the extremes to which most Unionists were prepared to go, nor the intensity of their feelings against the Government. His relations with both Kings had been unfortunate, and in his dealings with the Unionists in 1910 he had shown an alarming lack of sensitivity towards the feelings of his own followers.

Thus, the Liberals had won the Constitutional battle that had raged since 1906, and whose first rounds had been fought in 1892–5. But if ever there was a Pyrrhic victory in politics, this was it.

CHAPTER NINE

THE DARKENING SCENE, 1911-1914

SINCE THE defeat of the Second Home Rule Bill in 1893—and, indeed, since the death of Parnell in 1891—the Irish Question had been quiescant in British domestic politics. This calm was deceptive. As Professor Mansergh has written:

> The fall of Parnell marked the beginning of a period of profound disillusion in Ireland, a period in which is to be noted little of obvious interest or activity in the political field and which was yet a period of significant development in national consciousness.[1]

The ending of Parnell's domination—and the circumstances of his downfall—had heralded a return to the harsh faction-battles of Irish domestic politics. For a decade, in spite of the passage in the Commons of the second Home Rule Bill in 1893, the Nationalist movement remained in a state of shock, tormented by internecine feuds. It was not until 1900 that the Parliamentary Party was nominally reunited under the leadership of John Redmond.

Redmond was a gentle, civilised, attractive man. He had been an ardent admirer of Parnell, and he had stood by him resolutely to the end. Like Parnell, he believed that Home Rule must come from Westminster, and must be sought in the constitutional processes. But he did not have a comparable burning passion against England, nor did he ever manage to combine so effectively the militant and constitutional aspects of the Parnellite movement. Although he was capable of fierce statements, his kind personality removed any sting from them. In character and approach he was considerably closer to Isaac Butt than to Parnell.

The Unionist policy of 'killing Home Rule by kindness', combined with a firm application of the law seemed to have had a very considerable measure of success by 1905. The land question, which had lain at

[1] N. Mansergh: *The Irish Question.*

the heart of the Irish Question for the whole of the nineteenth century, had apparently been finally resolved in Wyndham's Land Purchase Act of 1903. It was believed that, with the solution of this hitherto intractable problem, the wider problem itself would be solved. This was not the case. Indeed, the cause of Irish Nationalism entered a new and more complex phase.

The formation in 1893 of the Gaelic League, and the remarkable Irish literary revival at the turn of the century, were manifestations of a new form of Irish Nationalism. Although it was less easy to quantify or identify than the previous forms, in many respects it was a far more serious threat to English domination. Gladstone had rightly said that Irish nationalism was not a passing mood but an inextinguishable passion. The Unionists, in the years 1886–1905, had treated it as a series of specific problems, of which the Land Question had been the most serious and the most important. In fact, the very solution of the Land Question had removed a problem which had obsessed Irishmen for generations, and left them more free to occupy themselves with the wider cause of Irish independence.

Sinn Fein ('Ourselves Alone') was founded by Arthur Griffith in 1905, who wrote in 1910 that:

> Ireland has maintained a representation of 103 men in the English Parliament for 108 years. The 103 Irishmen are faced with 567 foreigners. . . .
>
> Ten years from now the majority of Irishmen will marvel they once believed that the proper battleground for Ireland was one chosen and filled by Ireland's enemies. . . .

Sinn Fein achieved little of practical political importance before 1914, but its very creation, at a time when most Englishmen believed that the Irish Question was solved, was in itself significant. So were the strikes organised by the Irish Transport Workers' Union during 1912 and 1913, run by James Larkin and James Connolly. The differences between Irish Labour and Sinn Fein were those of priorities. Irish Labour believed that social reform must precede independence; Sinn Fein argued that independence must come first. In fact, as subsequent events were to demonstrate, the differences between Sinn Fein and Irish Labour were neither serious nor profound. After 1913 Irish Labour became more nationalistic in outlook, a fact signified by Connolly's increasing participation in the national movement.

Unionist satisfaction at the economic position in Ireland reads oddly when compared with the actual facts. The improvement was only relative. Rural poverty may have been reduced; urban poverty was still appalling. Housing conditions in Belfast and Dublin were among the worst in Europe. Wages were very low. The death rate in Dublin was 27·6 per 1,000 in 1911, the highest of any capital in Europe and higher than that of Calcutta. These were fertile breeding-grounds for sectarian bitterness. The old division between 'Constitutional' and 'violent' approaches to Home Rule in Ireland had become more sophisticated and complex. Sinn Fein had little connection with the Fenians, and scorned the efficacy of sheer physical force to defeat the British. Nevertheless, a far wider gulf separated the Sinn Feiners from the Irish Nationalists at Westminster. It was indeed ironical that these nationalist movements were in revival at a moment when it appeared that the 'Constitutional' approach was at last on the verge of success.

Any examination of the Irish Question from 1912–14 must be made in the context of the political temperature of Britain at the close of 1911. The relationship between the two major parties had deteriorated further, and there was a profound rancour and bitterness in the political battle. The political struggle in Britain rests, in the last analysis, upon mutual acceptance of certain conventions. In their use of the Lords between 1906 and 1911, the Unionists had broken at least one of those conventions. As it approached its culmination, the dialogue between the two parties was harsh, and often hysterical. In the Unionist ranks, the more extreme elements were now in the ascendant, but, in spite of the violence of the Constitutional struggle, it would have been difficult to anticipate the lengths to which the Unionists were prepared to go in their passionate vendetta against the Liberal Government.

This was a period of fever, of violence, and of extreme tensions. 1911 saw the most serious industrial unrest in modern British history; at Liverpool there was savage rioting, and two strikers were shot dead. Unrest flared violently in the South Wales coal fields. There was a railway strike, in the course of which Churchill called out troops without waiting for the local authorities to ask for them; Lloyd George saved what was developing into an ugly situation. Reaction in the Labour Party to Churchill's methods was extremely hostile, and prompted a memorable attack on the Home Secretary by Ramsay MacDonald. In reality, Churchill's conduct in the South Wales miners' dispute had been exemplary, and it was ironical that his name should be excoriated for 'Tonypandy' whereas his impetuous actions in the railway dispute were forgotten. But in Labour memories the two incidents became intermingled, and these episodes marked a significant change in the attitude of the Labour Party towards this colourful, dramatic figure. In the Liberal Party as well, Churchill was being regarded with increasing suspicion and apprehension; to the Unionists he was anathema. These shadows gathering over the most brilliant early career since that of Lord Randolph Churchill were to assume important proportions by 1914.

Tension was also growing abroad. As the Lords were debating the Parliament Bill, the Agadir Crisis was assuming very serious proportions. In September 1911 Italy declared war on Turkey and invaded Tripoli, and the long-delayed dismemberment of the Ottoman Empire began in earnest. The naval race between Britain and Germany maintained its menacing momentum. The Suffragettes developed new methods of violence.[1] It was a time of *sturm und drang*.

*

The recrudescence of the Irish Question in British politics coincided almost exactly with the accession of Bonar Law as Balfour's successor to the Unionist leadership. Balfour's resignation was announced on November 8th. The National Union was due to meet at Leeds the following week, and there was a remarkable concurrence of feeling in the Parliamentary Party that the issue must be resolved before then. A meeting of Unionist M.P.s was arranged for November 13th.

The principal contestants were Austen Chamberlain and Walter Long, the latter justly described by the former as 'a long-time Conservative, a typical country gentleman, and senior to me both in length of service in the House and in Cabinet rank, and he aroused none of the jealousies or doubts which were inseparable from my position'. The problem was not simply that Austen Chamberlain was a Chamberlain, nor that he was still a Liberal Unionist, while Long was a determined Tory squire with impeccable credentials and moderate intellect. The shadows of the Tariff Reform and the constitutional crisis hung over both of them, the Party was in a hectic and

---

[1] The Prime Minister was particularly unimpressed with their extreme methods. As Mr. Fulford has commented, 'The more the women marched, the less his reason marched with them.' (*Votes for Women*, 184).

vehement mood, and the two were personally on very bad terms. After a short period of fierce lobbying by their partisans, they agreed to step aside if a compromise candidate could be found.

As Amery has written of Chamberlain:

> The trouble with Austen was not undue humility or diffidence. He had quite a good opinion of himself. But he had an exaggerated fear of being regarded as pushful. . . . There was in him none of Churchill's ready assertion of a conscious fitness to lead. So he made no attempt to fight for his own hand.[1]

To the surprise of Law and Chamberlain, Bonar Law also came forward—in the view of many contemporaries, pushed forward by his Canadian adventurer friend and recently elected M.P. for Ashton-under-Lyne, Max Aitken, an interpretation not now accepted by historians. The matter was handled by a very small section of the party hierarchy, and Law was submitted to the party meeting as the only candidate for the new Leader in the Commons. Chamberlain, in seconding Law's nomination, admitted that 'there has been a little feeling that the matter has been taken out of the hands of the Party, and too much settled for you before you came to this gathering'. There were many who agreed wholeheartedly, yet in the circumstances they had little choice. Law was unanimously elected Leader.[2]

Law was a cautious and reserved man, 'meekly ambitious' in Asquith's phrase, and one who has been regarded without undue enthusiasm by most historians. He was in many respects an attractive man. He was modest, calm, and unassuming. He was utterly devoid of pomposity. He had no interest in political or social gossip. He was a total abstainer, and wholly unenamoured of the pleasures of the table.[3] The sudden death of his wife in 1909 had accentuated a habitually gloomy and pessimistic outlook on life. His habits were simple, although he was relatively wealthy, and his private character was absolutely beyond reproach. He was a kindly man, to whom his few close associates were utterly devoted. There was a gentleness, compassion and simplicity in his character which was rare and refreshing. As

[1] Amery: *My Political Life*, Vol. I, 386.

[2] For the best account of this curious episode see Robert Blake: *The Unknown Prime Minister*, pp. 71–86.

[3] 'The food on Bonar Law's table', as Beaverbrook has commented with feeling, 'was always quite execrable. Its sameness was a penance and its quality a horror to me.' This should not be taken too seriously. Beaverbrook's standards were not low.

J. M. Keynes—who subsequently served him at the Treasury—has written of him:

> Many politicians are too much enthralled by the crash and glitter of the struggle, their hearts obviously warmed by the swell and pomp of authority, enjoying their positions and their careers, clinging to these sweet delights and primarily pleasing themselves. These are the natural target of envy and detraction and a certain contempt. They have their reward already and need no gratitude. But the public have liked to see a Prime Minister not enjoying his lot unduly. We have preferred to be governed by the sad smile of one who adopts towards the greatest office in the State the attitude that whilst, of course, it is nice to be Prime Minister, it is no great thing to covet, and who feels in office, and not merely afterwards, the vanity of things.

It is necessary to probe further. Andrew Bonar Law had been born in New Brunswick in 1858, a child of the Manse, and something of his Scottish Presbyterian background seems to have remained with him all his days. He had made a considerable fortune as an iron merchant in Glasgow before entering Parliament in the 1900 Unionist victory, and had the misfortune to make his maiden speech on the same evening as the dashing son of Lord Randolph Churchill, for whom he developed an enduring antipathy. In an age when it was regarded as imperative that a political career should start very early, the observations of an unknown Scottish businessman in his forties were not regarded as of much moment. Such men are familiar to the House of Commons. They enter obscurely, make some speeches of practical common sense, earn a certain respect, are asked to undertake the most boring of Parliamentary chores, and then either die, lose their seats, or drift into the House of Lords. Cromwell approved of such men, and so has the House of Commons down the ages. But their station is lowly and is destined to remain so; they are the foot-soldiers of politics—and particularly Tory politics.

But Bonar Law was of a different calibre. He had not come to Westminster to drift into placid backwaters. The very frugality of his life and his quiet glumness soon earned him many, and exceptionally devoted, friends. He had trained himself in local mock Parliaments—a great feature of those times, and long gone—to speak at length without notes, his mastery of complicated statistics was notable, and his bluntness and direction of expression were only to be emulated sub-sequently by Clement Attlee, with whom he had much in common. Like Attlee, Bonar Law had his points of principle on which he would not be moved. Like Attlee, he was distrustful of more glittering politicians, while at the same time being fascinated by them. In appearance, the sombre Law appeared incongruous on a public platform with F. E. Smith and Sir Edward Carson—until he began to speak. A later generation witnessed a similar phenomenon when Attlee appeared with Stafford Cripps or Aneurin Bevan.

Law was an expert upon, and passionately concerned with, two subjects above all others—Tariff Reform and Ulster. Although he had served as a junior Minister in the Balfour Government, Joseph Chamberlain was his lode-star, and, after Chamberlain's disintegration in 1906, his most ardent advocate. On Ulster, he was not open to dis-cussion or argument, and believed implicity in the creed of Lord Randolph Churchill.

Law was a ruminative, somewhat introspective, lonely man. He had no vices—unless teetotallism, continuous pipe-smoking, lack of interest in food, and a mania for chess can be so described (and a case could be made out)—and he could certainly not be described as an intellectual. But he was thoughtful, serious, dedicated, and softly determined. He was also highly ambitious, but reticently so. The Unionist Party, after a surfeit of catastrophic brilliance, was in the mood for blameless reliability in 1911. In Lloyd George's words, 'the fools chose the right man by mistake'. But perhaps the reasoning was not as faulty as Lloyd George—who never comprehended Tories—appreciated until October 1922 when the modest iron-merchant from Glasgow struck him down as completely as he had Churchill and Asquith. Bonar Law has often been depicted as a dull man, a plodder. But a man who dully plods his way to the leadership of his party within ten years of entering politics, holds a position of commanding influence for six years, and ends up as Prime Minister is not to be casually treated. Bonar Law was shrewd, quick, professional, and with an inner hardness and craftiness which some crudely describe with the adjective 'tough'. The judgement of A. G. Gardiner was to the point:

He is as unimaginative as the ledger in his country-house. His speech is dry and colourless, his voice thin and unmusical. . . . He is as innocent of humour as a dirge and had never made an epigram.

But he can sting. His qualities are an unhesitating fluency, an orderly argumentative progression, a certain business-like exactness, and an unaffected sincerity.[1]

Asquith and his colleagues made the great mistake of regarding Law with considerable contempt and condescension. He was to the Liberal leader and many of his colleagues (particularly Churchill) 'the gilded tradesman'. Of the Liberals only Lloyd George seems to have appreciated the calibre of Bonar Law, his adroitness in debate, and the moral and political toughness that lay beneath the unprepossessing façade.

On the subject of Home Rule, Law was a deeply committed man, far more committed than Balfour. The prospect of handing over Protestant Ulstermen to the rule of the Catholic South genuinely repelled him. As his biographer has commented:

We may then safely take with a grain of salt Bonar Law's strictures upon such topics as Welsh Disestablishment or the Franchise Bill, but upon Irish Home Rule . . . he meant every word he said.[2]

One may perhaps be reminded of Disraeli's aphorism that 'a little sincerity is a dangerous thing, and a great deal of it is absolutely fatal.'

Meanwhile, Ulster had found a leader. Sir Edward Carson, who led the Ulster Unionists from February 1910, was as strange a man to find in that position as Parnell had been to lead the Catholic Southern Nationalists in the 1870s. Carson was a Southern Irishman who sat as Member for Dublin University until he accepted the Ulster leadership. Until he became the leader of Ulster he had had no connection with Northern Ireland that would have led men to anticipate his emergence. He was a hypochondriac, a serious and responsible constitutional lawyer, and in reality a moderate man. It was particularly difficult for a fellow lawyer like Asquith, who knew Carson so well, to take Carson's violent language too seriously.

This was another mistake. As George Bernard Shaw once remarked: 'We must also bear in mind that political opinion in Ulster is not a matter of talk and bluff, as it is in England . . . there is a strength in [the Ulsterman's] rancour which lifts it above rancour.' Carson knew this. His appearance was magnificent, his mien decisive and intimidating, and he had something of Parnell's quality of icy delivery. His

[1] A. G. Gardiner: *Pillars of Society*.
[2] Robert Blake: *The Unknown Prime Minister*.

merciless destruction of Oscar Wilde had demonstrated his forensic persistence and quickness. His assault on the Admiralty in the famous Archer–Shee case was a celebrated episode. But, up to February 1910, he had not made a deep impression upon the House. From that moment he was a changed man. Like Law, he meant every word that he said on the matter of Home Rule. Ulster was determined not to be coerced by the South. In Carson they had found what they had hitherto lacked, a real leader. Thus, Carson, the outsider, understood better, and was closer to, his followers than Redmond. And, whereas Redmond was deeply committed to constitutional methods, Carson was fully prepared to countenance extremist actions if need be. There were those who thought that this was all a gigantic bluff, and that he was at heart a moderate and a man of peace; but Carson's manner, methods and language made even the most sceptical begin to doubt. Carson was the leader, but his most effective lieutenant was Captain Craig, who demonstrated a flair for stage-management of Ulster demonstrations.

The Liberals embarked on Home Rule once again with little enthusiasm. Politicians on both sides steeled themselves for the wearying repetition of the old, long familiar arguments. Once again, and with greater justification than in 1892–3, the Unionists alleged the existence of a political deal between the Government and the Irish Nationalists. The facts spoke for themselves. From 1906 to 1910, with a comfortable independent majority, Home Rule had been ignored. Now, dependent upon the Irish vote for their existence, Ministers had no choice. 'Unless an official declaration on the question of Home Rule be made', Redmond wrote to Morley, 'not only will it be impossible for us to support Liberal candidates in England, but we will most unquestionably have to ask our friends to vote against them . . . as you know very well, the Opposition of Irish voters in Lancashire, Yorkshire and other places, including Scotland, would certainly mean the loss of many seats.' No formal compact was required; the situation was stark and clear to each party. On this basis, the Liberal Government was propelled unhappily forward.

The Third Home Rule Bill was introduced in April 1912. Its novelty was to embrace the federal conception of Home Rule, on which Asquith laid emphasis in the speech he made introducing it. But in essentials, it was not very different from the Bill of 1892, inasmuch as the Irish Parliament was to have powers severely circumscribed to the point when, as Sir Harold Nicolson has commented, it was nothing more than 'a glorified County Council'. But although it did not go far enough for Sinn Fein, it went far further than the Ulster Unionists were prepared to tolerate. The Session that opened in February 1912 was to be one of the most arduous in modern political history. With a break of eight weeks in the summer of 1912, and another early in 1913, Parliament sat virtually continuously until August 1913. Once again, 'all Parliamentary roads led to Ireland'.

The issues involved were at once simple and also complex. With the majority in the Commons, and with the Lords' powers cut, the passage of the Bill was virtually inevitable. This was the major difference between 1886 and 1893. Everything hinged on the position of Ulster. Historically, politically and economically the north-eastern corner of Ireland had little affinity with the rest of the country. Since the seventeenth century four of the Nine Ulster Counties— Antrim, Armagh, Down and Londonderry—had had populations which were overwhelmingly Scottish in origin and Protestant in religion. In two other counties—Fermanagh and Tyrone—the Catholics and Protestants were more or less equally divided. In the remaining three—Donegal, Monaghan, and Cavan—there was a Catholic majority numerically, but with a powerful and wealthy Protestant minority.

On the face of it, the case of the Ulster Unionists in claiming the Nine Counties was not a strong one. Indeed, in 1912 the Nine Counties were represented at Westminster by seventeen Unionists and sixteen Irish Nationalists, and a by-election at the beginning of 1913 actually gave the Nationalists a majority in the Nine Counties.

It was always the claim of the Irish Nationalists that Ireland was one, and that partition was unthinkable. In part, this was an emotional feeling. But it was also a practical one. The four north-eastern counties provided the only modern industrial plant in Ireland, and the wealth of Belfast was regarded as crucial to the economic existence of a future Irish State. Belfast was the centre of resistance to Home Rule. In 1886 it had welcomed Lord Randolph Churchill rapturously, and in 1893 it had been the scene of the great Ulster Convention at which one speaker had declared that 'as a last resort we will be prepared to defend ourselves'. By 1911, when the ill-fated *Titanic* was built there, Belfast had the largest shipyard in the world. The city also harboured, as Morley once wrote, 'a spirit of bigotry and violence for which a parallel can hardly be found in any town in Western Europe'. In September 1912, 417,444 Belfast citizens signed a 'Solemn Covenant' prepared by Craig 'never to recognise a Dublin Parliament'. It requires emphasis that the temper of Belfast, and of Ulster Nationalism, was militant long before Carson, Craig, Law and F. E. Smith—a very recent and opportunistic convert to the cause of Ulster—appeared on the scene. But their intervention gave the issue a new, and more ominous, dimension.

Law quickly made it plain that his attitudes towards the Government were different to those of Balfour. In his first speech as Leader, at the Albert Hall, he described Ministers as 'humbugs' and as 'artful dodgers', a manner derided by Asquith as the 'new style'. If it was somewhat rough and unsophisticated, it was greatly to the taste of the Unionists. And on the Irish Question, Law was in deadly earnest. 'It may seem strange to you and me', he remarked to Lord Riddell, 'but it is a religious question. These people are . . . prepared to die for their convictions'.

As the Home Rule Bill proceeded slowly through the House of Commons, the Ulstermen began to prepare. On January 5th 1912 they started drilling a Volunteer Force; on April 9th Carson, Lord Londonderry, Law and Walter Long took the salute of 80,000 Orange Volunteers. A counter-attack was launched. On October 3rd of the previous year Churchill had told his Dundee constituents that 'we must not attach too much importance to these frothings of Sir Edward Carson. I daresay when the worst comes to the worst we shall find that civil war evaporates in uncivil words'. To prove his point, with real courage, Churchill—now First Lord of the Admiralty—accepted an invitation to speak at a Home Rule meeting in Belfast in March, and in the Ulster Hall, the very place in which Lord Randolph Churchill had made his famous speech in January 1886. Eventually the venue was changed to the Celtic football ground—in the Nationalist part of the city. Feeling at this act of sacrilege was very intense. Troops—seven battalions of infantry and a squadron of cavalry—were brought in, but the meeting itself passed off without any serious incidents, in spite of the inevitable interruption by a suffragette. The visitor was then hastily dispatched to Larne and back to England by a circuitous route. Courage was required for this expedition, and it was a quality which Churchill possessed to the full. But the incident did nothing to soothe the passions of the situation.

The Ulster retort was a spectacular Easter Demonstration in Belfast, which included the breaking-out of a gigantic Union Jack— said to be the largest ever woven, forty-eight feet by twenty-five feet— an interminable march-past of Volunteers, and much violent speech-ifying, in which Law described Belfast as 'a besieged city'. This was, however, mild compared to what he said at a Unionist rally on July 12th, at Blenheim Palace:

I can imagine no length of resistance to which Ulster can go in which I should not be prepared to support them, and in which, in my belief, they would not be supported by the overwhelming majority of the British people.

This was coming very close indeed to encouraging defiance of the constitutional conventions. Just in case this point had not been taken, Law made it emphatically clear:

In our opposition to them we shall not be guided by the considera-tions or bound by the restraints which would influence us in an ordinary Constitutional struggle. We shall take the means, whatever means seem to us most effective, to deprive them of the despotic power which they have usurped and compel them to appeal to the people whom they have deceived. They may, perhaps they will, carry their Home Rule Bill through the House of Commons—but what then? *I said the other day in the House of Commons, and I repeat here, that there are things stronger than Parliamentary majorities.*

Law did not confine his threats to the Commons or to the public platform. He astounded King George by calmly informing him on May 12th that he would be fully justified in using the Royal Veto on the Home Rule Bill—constitutional usage since the death of Queen Anne notwithstanding—and implied that he would be liable to strong criticism if he did not exercise his duty.

Meanwhile, the Home Rule Bill debates were characteristically prolonged and rancorous, and included one suspension of the House and an occasion on which an Ulster M.P. accurately hurled a copy of the Standing Orders at Churchill. On January 16th 1913, the Bill was given its Third Reading in the Commons by 367 votes to 257. On January 30th it was thrown out by the Lords by 326 to 69. On March 10th a new Session began, and the Bill started all over again. On July 7th it received its Third Reading in the Commons; on July 15th the Lords rejected it once again. The exhausted Parliament adjourned on August 15th, and was in recess for the rest of 1913.

*

Home Rule, although the major political preoccupation at this time, was not the only one. Throughout 1912 and the early part of 1913 it was closely rivalled by the strange affair of the Marconi Scandal.

The broad outlines of what actually occurred are as follows. In March 1912 the Postmaster-General, Herbert Samuel, provisionally accepted a tender from the English Marconi Company for the construction of a chain of wireless stations in the Empire; this caused a sharp rise in Marconi shares, accentuated by the extensive publicity given to the importance of wireless communications after the disaster of the sinking of the liner *Titanic* after striking an iceberg on April 10th.

The managing director of the English Marconi Company was Godfrey Isaacs, a brother of the Attorney-General, Sir Rufus Isaacs, who was also managing director of the legally independent American Marconi Company. Godfrey Isaacs decided to expand the American company—in which the English company had a majority shareholding—by floating a new issue of shares on the British market on April 18th. On April 9th he invited two of his brothers—Harry and Rufus—to buy a large block of the new shares at a price considerably below the probable market price. Harry Isaacs bought 56,000; Rufus Isaacs at first did not like the idea, but a few days later bought 10,000 from Harry Isaacs at £2 a share. He then sold 1,000 to Lloyd George and another 1,000 to the Liberal Chief Whip, the Master of Elibank, at no profit to himself.

On the next day—April 18th—the new issue was floated and the shares jumped to £4 each. All three Ministers promptly disposed of their shares at a handsome profit. Subsequently they bought more shares, and, as the value of the shares dropped, they made a net loss. For some strange reason, this fact has been often cited in defence of the Ministers, as though the purpose of making a profit had been far from their thoughts, and their losses in some way made their offence innocuous. The fact remained that three senior Cabinet Ministers had bought shares on a privileged basis from a major Government contractor and had made a considerable initial profit on the transaction. The fact that, encouraged, they subsequently tried again and got their fingers burnt is hardly to be regarded as a convincing defence of their activities. Viewed in the most charitable possible light, they acted with great imprudence. A more realistic assessment would be harsher.

Well-informed rumours began to circulate in the City, and at length emerged in a violently anti-Semitic journal called *Eye Witness*, edited by Hilaire Belloc and Cecil Chesterton (brother of 'G.K.'). (A somewhat ironical development, when Lloyd George's anti-Semitism in his Boer War period is recalled.) Samuel, who was wholly uninvolved, was also mentioned in these attacks; he wanted to bring an action for libel, but was dissuaded by Asquith. In August Isaacs was also persuaded by Asquith not to take legal action.[1] Asquith, indeed, wrote to him:

> I expect [it] . . . has a very meagre circulation. I notice only one page of advertisements and that occupied by books of Belloc's publishers. Prosecution would secure it notoriety, which might yield subscribers. We have broken weather [*he went on somewhat irrelevantly*], and but for Winston there would be nothing in the newspapers.

In private, Asquith was very angry. But either he was very much implicated in a serious attempt to mislead the House of Commons later in the year or he did not fully ascertain the facts at this early stage. Neither conclusion reflects to his advantage.

On October 11th Samuel moved to appoint a Select Committee to investigate the whole story of the Marconi contract. In the debate, both Isaacs and Lloyd George specifically, and with much heat, disclaimed any dealing in the shares of 'the Marconi Company'. They were careful to word these denials so as to cover only the English Marconi Company, but the impression given was that they had not had dealings in any Marconi shares at all. In spite of the torrid atmosphere of politics at the time, these denials were accepted by the House of Commons and by the Opposition, and the matter appeared to be concluded.

This conclusion was abruptly amended when it was learned early in 1913 that Samuel and Isaacs proposed to sue the French newspaper

---

[1] It is, however, open to doubt whether Asquith—as Samuel has stated in his *Memoirs*—knew of the full details before January 1913. The latter is the date given by Asquith in his account to the King, but the matter remains in doubt. It is, however, an important point, as it concerns the extent of Asquith's involvement in the Lloyd George–Isaacs disclaimers in the Commons in October 1912.

Le Matin and that Isaacs would admit that he and Lloyd George had bought shares in the American Marconi Company. Hardly less startling was the news that F. E. Smith and Carson would defend the Ministers at a time when they were the foremost advocates of extreme measures in Ulster and were making violent inflammatory speeches against the Government. Smith defended his decision in characteristically majestic terms, invoking the hallowed traditions of the English Bar at a time when he was defying and deriding certain fundamental tenets of English Law, thereby giving rise to the justified conclusion that although he was very clever he was not very intelligent (or, alternatively, that he was morally and professionally schizophrenic). Perhaps the truth lies in Arthur Lee's reminiscence: 'He once said to me jestingly: "At least I can say this, that never in my life have I attempted to resist temptation", and he pressed his reckless course without illusions and certainly without fear.' Bonar Law was not the only Unionist who found this performance stupid and totally incomprehensible, and the episode marked a decisive turning-point in Smith's fortunes with his party.

But matters now became much more serious for the Government. It transpired that the Master of Elibank had not only invested some £9,000 of Liberal Party funds in the Marconi shares but had left the country to go to the remote township of Bogota and accordingly would not be available to give evidence before the Select Committee. Colombia was far distant from Westminster, and caustic references to this fact became frequent at Unionist meetings. Matters were hardly improved by the blatant partisanship of both sides on the Select Committee. After much fury and other disagreeableness, the Committee eventually reported on purely party lines, and a very fierce debate in the Commons ensued. The Ministers not only survived, but Asquith appointed Isaacs to the highest judicial post in the land, Lord Chief Justice, an act which provoked Kipling to pen one of the most vitriolic political verses in modern politics. Isaacs' career prospered thereafter. He became, as Lord Reading, British Ambassador in Washington and subsequently Viceroy of India. If he never quite succeeded in escaping from the shadows cast by the Marconi affair, his sufferings were minimal. Lloyd George's career received only a very temporary setback. Within a very short time he was even posing as the victim of a conspiracy to malign his character. Nerve was one of Lloyd George's most remarkable political attributes. Lloyd George and

Isaacs were lucky in their Prime Minister, but their gratitude took a strange form.

Not altogether surprisingly, this episode did little to elevate the stature of the Government nor to reduce the political temperature. Moral strictures by Lloyd George became even less supportable for the Unionists, aware as they were of other aspects of his private life. The antagonism between the parties, which had been accelerating since 1906, was now greater than anyone in English public life could recall.

*

Marconi was a symptom of a much deeper bitterness. By the end of the Session in August 1913 the Home Rule Bill had been twice passed by the Commons and twice rejected by the Lords. Under the terms of the Parliament Act, its final passage could not be long delayed. The Ulster Volunteers were drilling and preparing for armed resistance; plans for an alternative government were far advanced; weapons were being purchased, and by various methods being brought into Ulster. On Roberts' personal recommendation, a retired officer, Lt.-Gen. Sir George Richardson, K.C.B., a veteran of Afghanistan and the Boxer Campaign, was in command in Belfast. The Government was not well served by the Chief Secretary, Augustine Birrell, a man of great charm but consistently out of touch with reality in Ireland, and who declined to regard the situation with adequate seriousness.

Up to this point, it must be emphasised, there had been no serious discussion about treating Ulster separately. The Unionist case was that Home Rule was impossible because of the special position of Ulster. Carson's line, however, was somewhat different. He recognised that Ulster could not prevent Home Rule; but he was determined that Home Rule should not include Ulster; he was fully prepared to come to an arrangement on these lines with the Government.

The King was, by this stage, becoming justifiably alarmed, particularly when Law had advised him that he ought to dissolve Parliament on his own responsibility. While the King was fully aware of the fact that no Monarch had dismissed a Prime Minister since 1834, that the precedent was not promising, and that much had happened since then,[1] he was justifiably agitated. But Law had also raised another very disconcerting possibility: If Home Rule had to be imposed on

---

[1] Rosebery was among those who, when their advice was sought, pointed out the dangers involved in the Monarchy in taking such an action.

Ulster by military force, would the Army obey such an order? The King laid these dilemmas before Asquith on August 11th in the form of a handwritten memorandum, in which he described his personal position and raising the possibility of 'a settlement by consent'. Asquith dismissed the King's arguments somewhat briskly, and on September 22nd the King wrote to Asquith again:

> Will it be wise, will it be fair to the Sovereign as head of the Army, to subject the discipline, and indeed the loyalty of his troops, to such a strain?

Asquith replied that there were 'no sufficient grounds for the fears— or hopes—expressed in some quarters, that the troops would fail to do their duty'.

Nevertheless, as the King urged, it was necessary at least to attempt a negotiated settlement of the crisis. In the late autumn of 1913 it was begun in an atmosphere of distinct coolness between Bonar Law and Asquith. Although it came to nothing, the ingenious mind of Lloyd George produced a scheme whereby the Home Rule Bill would not come into effect in Ulster for five or six years. This eventually emerged in the following March in an offer by Asquith that any County in Ireland could vote itself out of Home Rule for six years. This merely succeeded in enraging both sides. 'We do not want sentence of death with a stay of execution for six years', as Carson retorted; the National- ist dismay and resentment was equally strong. The latter was increased by the decision of the Government in December to forbid the embargo on importing arms into Ireland that had been relaxed since 1906, and which had enabled the Ulstermen to arm themselves.

Passions on both sides were now rising to a very dangerous level. Lord Roberts drafted a letter for publication (in fact never published), approved by Carson and Bonar Law, to the effect that in the event of Civil War the normal rules of military discipline did not apply. Excitement was also growing in the Empire. The Orange Association of Manitoba prepared to send a regiment of volunteers to Ulster, and other Canadian states—notably Winnipeg, Saskatchewan, Alberta and Vancouver—pledged support to the same cause. Nationalist movements sprang up in New Zealand, South Africa, and the United States. At Dublin, in November 1913, Law made a clear appeal to the Army to disobey orders. Matters were further complicated by the attitude of Ministers. Many—particularly Asquith—did not take the

Ulster threats seriously; few were enthusiastic about Home Rule. By the beginning of 1914 they had succeeded in disillusioning and infuriating both sides. Their subsequent actions made the situation, if anything, even worse.

In March 1914 Churchill—whose prestige with his own party was in marked decline—made another hapless intervention in the Irish Question with the purpose, as he subsequently frankly admitted, 'to ingratiate myself with my Party'. On March 14th he made a highly belligerent speech at Bradford in which he declared that there were 'worse things than bloodshed even on an extended scale', that Britain must not be reduced to the condition of Mexico, and that if her civil and Parliamentary institutions were to be brought to the crude challenge of force he could only say 'Let us go forward together and put these grave matters to the proof.' The Cabinet had set up a small Committee to handle the Ulster problem on March 11th, which consisted of Crewe (who, through illness, took no part), Churchill, Birrell, J.E.B. Seely (Secretary for War) and Simon. On March 17th it reported with recommendations for increased guards on depots and movement of troops. Churchill reported that 'the forthcoming practice' of the Third Battle Squadron would take place off the Isle of Arran. In fact, the naval movements to Lamlash had already been ordered. To the Unionists this seemed clear evidence of attempts to coerce the Ulstermen, and even to countenance the use of force.

Meanwhile, Seely ordered Major-General Sir Arthur Paget, Commander-in-Chief Ireland, to concentrate and reinforce his troops at a number of important points. Asquith cancelled the warship movement to Lamlash—although not before much political damage had been done—but Seely's order to Paget was the vital spark.

Seely—later Lord Mottistone—was a lively, dashing, cheerful man of action, whose career had many points in common with that of Churchill. Like him, he had distinguished himself in the Boer War, had entered the Commons as a Conservative and had joined the Liberals over the Free Trade issue. But if Churchill was impetuous, Seely's impetuousness was in a different class. It is difficult to consider that he was very intelligent, and he was a strange successor to Haldane at the War Office.

Paget came to London and obtained several undertakings from Seely, of which the most important was that any officer whose domicile was in Ulster could 'disappear' if ordered north. Paget informed his senior officers of this concession and also told them that any not domiciled in Ireland but who refused to undertake active operations against Ulster should send in their resignations. This was a subtle, but crucial, extension of Seely's orders. General Sir Hubert Gough and sixty of the seventy officers of the Third Cavalry Brigade said that they would prefer dismissal if ordered north. The War Office ordered Gough and his three colonels to London. They proceeded to negotiate with Seely, demanding a written assurance that they would not be called upon to enforce Home Rule upon Ulster. Asquith, on March 23rd, wrote out a cautious letter to Gough exonerating him from the charge of disobeying orders. Disastrously, Seely—with Morley's assistance—added two paragraphs of which the second one stated that the Government 'have no intention whatever of taking advantage of the right to crush political opposition to the policy or principles of the Home Rule Bill'.

Gough returned to the Curragh, the hero of the hour. The Liberals and the Nationalists were enraged, and Asquith's removal of Seely could not materially change the situation. The Unionists were convinced that Seely and Churchill had planned a massive use of force against the Ulstermen which they had been compelled to abandon. Unionist feeling against Churchill ran very high, and Asquith's position was seriously affected. As Ensor subsequently wrote: 'His followers supposed that this betokened a drastic policy, such as only a prime minister could put through; in fact, it heralded a policy of surrender, such as only a prime minister could put over.' The long-term effects of the so-called 'Curragh Mutiny' were to be substantial. But the immediate were also significant. In May the Ulster Volunteers smuggled in at Larne some 30,000 rifles and three million rounds of ammunition without military or police interference. The feeling in the South that the Government was in effect condoning the Ulster cause and bowing to Ulster pressure was greatly augmented. There was a rush to join the Irish Volunteers. Ireland advanced rapidly closer to Civil War.

The inter-party discussions continued throughout the summer. On July 18th, advised by Asquith, the King summoned a formal conference under the chairmanship of the Speaker at BuckinghamPalace; it opened on July 21st. The differences were irreconcilable, and no progress was made after four days in which, as Churchill has related, the conference 'toiled round the muddy byways of Fermanagh and

Tyrone'. A proposal by Asquith to exclude six of the Nine Counties from Home Rule was rejected by both Redmond and Carson. On July 26th the National Volunteers carried out a gun-running at Howth. Soldiers were called out, and, in Dublin, were stoned by an angry crowd. They fired, killing three civilians and wounding thirty-eight. Civil War seemed imminent. All plans were ready. Lord Milner was urging the immediate setting up of an Ulster Provisional Government.

But on July 24th, at the end of a Cabinet meeting concerned with the breakdown of the Buckingham Palace Conference, just as Ministers were rising to depart, Grey informed them of the text of an ultimatum sent to Serbia by Austria-Hungary. To quote Churchill's account:

> The parishes of Fermanagh and Tyrone faded back into the mists and squalls of Ireland, and a strange light began immediately, but by perceptible gradations, to fall and glow upon the map of Europe.

BIBLIOGRAPHY

The quantity of books, monographs and articles concerned with the period 1880–1914 is very substantial indeed, and as this bibliography is intended for the guidance and assistance of the reader who wishes to study the period further rather than a comprehensive list of all the works consulted, it is kept as brief as possible.

1 Political Papers

The principal collections that I have used during the preparation of this volume are, in alphabetical order, the papers of Sir Henry Campbell-Bannerman (British Library), Lord Randolph Churchill (Chartwell and Blenheim Palace), Sir Charles Dilke (British Library), Herbert and W. E. Gladstone (British Library), Sir Edward Hamilton (British Library), W. V. Harcourt (then in the possession of the present Lord Harcourt, and now in the Bodleian Library, Oxford), Lord Kitchener (Public Record Office), Sir Stafford Northcote (then in private possession, now in the British Library), Lord Rosebery (now in the National Library of Scotland), Lord Salisbury (Christ Church, Oxford, and Hatfield House), Lord Ripon (British Library), and W. H. Smith (British Library). I have also made use of the complete correspondence between Prime Ministers and the Sovereign (Public Record Office) and the Cabinet papers.

2 Public Works

On general histories of the period, R. C. K. Ensor: *England 1870–1914* (1936), in spite of much subsequent research and discoveries, still holds the field, and is a work of abiding quality. Halévy's: *The Rise of Democracy* (1943) is certainly in the same class. Of more recent books, particular note must be taken of H. Pelling: *Popular Politics and Society in Late Victorian Britain* (1968), R. Shannon: *The Crisis of Imperialism 1865–1915* (1974), and S. Maccoby: *English Radicalism 1886–1914* (1953). R. T. Mackenzie's *British Political Parties* (1955; revised editions 1964 and 1970) covers a considerable part of this period, while on economic matters the best single work is W. Ashworth: *Economic History of Modern England 1870–1939* (1960). On the parties, R. Blake's *The Conservative Party from Peel to Churchill* (1970), although exhilirating, is not the substitute for the detailed history of this remarkable confederation that is urgently needed. P. Smith: *Disraelian Conservatism and Social Reform* (1967) is a step in the right direction. Lord Chilston's *Chief Whip* (1961) throws some further light, and E. J. Feuchtwanger: *Disraeli, Democracy and the Tory Party* (1968) is good on the 1870s and 1880s. H. Pelling's work on the Labour Party—particularly *The Origins of the Labour Party* (1965) and *A Short History of the Labour Party* (1965) are excellent, as are A. M. McBriar: *Fabian Socialism and English Politics 1884–1918* (1962) and R. McKibbin: *The Evolution of the Labour Party 1910–1924* (1975); R. Harrison: *Before the Socialists—Studies in Labour and Politics, 1861–1881* (1965) is an indispensable work. The Liberals have also been better served by historians than the Conservatives, notably in D. Southgate: *The Passing of the Whigs* (1962), J. R. Vincent: *The Formation of the Liberal Party 1857–1868* (1966), D. A. Hamer: *Liberal Politics in the Age of Gladstone and Rosebery* (1972), P. Stansky: *Ambitions and Strategies—The Struggle for the Leadership of the Liberal Party in the 1890s* (1964) and R. B. MacCullum: *The Liberal Party from Earl Grey to Asquith* (1963). H. J. Hanham: *Elections and Party Management—Politics in the Time of Disraeli and Gladstone* (1959) was a pioneering work of high quality, as were M. Cowling's *Disraeli, Gladstone and Revolution: The Passing of the Second Reform Bill* (1967), C. O'Leary's *The Elimination of Corrupt Practices in British Elections 1868–1911* (1962), R. T. Shannon's *Gladstone and the Bulgarian Agitation, 1876* (1963), and N. Blewett: *The Peers, The Parties and The People,* (1972).

On specific episodes, attention should be given to several excellent studies, notably F. B. Smith: *The Making of the Second Reform Bill* (1966), T. Lloyd: *The General Election of 1880* (1968), A. Jones: *The Politics of Reform, 1884* (1972), A. B. Cooke and J. R. Vincent: *The Governing Passion, Cabinet Government and Party Politics in Britain 1885–86* (1974), R. Jenkins: *Mr. Balfour's Poodle* (1954), A. K. Russell: *Liberal Landslide—The General Election of 1906* (1973) and W. L. Arnstein: *The Bradlaugh Case* (1965).

For the House of Commons, the best accounts are those of H. W. Lucy, whose 'diaries' of the Parliaments from 1874 to 1906—in fact the compilation of his weekly columns as a lobby correspondent—provide the best contemporary portrait available to us.

It is when the historian comes to biographies that he begins to fell overwhelmed by the sheer mass of published material. On Disraeli, the volumes of F. W. Monypenny and G. E. Buckle, published between 1910 and 1920, still have a powerful attraction and much interest. R. Blake's long, but in comparison brief, biography published in 1966 is by far the best biography yet published. On Gladstone, the publication of his Diaries has proved a most lengthy process, and have not yet begun to approach the period covered by this volume. Morley's classic three volume biography (1903) maintains its position, but is now greatly supplemented by J. L. Hammond and M. R. D. Foot: *Gladstone and Liberalism* (1952) and Sir Philip Magnus's *Gladstone* (1954). An admirable brief study was published by E. J. Feuchtwanger in 1975. One of the best sources is *The Political Correspondence of Mr. Gladstone and Lord Granville*, edited by Agatha Ramm, that covers the years 1868–76 (published in 1952) and 1876–86 (1962).

J. L. Garvin's huge and idiosyncratic biography of Joseph Chamberlain first began to appear in 1932, and was greeted with warm praise. Later evaluations, however, have been less admiring. Now that the work has been completed by J. Amery, it is evident that a new single volume biography is very much needed. P. Fraser: *Joseph Chamberlain, Radicalism and Empire, 1868–1914* (1966), although of interest, does not really meet this requirement. M. Hurst's *Joseph Chamberlain and Liberal Reunion: The Round Table Conference of 1887* (1967) deals with one episode in Chamberlain's career (at great length). Chamberlain's *A Political Memoir 1880–1892* (1953), edited by C. H. D. Howard, is a valuable source, but should be approached with considerable caution.

Lord Randolph Churchill was (at least initially) more fortunate. Winston Churchill's biography (1906) and Lord Rosebery's memoir, published the same year, are classics of British political literature. Rosebery's vignette tells us much more about the man. R. Rhodes James's biography, published in 1959, added new material from sources not available to the earlier biographers. Lord Randolph's fascination, not only for his contemporaries but later generations, is evident in each of these biographies. Lord Randolph not only 'forgot Goschen', but so have historians, apart from A. D. Elliot's sombre biography (1911) and P. Colson's *Lord Goschen and His Friends* (1946).

Lady Gwendolen Cecil's uncompleted biography of Salisbury (published in four volumes between 1921 and 1931) is a superlative work of political biography, but a single-volume new biography is very much needed. A. L. Kennedy: *Salisbury* (1953) does not adequately supply this. R. Taylor's brief biography (1974) is an excellent short study but necessarily limited in scope. Campbell-Bannerman received massive treatment by J. A. Spender in 1923, and an admirable—if perhaps rather too admiring—biography by J. Wilson in 'C-B' (1973). Milner—like Curzon—has been heavily assailed by biographers. *The Milner Papers*, edited by C. Headlam (1931, 1933) were, we can now see, rather too well edited. J. E. Wrench: *Milner* (1958), V. Halperin: *Lord Milner and the Empire* (1952), E. Crankshaw: *The Forsaken Idea: A Study of Lord Milner* (1952) and A. M. Gollin: *Proconsul in Politics* (1964) view this intriguing man from varying angles and with sympathetic skill.

A really satisfying biography of Lloyd George has yet to be written but J. Grigg: *The Young Lloyd George* (1973) is a first-rate study of his early career. H. du Parcq's *Life of David Lloyd George* (1911–13), although written before the most dramatic part of his career and with all the disadvantages of contemporary biography, remains an indispensable source. F. Owen's *Tempestuous Journey* (1954) has been consistently underrated; its style is certainly an acquired taste. W. George: *My Brother and I* (1958) and K. Morgan: *Lloyd George, Family Letters 1885–1936* are of considerable value and interest. The biography by T. Jones (1951) is more illuminating on Lloyd George's later career than the earlier; M. Thompson's *David Lloyd George: The Official Biography* (1948) is not very illuminating on any period. K. O. Morgan: *Wales in British Politics 1868–1922* (1963) is essential reading in its own right, but is invaluable in the context of Lloyd George's rise.

A. J. Balfour similarly lacks a biography that does full justice to his complex character and career. Mrs. Blanche Dugdale's biography (1939) provided some excellent family glimpses, but was too admiring and deficient on certain vital episodes to be an acceptable political biography. K. Young's new biography (1963) was a bold attempt to remedy the situation, but was not wholly successful. A. M. Gollin's *Balfour's Burden* (1965) deals with the 1903–5 crisis in the style of Lord Beaverbrook—a somewhat startling metamorphosis, and not convincing. D. Judd: *Balfour and the British Empire* (1968) has good material and interesting insights, but Balfour remains as inscrutable as ever.

Asquith published his own *Memories and Reflections* in 1928, which have occasional flashes of real interest. Margot Asquith's *Autobiography* (1920–2) also has the same characteristic, but is much more fun. The official biography by J. A. Spender and C. Asquith (1932) is a solemn work of veneration; R. Jenkins's biography (1964) is the best study yet provided, although not devoid of flaws, and rather more sympathetic than is required in a revising biography.

The list of biographies of Curzon, started by Lord Ronaldshay (1928), seems endless. Of the recent attempts the best are D. Dilks: *Curzon in India* (1969–70), M. Edwardes: *High Noon of Empire—India Under Curzon* (1965) and K. Rose: *Superior Person* (1969). None, however, is really a biography; L. Mosley: *Curozn—The End of an Epoch* (1960) is a caustic and somewhat dramatised study, but with many virtues.

On Sir Edward Grey, the only complete biography is that by K. Robbins, published in 1971, but his own *Twenty-Five Years* (1925) should not be neglected. The biography of C. F. G. Masterman by his wife Lucy (1939) and Masterman's own *The Condition of England* (1910) emphasise the significance of this now virtually unknown man, whose career ended so prematurely. John Morley's *Recollections* (1921) are highly haphazard and not easy to follow, but of great value. D. A. Hamer's biography (1968) is a major attempt to portray Morley, but hampered—as in the case of Grey—by the disappearance and scattering of his papers. J. Pope-Hennessy: *Lord Crewe—The Likeness of A Liberal* (1958) gives belated justice to a minor but far from unimportant public personality, as does C. Cross: *Philip Snowden* (1966). The biography of Beatrice Webb by K. Muggeridge and R. Adam (1967) only tends to emphasise the need for more full treatment. Lord Zetland's biography of Cromer (1932) has been supplemented most interestingly by Afaf Lutfi Al-Sayyid's *Egypt and Cromer* (1968). Sir Philip Magnus's biography of Kitchener (1958) is a vast improvement on the previous attempt by Sir George Arthur, but leaves the reader vaguely unsatisfied. The same can be said of the biography of Northcliffe by R. Pound and G. Harmsworth (1959). In contrast, A. M. Gollin's *The Observer and J. L. Garvin* (1960) and A. J. P. Taylor: *Beaverbrook* (1972) are excellent studies of two other major journalistic and political figures. C. Mallet: *Herbert Gladstone—A Memoir* (1932) is an important book, but subsequent research on his papers demonstrates that a new biography would be of value. Lord Newton's biography of Lord Lansdowne (1929), falls into the same category. Haldane's *Autobiography* (1929) has been supplemented by Sir Frederick Maurice's official biography (1937), and by D. Sommer's rather disappointing *Haldane of Cloan* (1960). S. E. Koss: *Lord Haldane— Scapegoat for Liberalism* (1969) is excellent in its early chapters, but thereafter must be treated with reservations. Austen Chamberlain wrote his own memoirs (*Politics From The Inside* (1936)) and his biography was written by Sir Charles Petrie in 1939. Now that his papers are available it is to be hoped that a new study may be attempted. R. Blake's biography of Bonar Law (1955) is difficult to fault on any count.

Lord Birkenhead's biography of his father, first published in 1933, and revised in 1960 under the title 'F.E.', has many of the virtues, but also many of the deficiencies, of filial biography. Randolph Churchill's biography of his father Winston (Vol. I 1966, Vol. II 1967) was a project flawed both in conception and execution, excessively documented and excessively admiring. Volume One made a good beginning, but the second was a sad disappointment. Churchill's own autobiography: *My Early Life* (1930) and his *Great Contemporaries* (1937), and Lady Violet Bonham Carter's *Winston Churchill As I Knew Him* (1965) should be read in conjunction with the Randolph Churchill volumes. H. Pelling's single volume biography (*Winston Churchill* (1974)) is surprisingly uncritical and rather bland. R. Hyam: *Elgin and Churchill At the Colonial Office 1905–08* (1968) is essential reading both in the context of the South African policies and in Churchill's development and characteristics as a young Minister. The essays in *Churchill—Four Faces and the Man* (1969) provide a more critical appraisal than was then fashionable, as did R. Rhodes James: *Churchill, A Study In Failure 1900–1939* (1970), whose ironically intended sub-title deluded those who read no further into the belief that this was a denigratory biography. But it may be stated with confidence that, even after M. Gilbert has completed the gargantuan task which he assumed on the death of Randolph Churchill, this extraordinary career will continue to fascinate historians and biographers.

Other biographies that merit attention are E. Marjoribanks and H. M. Hyde on Carson (1932 and 1953 respectively), Lord Askwith's *Lord James of Hereford* (1930), Viscount Chilston: *W. H. Smith* (1965), K. Morgan: *Keir Hardie* (1975), and R. Rhodes James: *Rosebery* (1963).

On Ireland, the list of books and studies is so substantial—and of such high quality—that only a very limited selection can be given. N. Mansergh: *The Irish Question 1840–1921* (1965) is perhaps the best single study of the period. On Parnell, the best studies by far are R. Barry O'Brien's magnificent biography, published in 1898, Conor Cruise O'Brien's *Parnell and His Party* (1957), and F. S. L. Lyons: *The Fall of Parnell* (1960). There have been many other biographies and studies of Parnell, but none of this quality. D. Thornely: *Isaac Butt and Home Rule* (1964) L.P. Curtis: *Coercion and Conciliation In Ireland 1880–1892* (1963), F. S. L. Lyons: *The Irish Parliamentary Party 1890–1910* (1951) and *John Dillon* (1968) are fully up to the high standard of modern Irish histories. J. L. Hammond: *Gladstone and the Irish Nation* (1938) still holds its eminence as a work of outstanding scholarship and literature. M. Davitt's *The Fall of Feudalism In Ireland* (1904) should be read in conjunction with F. Sheehy-Skeffington's biography of Davitt, published in 1908 and deservedly republished in 1967. J. C. Beckett: *The Making of Modern Ireland 1603–1923* (1966) covers a large canvass with skill and objectivity.

The same dilemma confronts the historian of the Empire. The *Cambridge History of the British Empire, Volume III, 1870–1919* (1959) in a basic work. On African matters the indispensable works are E. A. Walker: *A History of Southern Africa* (3rd edition, 1957), the Cambridge History of the British Empire, Volume VIII—South Africa (1963), R. Robinson, J. Gallagher, and A. Denny: *Africa and the Victorians* (1963), D. M. Schreuder: *Gladstone and Kruger* (1969), J. S. Marais: *The Fall of Kruger's Republic* (1961), G. H. Le May: *British Supremacy in South Africa 1899–1907* (1965). Also of value are E. Pakenham (Lady Longford): *Jameson's Raid* (1960), P. Mansfield: *The British in Egypt* (1971), J. L. Lockhart and C. M. Woodhouse: *Cecil Rhodes* (1962), J. E. Flint: *Sir George Goldie and the Making of Nigeria* (1960) and M. Perham: *Lugard* (1956, 1960). On the South African War, L. S. Amery's history for *The Times* (1905–9²) is detailed, but heavy going. D. Reitz: *Commando* (1929) is a classic of military autobiography: W. B. Pemberton: *Battles of the Boer War* (1964) is clear and well written, as are J. Symonds: *Buller's Campaign* (1963) and the appropriate chapters of W. K. Hancock's excellent biography of Smuts (1962). R. Kruger's *Good-bye, Dolly Grey* (1959) gives a lively account of the war, as does E. Holt: *The Boer War* (1958). An interesting study of domestic reactions is given in R. Price: *An Imperialist War and the British Working Class* (1972). The best account of the Sudan Campaign of 1897–8 is to be found in Winston Churchill's superb *The River War* (1899, 1900), and no student of this area should ignore R. Slatin's: *Fire and Sword in the Sudan* (1896) nor G. Brook-Shepherd's biography of Slatin, *Between Two Flags* (1973), and R. Wingate: *Wingate of the Sudan* (1955). A new account of the Sudan campaign is given in P. Ziegler: *Omdurman* (1974). Although a good history, it is written in a colourful style that reads oddly from the sombre biographer of King William IV and Addington.

On the wider subject of Imperialism, J. R. Seely: *The Expansion of England* (1883, and in print until 1956) and the counter-attack in J. A. Hobson: *Imperialism: A Study* (1902) are essential, as is C. A. Bodelsen: *Studies in Mid-Victorian Imperialism*(1924). Also strongly recommended are M. Beloff: *Imperial Sunset, Vol. I 1897–1921* (1969), I. M. Cumpston: *The Growth of the British Commonwealth 1880–1932* (1973), A. P. Thornton: *The Imperial Idea and Its Enemies* (1959), R. Koebner and H. D. Schmidt:

Imperialism (1964), C. J. Lowe: *The Reluctant Imperialists* (1967), and C. C. Eldridge: *England's Mission. The Imperial Idea in the Age of Gladstone and Disraeli* (1974).

The period has produced a very considerable number of published memoirs, diaries and letters. The most important single collection is G. E. Buckle (ed.): *Letters and Journals of Queen Victoria* (Second and Third Series, 1928–30). On Queen Victoria herself, the best studies of her during this period are F. Hardie: *The Political Influence of Queen Victoria* (1938) and E. Longford: *Victoria R.I.* (1964), but this historian feels that much more work could and should be done on the Queen in the latter part of her reign. The publication of Sir Almeric Fitzroy's *Memoirs* (1925) caused Royal displeasure; of value also are Sir Frederick Ponsonby's delightful *Recollections of Six Reigns* (1951). The almost total destruction of the papers of King Edward VII by Lord Knollys and others has probably hurt rather than improved his subsequent treatment by historians. Sir Philip Magnus's biography (1964), although of characteristic quality and insight, certainly suffered from this lamentable incendiarism. Lord Ponsonby's *Henry Ponsonby; His Life From His Letters* (1942) and H. G. Hutchinson: *The Private Diaries of Sir Algernon West* (1922) are of considerable value and interest. Sir Harold Nicolson's *King George V—His Life and Reign* (1952) is by far the best modern Royal biography.

On political memoirs, in addition to those already mentioned, particular note should be taken of M. V. Brett: *Journals and Letters of Viscount Esher* (1934), G. P. Gooch: *Under Six Reigns* (1958), Lady St. Helier: *Memoirs of Fifty Years* (1909), Lord Kilbracken: *Reminiscences* (1931), F. E. Hamer (ed.): *The Personal Papers of Lord Rendel* (1931), J. A. Spender: *Life, Journalism, and Politics* (1927), Lord Winterton: *Orders of the Day* (1953), and A. Clark: *A Good Innings, The Private Papers of Viscount Lee of Fareham* (1974). Parts of the copious diaries of Sir Edward Hamilton have now been published, edited by D. W. Bahlman (1972), and Lord Carlingford's Journal for 1885, edited by A. B. Cooke and J. R. Vincent (1971).

On military matters, there is nothing to compare with A. J. Marder: *From the Dreadnought to Scapa Flow*, in five volumes (1961–70), although D. E. Morris's *The Washing of the Spears* (1966), a brilliant and sensitive history of the Zulu Wars, Churchill's *The River War*, and Reitz's *Commando* describe individual episodes with exceptional skill.

On foreign affairs, which do not occupy a substantial part of this volume, in addition to the biographies of Gladstone, Disraeli, Salisbury, Rosebery, Balfour, Grey, Campbell-Bannerman, Churchill and Asquith to which reference has been made, two works by A. J. P. Taylor, *The Troublemakers* (1957), and *The Struggle for Mastery in Europe 1848–1918* (1954) should be particularly mentioned, as should G. Monger: *The End of Isolation* (1963) and W. Langer: *The Diplomacy of Imperialism* (1951).

INDEX